EARLY CHILDHOOD EDUCATION SERIES
Sharon Ryan, Editor

ADVISORY BOARD: Barbara T. Bowman, Harriet K. Cuffaro, Stephanie Feeney, Doris Pronin Fromberg, Celia Genishi, Stacie G. Goffin, Dominic F. Gullo, Alice Sterling Honig, Elizabeth Jones, Gwen Morgan

(continued)

Young Investigators

The Project Approach in the Early Years

SECOND EDITION

• • •

Judy Harris Helm

Lilian G. Katz

Teachers College
Columbia University
New York and London

National Association for the
Education of Young Children
Washington, D.C.

The Project Planning Journal (beginning after page 120) is available for free download and printing from www.tcpress.com.

Published simultaneously by Teachers College Press, 1234 Amsterdam Avenue, New York, NY 10027, and the National Association for the Education of Young Children (NAEYC), 1313 L Street NW, Suite 500, Washington, DC 20005.

Library of Congress Cataloging-in-Publication Data

Helm, Judy Harris.
    Young investigators : the project approach in the early years / Judy Harris Helm, Lilian G. Katz. — 2nd ed.
        p.   cm. — (Early childhood education series)
    Includes bibliographical references and index.
    ISBN 978-0-8077-5153-4 (pbk. : alk. paper)
        1. Project method in teaching.   2. Early childhood education—Curricula.   I. Katz, Lilian G. (Lilian Gonshaw), 1932–   II. Title.

    LB1139.35.P8H46 2010
    372.13'6–dc22   2010026439

ISBN 978-0-8077-5153-4 (paperback)

NAEYC Item #244

Printed on acid-free paper
Manufactured in the United States of America

18 17 16 15 14 13   8 7 6 5 4 3

To our husbands, Richard Helm and the late Boris Katz, who have supported and encouraged us to take our own journeys and do our own project work, and to the teachers and children who have opened their classrooms and minds and by whom we have been instructed, inspired, and enriched.

Contents

Preface

IN PREPARING THE SECOND EDITION of this book, we have taken into account the questions raised and issues presented in the course of our work with many teachers of young children as we have helped them implement the project approach described in *Young Investigators*.

Many of the questions concerned how best to involve young children in project work who had not yet achieved mastery of basic literacy skills. Many resources for teachers that are currently available on the project approach are most useful for older children who have verbal fluency and beginning literacy and numeracy skills. These children, who often have a large vocabulary, can easily talk about their previous experiences related to the topic being investigated and can begin to formulate questions to which the investigation will seek answers. In addition, mastery of literacy skills (reading and writing) provides older children with ways of researching the topic, recording their thoughts, and representing their growing understanding of the topic that are not usually part of the young child's repertoire. Children who are 3 and 4 years old are still developing verbal fluency and the ability to organize their thoughts for communication. Formulating questions for investigation is often a challenge for young children. Five- and 6-year-olds are in the process of learning what the reading and writing process is all about. Research and representation take a different direction with these young learners. In addition, children with special needs in classrooms often present challenges with respect to communication and representational skills that are part of project work. This book provides a resource that specifically addresses some of these issues.

In our work with teachers we have also encountered doubts and concerns about whether children whose early experiences seemed to put them at risk for difficulties in school might respond to the exploratory and child-initiated nature of project work. In such cases also, many school officials and teachers expressed the view that children coming to school with less than optimal school readiness and from low-income homes were most in need of formal academic exercises, and that experiences like project work were most appropriate for wealthy and gifted children. As if these kinds of concerns were not sufficient to inhibit teachers' temptations to try project work in their curriculum, recent developments have placed them under increasing pressure to meet state and local performance and content standards. Many educators believe that such standards cannot be addressed in any way other than with formal instruction. These concerns are addressed throughout this book.

Interest in the project approach has been growing fairly consistently over the last two decades as more and more teachers have reported their experiences in journals, at conferences, and on the Project Approach Listserv offered by the Early Childhood and Parenting Collaborative, University of Illinois (http://ecap.crc.uiuc.edu/listservs.html). For example, several major programs have been implemented in Chicago Public Schools in cooperation with Kohl Children's Museum. The Illinois Project Group continues to meet yearly to share project work and is continuing to increase in number of participants. Methods of project work besides the project approach (such as problem-based learning and place-based learning) are growing rapidly and have become integral parts of plans for 21st-century schools. Projects from schools throughout the country and with all ages of students are featured on forward-thinking websites such as Edutopia.org.

A major influence on educators of the under-7-year-olds has been exposure to a great deal of information about the cutting-edge developments in early childhood education in the small northern Italian city of Reggio Emilia, including the extended projects done by the young children. The approach to project work taken in Reggio Emilia is more informal and flexible than the strategies we recommend and describe (see Hendricks, 1997). Nevertheless, all of us in the field have been inspired and motivated by examining their work, especially in the use of "graphic languages" and the power of careful documentation to enrich the work of young children and their teachers (Cadwell, 2003; Gandini, Hill, Cadwell & Schwall, 2005).

Several changes will be evident in this second edition of *Young Investigators.* The rapidly accumulating evidence of children's lack of connection with the natural world has led us to include special features in Chapters 1–5 on doing projects with nature topics. It has been a joy to see teachers become co-learners in the exploration of the natural world. Two new projects are shared by the teachers who guided them. Chapter 6 presents Lora Taylor's work on the Camera Project, and Chapter 7 presents Sallie Sawin's wonderful adventure of toddlers investigating a fire hydrant.

Finally, this book is dedicated to the proposition that all children are natural-born investigators. Our experience confirms the related proposition that the preschool years are an ideal time to support and strengthen the inborn dispositions of all children to observe and to investigate their experience and environments by incorporating the project approach in the early childhood curriculum. As readers will realize throughout the following chapters, our confidence in this proposition is supported by a wide range of experiences with teachers and children by whom we have also been instructed, inspired, and enriched.

Acknowledgments

WE ARE DEEPLY INDEBTED to our good colleagues, past coauthors, and personal friends Sylvia Chard and Sallee Beneke, with whom we have each shared research and dialogue about projects. This book would not have been possible without the extensive conversations and consultation with them that preceded the writing of this book. We are also grateful to the early childhood centers and schools where project work flourishes and inspires us, and whose work is included in this book. These include Bing Nursery School, Don C. Parker Early Education Center, Holy Trinity Lutheran Church Preschool, Illinois State University Child Care Center, Little Friends Learning Center, St. Ambrose University Children's Campus, University Primary School at the University of Illinois, Valeska Hinton Early Childhood Education Center, and Woodford County Special Education Association.

Since the first edition, we have been blessed with our involvement with Northminster Learning Center in Peoria, Illinois. Under the direction of Stacy Berg and Pam Scranton, this center and its teachers have inspired countless educators throughout the country to do project work through their Open Door conferences and writing. They continue to inspire us to learn more. The Center for Early Education and Care (CEEC) at the University of Massachusetts has provided much impetus for deep thinking with their thought-provoking questions and discussions. We are grateful to the staff at STARnet of Western Illinois University, especially Char Ward and Sharon Doubet, who have been tireless in their commitment to capturing and sharing good project work. Jan Deissler and Brenda Smith of Child Care Connection at Illinois Central College have enabled many of the teachers described in this book to learn about the project approach and documentation through their support of training and dissemination. We also thank the staff of the Early Childhood and Parenting (ECAP) Collaborative at the University of Illinois for sharing reflections about projects and consistently encouraging our work. Kohl Children's Museum of Greater Chicago, under the direction of Erika Miller and Mary Trieschmann, has worked tirelessly to bring project work to Chicago Public Schools and has sponsored two wonderful project conferences. We are thankful also for the consistent group of teachers and directors who have encouraged project work in Illinois through the annual Illinois Project Day, a teacher-to-teacher greet and share event that encourages quality project work.

In addition to the staff of the schools and centers listed above we want to acknowledge individually the competent, caring, and inspirational teachers who have shared their experiences guiding projects and their children's work through personal interviews and documentation. These include Jolyn Blank, Scott Brouette, Judy Cagle, Mary Jane Elliott, Natalya Fehr, Barbara Gallick, Johnna Gerlach, Mary Ann Gottlieb, Ruth Harkema, Jean Lang, Lisa Lee, Linda Lundberg, Lora Taylor, Sallie Sawin, Brenda Wiles, and Rebecca Wilson. They were all extremely generous in sharing their thoughts, their documentation, and their time. Cathy Wiggers shared her experiences as an administrator supporting projects. It is their work that will enable readers to see how projects can occur in real classrooms and will help teachers build the bridge between theory and implementation.

Last, but not least, we thank Marie Ellen Larcada, Susan Liddicoat, and Karl Nyberg, our editors at Teachers College Press. Marie Ellen nurtured us, while Susan worked wonders with our words. We also appreciate the work of Lynne Frost, who, as production editor, brought new ideas for layout and careful attention to detail to the task. Karl brought it all together. Their patience and encouragement enabled us to finish the task.

CHAPTER 1

· · ·

Projects and Young Children

I love project work because it enables my children to go in depth with their learning. They really like to investigate and really like to explore. Project work allows me to meaningfully bring real artifacts into the classroom for them to get down, get their hands into their learning . . . just a real in-depth exploration of the topic. I like project work too because it covers all areas of curriculum and does not just focus on one thing such as literacy. A project can help me integrate all areas of the curriculum in an engaging way.

—Lora Taylor, prekindergarten teacher

LORA TAYLOR has been doing project work for more than 10 years. Over the course of those years, circumstances have changed for Ms. Taylor and other teachers in the early childhood field. Concerns about students not doing well in school and increasing accountability issues have intensified the emphasis on standards and required curricula, both of which impact what occurs in classrooms, even those of 3- and 4-year-olds. A decade ago teachers were considered "good" if their classrooms were lively and offered an assortment of meaningful and developmentally appropriate learning experiences for young children. Good kindergartens and first grades were those that encouraged play and socialization and brought literacy to life through active engagement with books. Many children did well in such classrooms and went on to become successful students in the upper grades. However, some children did not. Those children faced specific challenges that can affect learning, such as poverty and learning a second language (Berliner, 2009). Today's early childhood and school environment is changing rapidly, as the numbers of children facing these challenges have increased. In 2008, 14.1 million children, or 19.0%, were poor (U.S. Bureau of the Census, 2008). The number of English language learners has also increased. A survey of state education agencies in 2000–2001 found that almost 10% of the total prekindergarten through 12th-grade public school enrollment had limited proficiency in English (Kindler, 2002). Because of these changes in the student population, there has been increased concern with accountability, which has also brought about an increased focus on discrete knowledge and skills that are testable (Ravitch, 2010).

At the same time, we are realizing that children in our schools today will exist in a world that we can only imagine (Darling-Hammond, 2010). Technological change and the development of a global economy require that our children develop 21st-century skills (Partnership for 21st Century Skills, 2010). To be successful students, our children will need to be technologically literate and to feel comfortable communicating electronically. They will need to be critical and creative thinkers and be able to work on teams collaborating within organizations with a diverse membership. They will need to be able to take initiative and integrate what they are learning from different disciplines. Most of all they will need to be flexible and eager to learn new skills and adapt to rapidly changing challenges.

Although we know that projects fit into those active, engaging classrooms of Ms. Taylor's past, do they also fit into the classrooms of today with the increased emphasis on standards, and, more importantly, do they prepare children for their lives in the 21st century? The answer on both counts is yes. Because many other educators agree with this assessment, interest in project work is increasing, and project work is now included in most recommendations for educational reform. For example, the George Lucas Foundation, an organization dedicated to creating a vision for this new world of learning through leading-edge interactive tools and resources (Edutopia.org), endorses project work as one of its Core Concepts. Teachers like Ms. Taylor—as well as kindergarten and first-grade teachers who now do much of their planning around standards—are discovering that project work enables them to integrate knowledge and skills in meaningful ways.

THE PROJECT APPROACH

Many teachers of young children have been challenged by the work of Lilian Katz and Sylvia Chard (2000; Chard, 1994) on the project approach to introduce opportunities for children to engage in investigation as part of the studies undertaken in their classrooms. The early years are important years for all aspects of development. Children's natural dispositions to be intellectually curious and to investigate their environments emerge (Katz, 1995). They learn about tools such as reading and writing and become motivated to develop and use a wide variety of related skills. It is important that they have an opportunity to experience active, engaged learning.

However, research and investigations are easier to incorporate in a curriculum for older students, who have mastered reading and writing, than in early childhood programs. This book presents the teaching strategies and project stories of Lora Taylor and other teachers who are successfully using the project approach with 3-, 4-, and 5-year-olds and with first-graders who are beginning to read and write. Even toddlers are doing project work. In this volume we summarize the knowledge gained as projects have been undertaken in schools, childcare centers, and early intervention programs in rural and urban areas and in small towns. These projects are described with step-by-step explanations of how young children's projects are guided by teachers and caregivers. Also included are strategies and project stories of teachers doing project work with toddlers.

Defining Project Work

The project approach is not a new way to teach children. It was a central part of the Progressive Education movement and was used extensively in the British Infant Schools in the 1960s and 1970s (Smith, 1997). Interest in the potential value of project work was renewed with the publication in 1989 of the first edition of *Engaging Children's Minds: The Project Approach* (Katz & Chard). Even greater interest in the project approach was stimulated by the impressive reports and displays of group projects conducted by children in the pre-primary schools of Reggio Emilia (Edwards, Gandini, & Forman, 1993, 1998; Gandini, 1993; New, 1990, 1991; Rankin, 1992). According to Gandini (1997):

> Projects provide the backbone of the children's and teachers' learning experiences. They are based on the strong conviction that learning by doing is of great importance and that to discuss in group and to revisit ideas and experiences is the premier way of gaining better understanding and learning. (p. 7)

Although the word *project* has many meanings, when used in the "project approach," it has a specific meaning:

A project is an in-depth investigation of a topic worth learning more about. The investigation is usually undertaken by a small group of children within a class, sometimes by a whole class, and occasionally by an individual child. The key feature of a project is that it is a research effort deliberately focused on finding answers to questions about a topic posed either by the children, the teacher, or the teacher working with the children. (Katz, 1994, p. 1)

There are other approaches to curriculum that are similar to the project approach. These also involve deep investigation and student initiation and guidance of learning; some are more content-based or have additional goals. These approaches are often used in classrooms with older children. They include project-based learning (Polman, 2000) and problem-based learning, often called PBL (Barrell, 2006). Project-based learning, like the project approach, is centered on the learner and affords learners the opportunity for in-depth investigations of worthy topics. Another project method that centers project work on the neighborhood and community near the school is place-based education (Smith, 2002; Sobel, 2005). In all of these approaches to project work, learners are more autonomous as they construct personally meaningful artifacts that are representations of their learning (Grant, 2002).

Projects, Units, Themes, and Learning Centers

Many teachers use units or themes for organizing the activities they provide. A theme is a broad concept or topic, such as "seasons" or "animals." When using a theme, teachers assemble books, photographs, and other materials related to the theme. Experiences in most content areas or domains of development (such as language, math, or science) are then related or connected to the theme.

Units usually consist of preplanned lessons and activities on a specific topic that the teacher considers important for the children to know about, such as "magnets" (Harlan, 1984). When providing information in units, the teacher typically has a clear plan about what concepts and knowledge he or she wants the children to learn.

Many teachers also use learning centers as a way to organize their teaching. Areas of the room are designated for the investigation or development of certain knowledge and skills, such as "block area" or "music and movement area" (Dodge, Colker, & Heroman, 2002). Materials and equipment for each area are selected to teach concepts and provide practice in skills that the teacher wishes the children to develop.

In all of these methods, however, the focus is not to help children pose questions to be answered or take the initiative for investigation. Many of these methods have an impor-

FIGURE 1.1 • Degree of child initiation and decision-making in different approaches to teaching

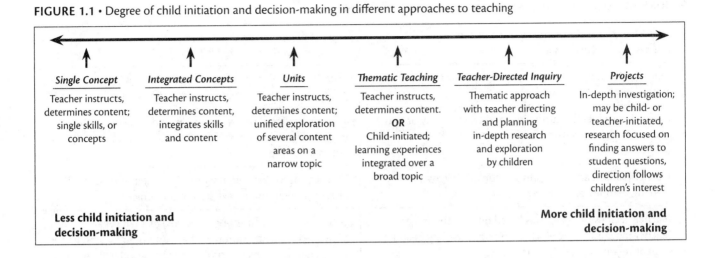

Single Concept	*Integrated Concepts*	*Units*	*Thematic Teaching*	*Teacher-Directed Inquiry*	*Projects*
Teacher instructs, determines content; single skills, or concepts	Teacher instructs, determines content, integrates skills and content	Teacher instructs, determines content; unified exploration of several content areas on a narrow topic	Teacher instructs, determines content. **OR** Child-initiated; learning experiences integrated over a broad topic	Thematic approach with teacher directing and planning in-depth research and exploration by children	In-depth investigation; may be child- or teacher-initiated, research focused on finding answers to student questions, direction follows children's interest

Less child initiation and decision-making

More child initiation and decision-making

tant place in the early childhood curriculum. However, there are additional opportunities for growth of knowledge, skills, and dispositions when children ask their own questions, conduct their own investigations, and make decisions about their activities. Projects provide contexts in which children's curiosity can be expressed purposefully, and that enable them to experience the joy of self-motivated learning. Teachers do not always know what direction a project will take or what aspects of a topic will interest a particular group. Well-developed projects engage children's minds and emotions and become adventures that teachers and children embark on together. The continuum in Figure 1.1 represents the degree of child initiation and decision-making in the learning process with different approaches to teaching. Projects are on the far right of the continuum because a child or children in a classroom often initiate the project topics. Projects also involve the child in making decisions about topic selection, investigation, and how to culminate the project. There are many valuable learning experiences that can and do occur at all points along the continuum. Teachers who use the project approach often also teach single concepts and employ units, themes, and directed inquiry. A classroom may have project work as well as thematic and single-concept teaching happening in the same day. Some topics, by their nature, do not make good project topics and are more effectively taught as single concepts, units, or themes.

We believe, however, that projects provide experiences that involve students intellectually to a greater degree than the experiences that come from teacher-prepared units or themes. It is the children's initiative, involvement, and relative control over their own activities and participation in what is accomplished that distinguish projects from units or themes. Additional differences between projects and units or thematic teaching include the length of time devoted to

the topic, the teacher's role, the timing of field trips, and the use of a variety of resources. These differences are summarized in Figure 1.2.

Academic Tasks and Intellectual Goals

In understanding the role that projects play in an early childhood and primary curriculum, it may be helpful to look at the difference between academic tasks and intellectual goals. Academic tasks are typically carefully structured, sequenced, and decontextualized small bits of information and discrete skills that often require some small-group or individual instruction by a knowledgeable adult. The academic tasks in the early childhood curriculum usually address facts and skills that the majority of children are unlikely to learn spontaneously or by discovery, though, under favorable conditions, many children do so. For example, under the right environmental conditions, many young children can "pick up" the names of colors and shapes and need little in the way of didactic or systematic formal instruction to learn them. These items of knowledge may be spontaneously "constructed" by some children, as can be seen in invented spelling. However, in such cases these bits of knowledge are often misconstructed and require assistance to reconstruct correctly.

Similarly, the alphabet, an arbitrary sequence of symbols developed over a long period of human history, has no inherent discoverable logic. It simply has to be mastered with the help of knowledgeable others who encourage frequent repetition and who correct errors until mastery is achieved. In the case of most young children, it would be wasteful and inefficient for them to have to "discover" such things as the alphabet, punctuation rules, the pledge of allegiance, the national anthem, or other conventional knowledge by self-initiated discovery processes.

FIGURE 1.2 • Differences between teacher-planned experiences and the project approach

In teacher-planned experiences such as units you are more likely to see	In projects you are more likely to see
Length of learning experience predetermined; shorter time periods, such as 1 or 2 weeks.	Length of learning experience determined by project progression; usually several weeks, sometimes months.
Topics determined by curriculum and teacher, may or may not be of interest to students.	Topics negotiated between students and teacher with integrated curriculum goals; children's interest a major criterion for topic selection.
Teacher plans in advance, presents topics, designs and prepares learning experiences.	Teacher observes children's investigation, uses student interest to determine next step of the project.
Teacher decides on objectives based on curriculum goals. Teacher may or may not include inquiry experiences and student research to achieve objectives.	Teacher webs to assess prior knowledge, then organizes project so students learn what they do not know; integrates curriculum objectives as project progresses; always involves child investigation.
Knowledge gained through teacher-planned experiences, resources brought into the classroom, small- and large-group activities, and events.	Knowledge gained by finding answers to questions or investigation; children involved in determining the activities and events and in how to find answers.
Resources are provided by the teacher, but students may also bring in resources.	Resources are brought in by students, the teacher, and experts who visit the classroom or are gathered on field-site visits.
A field trip may or may not be included. If included, field trips may occur at any time but often near the end of the unit to culminate the study.	Field-site visits are an important part of the project process. Students may do several site visits for one project. Field-site visits usually occur early in project.
Topic often taught at specific teacher-determined times of the day, or it may be integrated into many content areas and permeate the day.	Project permeates the day and the classroom, involving many different curriculum areas and skills.
Activities (such as making a craft, doing a science activity) are planned by the teacher to teach specific concepts.	Activities focus on investigation, finding answers to questions, and using resources. Teacher supports integration of concepts during debriefing and discussion.
Representation relates to specific activities—drawing to show observations in a science experiment, creating maps, drawing a picture, or writing a play, for example. Representation activities are not usually repeated.	Representation (drawing, writing, building, constructing) challenges children to integrate concepts. Representation documents what children are learning. Activities are repeated to show growth in knowledge and skills as the project progresses.

While academic goals address small units of knowledge and skills, intellectual goals address dispositions—that is, habits of mind that include a variety of tendencies to interpret experience (Katz, 1993). Some habits of mind that relate to intellectual goals include the disposition to

• Make sense of experience
• Theorize, analyze, hypothesize, and synthesize
• Predict and check predictions
• Find things out
• Strive for accuracy

• Be empirical
• Grasp the consequences of actions
• Persist in seeking solutions to problems
• Speculate about cause–effect relationships
• Predict others' wishes and feelings

Along with many others not mentioned, these dispositions are all intellectual rather than academic in focus. It is reasonable to assume that the most important intellectual dispositions are inborn in all humans and are likely to be fairly robust in very young children. For example, the dispositions to make sense of experience, to be curious, and to be empirical can be observed in virtually all very young children, regardless of family income and environment.

Intellectual dispositions deserve explicit attention in curriculum planning and teaching methods so they can be manifested, appreciated, and thereby further strengthened and developed. Unless the curriculum provides contexts in which the intellectual dispositions can be strengthened by being used and applied meaningfully, they may be weakened or even lost. Once lost, they may be very difficult to reinstate. Margaret Donaldson (1978) noted that all children seem to begin their school experiences with eagerness to find things out and to pose questions, and to do what is asked of them in school. She also notes that "the problem then is to understand how something that begins so well can often end so badly" (p. 14).

Unfortunately, what happens in some classrooms promotes neither academic nor intellectual goals. Some children spend much time on relatively mindless activities (such as cutting and pasting pre-cut Valentine hearts) and in group discussions from which the majority of the participants withdraw psychologically within minutes. Such pursuits involve limited academic skills and do not provide for the development of intellectual dispositions. These activities do not sufficiently challenge children to identify and solve problems but instead emphasize passive following of instructions or being entertained. These experiences are often justified on the basis of their being "fun." While such activities may not harm anyone and may be beneficial in a few ways, they lack sufficient intellectual vitality to support or strengthen the intellectual dispositions.

The Project Approach and the Larger Curriculum

Involving young children in project work is unlikely to offer all of the learning experiences that should be included in their curriculum. There are many other learning activities that are beneficial for the young child.

However, classrooms where children are actively engaged in projects are also classrooms where children sing, listen to stories, build block structures, paint, participate in dramatic play, and learn and practice emerging skills. Projects are compatible with many different curriculum approaches and classroom structures and environments. Units, thematic teaching, and direct instruction can provide good learning experiences for some skills and some topics. In many of the classrooms described in this book, units and projects were progressing at the same time. Projects are unlikely to constitute the whole childcare, preschool, kindergarten, or first-grade curriculum.

Teachers who are comfortable with the project approach often very effectively incorporate features of the project process (such as construction, observational drawing, and documentation) into other types of learning experiences. Because of this, some units or thematic learning experiences look like projects. However, unless the elements of child initiation, child decision-making, and child engagement are present in a learning experience, it is not a project, and it is less likely to provide the unique benefits of project work.

It is only when children are curious, absorbed, and interested in a topic that the benefits of projects are realized. Children benefit from the added opportunity to initiate, investigate, and follow through on their interests.

BENEFITS OF PROJECTS IN THE EARLY YEARS

Projects and Academic Achievement

With 65% of mothers of children under 6 in the labor force (Children's Defense Fund, 2005), a significant proportion of children's growing and learning time is spent outside the home. Many of these children are in group-care settings in which a large portion of the day is devoted to teacher-directed learning experiences. These experiences often do not provide opportunities to take initiative and responsibility for the work undertaken, as in the experiences of project work. A number of studies have documented the benefits of opportunities for children to direct their work and to follow their interests by self-selection of activities and exploration of materials (Schweinhart, 1997):

> The relevant evidence from these studies suggests that preschool programs based on child-initiated learning activities contribute to children's short- and long-term academic and social development, while preschool programs based on teacher-directed lessons obtain a short-term advantage in children's academic development by sacrificing a long-term contribution to their social and emotional development. On this basis, research supports the use by preschool programs of a curriculum approach based on child-initiated learning activities rather than one based on teacher-directed lessons. (p. 2)

The benefits of children's having substantial control over the work undertaken extend beyond the early years. Marcon (1992, 1995, 2002) found that children from preschool classes that offered ample opportunity for child-initiated, as opposed to teacher-directed, activity showed the greatest mastery of basic reading, language, and mathematics skills. At fourth grade, children who had experienced self-initiated learning also had higher overall grade-point averages and higher grade-point averages in most individual subject matter areas. Boys especially may fare better in school in the long run when they have experienced a preschool that emphasizes self-initiated learning (Marcon, 1992; Miller

& Bizzell, 1983). By the end of their fifth year in school, there were significant differences in academic performance among children who had experienced three different preschool models. Even into their sixth year of school, the effect of the academic-oriented preschool experiences could be seen, as those children had significantly lower grades compared with those who had attended the child-initiated preschool classes. This is a strong argument for the value of more active, child-initiated early learning experiences (Marcon, 2002).

Too often, schools and childcare centers, especially those with high concentrations of children from low-income families, compound the problem by limiting experiences to large-group instruction in isolated subskills and extensive drill and practice (Knapp, 1995). An opportunity to follow their interests, to acquire new interests, and to investigate a topic in depth can be highly beneficial for the academic achievement of children in these environments. It can also assist social and emotional development.

Projects and Social and Emotional Development

Children of all socioeconomic backgrounds can benefit from emotional involvement in and commitment to finding things out and mastering new knowledge and skills. Missed opportunities to become meaningfully engaged in a topic of interest may affect the development of dispositions to achieve and learn. If a school or a childcare center fails to provide opportunities for emotional involvement in learning experiences, children's inborn curiosity and desire to learn may not be sufficiently strengthened. Parents who have ample time and financial resources may provide these experiences for their own children within the family setting. They may watch for their children's emerging interests and then encourage them by buying books, taking trips, and providing resources for acquiring further knowledge about the topic. These parents model emotional involvement in learning for the child. Children who spend extended periods of time in group care may not have sufficient experience of this type of support for their individual interests.

Research suggests that there is a relationship between the role that children have in determining their own learning experiences and the development of social skills. A study of kindergarten classes that used three different teaching approaches (direct instruction, a constructivist approach based on child-initiated activities, and an eclectic approach) found that the children from the constructivist class were more interpersonally interactive. They exhibited a greater number and variety of negotiation strategies and shared more experiences (DeVries, Reese-Learned, & Morgan, 1991).

Considerable interest continues to be focused on the concept of engaged learning. Engaged-learning experiences are defined by Jones, Valdez, Norakowski, and Rasmussen

(1994) as learning experiences in which learners take responsibility for their own work, are self-regulated, and are able to define their own goals and evaluate their own accomplishments. When students are energized by their own work, their disposition to solve problems and to seek deeper understanding can be developed and strengthened. Learning experiences that engage children are especially important during the early years, when children's approaches to learning (motivations, attitudes, and behaviors) are developing. According to Hyson (2008), challenges of poverty, violence, and instability in families, combined with high-stakes testing that emphasizes extrinsic rewards and sanctions, make it especially important to use approaches that emphasize children's engagement in the learning experience.

It is this engaged learning that occurs in the project approach when children have the opportunity to initiate, investigate, and follow through on their interests. Because these activities are so similar to the investigative process of adults, we began to call young children doing these activities "young investigators." In this book, we use the term young investigators to refer to children toddler through age 6 who are engaged in active investigation of a topic through the project approach, although they have not yet achieved verbal fluency or mastery of basic literacy skills.

Projects and Parent Involvement

Another potential benefit of the project approach for young children is the readiness and ease with which parents become involved and interested in the children's work. Parents' involvement in their children's education is significantly related to children's success in school (Henderson & Berla, 1994).

There are many ways in which parents can become involved in projects. Epstein (1995) has specified six types of parent involvement that are valuable and can have an impact on student success. Four of these six key types can occur through parent involvement in projects. These include volunteering, learning at home, communicating with the home, and collaborating with the community. Teachers who implement the project approach in preschool, kindergarten, and first grade frequently report how interested and involved parents become in the projects. When young investigators talk extensively and enthusiastically at home about the projects and what they are learning, communication about school in general increases.

When teachers carefully document the young investigators' experiences and share what children are learning through their investigations, parents are often amazed and delighted to see the level of thinking revealed. It is common for parents to become so interested that they take children to field-sites outside of school hours, purchase books or materials that relate to the topic, or bring resources and materials from home into the classroom. Parents often serve as visiting experts and enjoy answering young investigators' questions or assisting in the teaching of relevant skills during a project. Sometimes parents participate in the investigation and accompany young investigators to community sites, where they learn about the topic alongside their children. Most projects end with a culminating event that includes a display of children's work, which also involves parents. During these events parents frequently comment on their surprise at how much learning has occurred.

As parents observe projects develop, they see engaged learning experiences and observe techniques for fostering engaged learning in the home. For example, a parent accompanying a class on a field-site visit may observe how the teacher encourages young investigators to ask questions and how he or she draws the children's attention to observing and recording. The parent may see very young investigators draw, write, and photograph. These are skills that many parents may not even be aware that young children can acquire. The parent will also see how the teacher listens carefully to children's comments and questions and responds to them respectfully.

The project approach can also be taught directly to parents through a series of parent workshops in which parents complete "home projects" following a format similar to that outlined in this book (see Helm, Berg, & Scranton, 2004; Helm, Berg, Scranton, & Wilson, 2005).

OPPORTUNITIES AND CONSTRAINTS OF THE EARLY YEARS

Developmental Milestones

Projects are especially valuable for children in the early years because this is a period of rapid intellectual growth that can have important long-term consequences. Berk (2008) discusses the competencies of intellectual development that emerge in the age range 2 through 4 years. These include:

- Representational activity (development of language, make-believe play, meaningful drawings, and understanding of spatial symbols such as photographs, simple maps, and models)
- Taking the perspective of others in simplified, familiar situations and in everyday communication
- Distinguishing animate beings from inanimate beings
- Categorizing objects on the basis of common function and kind of thing, not just perceptual features
- Classifying familiar objects hierarchically. (p. 237)

These competencies continue to develop during kindergarten and first grade. Competencies such as those above have been identified through observation and children's performance on cognitive tasks.

BUILDING MIND/BRAIN CAPACITY

Another way to look at project work is to consider research from the field of neuroscience. A common understanding emerging from this research is that the brain and the ability to think are shaped by experiences (Zull, 2002). The capacity of the brain to think in different ways—the ability to problem solve, reflect, and be open to new ideas—is built over time and exposure, with the greatest plasticity and potential in the beginning years of life (Wexler, 2008). Additional insight into intellectual development is now coming from recent experimental developments in the study of early cognition, such as observing the activity of the brain during cognitive activity and growth, and from computer-assisted models of the brain's development of networks of information during early learning (Blakemore & Frith, 2005). Although it is too early to draw many conclusions from this new research, Catherwood (2000), in a review of these new views of the young child's growth and development, came to the conclusion

> that experiences that support the child in making connections amongst domains of knowledge (e.g. as in 'event-based' programmes in which children develop activities around conceptual themes) are likely to impact on and enhance the richness of neural networks in the child's brain. (p. 33)

There are many experiences in project work that are consistent with Catherwood's conclusion. These include the focus of projects on topics in which the child has some background knowledge and interest, the integration of many domains of learning, the opportunity and purpose for verbal communication that emerges in project work, the "events" of field-site visits and visits by experts, and the development of activities by children.

In addition to the rapid general cognitive growth, a variety of skills related to competence in literacy begin to emerge, as well as an understanding of the importance and usefulness of numerical concepts and skills. Children begin to learn about scientific inquiry. In a classroom that provides opportunities for project work, these intellectual dispositions and academic skills can be applied in ways that are clearly useful in the eyes of young investigators.

Projects and Literacy Development

The prekindergarten, kindergarten, and first-grade years are recognized as key years for the development of communicative competence, including language and understanding of symbol systems (Machado, 1995). While in the past teachers were sometimes discouraged from introducing reading and paper-and-pencil activities into the prekindergarten, teachers are now strongly encouraged to a provide a

A CLOSER LOOK   • HOW PROJECTS CAN CONNECT CHILDREN WITH NATURE •

Recognizing the Problem

Children's connection with nature is diminishing even as we are beginning to realize its effect on their intellectual, emotional, social, and physical development (Kellert, 2005). In one study, although 70% of mothers reported playing outdoors every day as a child, only 31% of their children did (Clements, 2004). Children's contact with the out-of-doors and with living things has an impact on their well-being, and more and more educators and parents are becoming aware of the resulting problems of diminished contact with nature (American Academy of Pediatrics, 2006; Louv, 2008; Taylor & Kuo, 2006). A movement to reconnect children with their natural world, which has mushroomed since 2005, has been documented by the Children and Nature Network (Charles, Louv, Bodner, Guns, & Stahl, 2009). Some of the benefits of outdoor play include concentration and impulse control, emotional coping and stress reduction, more creative play, increased fitness and reduction in childhood obesity, and resiliency. Not all out-of-doors experiences result in contact with nature. Although we may provide playground space and play equipment, both are often devoid of contact with living or natural things. Many of these outdoor spaces—with their plastic and metal climbing equipment, rubber cushioning surface, and concrete wheeled-toy areas—are more like outdoor workout gyms than play areas.

How Project Work Can Help

Opportunities for contact with nature and discussions about nature topics have been relegated to instructional time. We may read books about nature, show videos, or have large posters in the classroom. These, however, have limited impact on children's understanding of nature and the benefits that come from experiencing nature. All experiences with nature are not alike. Kellert (2005) discusses the differences in children's experiences. *Abstract or Vicarious Experiences* occur when we are limited to videos, photos, and books to introduce nature to children. These vicarious experiences do not involve contact with actual living organisms or the natural environment but instead with images or representations of them created by others. In this way they are less engaging, but they also provide opportunities for developing misconceptions. For example, seeing an elephant on a computer screen usually does not produce an understanding of how big an elephant really is. *Indirect Experiences* provide structured interaction in carefully prepared spaces such as zoos, playgrounds, or groomed parks. These experiences are dependent on human management and intervention. Indirect experiences can occur at a school with the addition of a garden or nature walk area. *Direct Contact* with nature provides experiences for children with living things and parts of the environment that are self-sustaining. These experiences connect children to plants, animals, and habitats that function independently of human activity. Children are free to climb, poke, build, take apart, and experiment. We have found Kellert's framework helpful in understanding the importance of children's own investigations and have summarized these ideas in a chart.

Although providing all three types of experiences that connect children with nature is beneficial, it is the direct contact experiences that are critical because these experiences are disappearing from children's lives. One solution is to provide rich outdoor play areas within our programs. The Arbor Day Foundation has established guidelines for nature exploration areas for young children. The recommendations include providing messy areas, gardening spaces, building areas for construction, and presentation areas (Rosenow, Wike, & Cuppens, 2007). These outdoor classroom spaces can provide indirect experience in a controlled area and in some cases actual direct contact experience.

Another way to increase children's direct contact with nature is to focus some of our projects on nature. The activities and events in project work can make a unique contribution to connecting children with nature. As children do project work, they collect artifacts, study them closely, and represent what they learn by drawing, painting, constructing, writing, or even through play. Nature is highly stimulating and engaging, and invites study and deep thinking. In doing projects with nature, children form basic understandings of facts and terms, they learn the importance of differentiating terms and develop rudimentary classifications, and they begin to develop a sense of cause and effect. Nature provides many opportunities to learn the names of things, extend and elaborate knowledge, define precisely,

Kellert provides a framework for examining the characteristics of children's experiences with nature. Direct experience is waning.

Children's Connection with Nature		
Vicarious Experiences	Indirect Experiences	Direct Experiences
Abstract *Learning about nature*	*Going to prepared spaces*	*Unstructured, imaginative play* *Explorative contact*
Books, videos, media	Interaction with groomed and controlled nature in places such as zoos and parks	Children manipulate, arrange, and plan their own experiences

Kellert, S. R. (2005). Nature and childhood development. In *Building for life: Designing and understanding the human–nature connection* (p. 65). Washington, DC: Island Press.

and categorize. For example, children studying a meadow will learn about the birds and about the flowers and other plants that grow there—and about how they are alike and different. Instead of just learning the meaning of "tree," they may also learn the differences between evergreens and deciduous trees. They may learn that crows are different from songbirds. They will have an opportunity to develop deep understanding—not just knowledge of isolated facts and identification but a sense of why things happen. For example, birds peck on trees to eat insects that live there. Snow falls from the sky only at certain temperatures. Butterflies fly but caterpillars do not. Project work on nature also supports problem-solving and creative thinking. How can we capture that dragonfly without hurting it? How can we make sure our plants get enough water? Just interacting with nature can provide challenges. As children focus their investigation on nature topics, they also learn that nature and a natural environment are interesting and valuable. They learn to be protective and supportive of the natural environment.

literacy-rich environment in kindergarten as well as preschool classes (Dickinson, 2002). Although whole-group, formal instruction in reading and writing is still difficult for children from 3 to 5 years of age, they begin to represent concepts and ideas through drawing and early writing.

Our experience of working with many teachers who implement the project approach suggests strongly that among its many advantages is how it appears to strengthen young children's motivation to master a wide variety of skills, including reading and writing. This response to project work seems to be related to the children's sense of purpose for the work undertaken. For example, the purpose for their early efforts to read signs, pamphlets, or books is to find answers to the questions generated in Phase I of the project. The purpose of writing may be to send messages, or to record observations made during fieldwork, rather than just to please the teacher, complete an assignment, or finish a chore whose purpose may be obscure to them.

Young investigators are often highly motivated to show others what they have learned about a topic. Young investigators create play environments, block structures, buildings, and other products related to the project. Often children want to show what they know about a topic by writing

about it. As children build block structures related to a topic (e.g., a barn, during an investigation of a local farm), they often write signs to identify the parts of their structure (e.g., hay loft). When they make a dramatic play environment such as a restaurant, they may create signs or other literacy items to make their play environment more realistic (e.g., menus or notices of opening hours).

During the first phase of a project, when the teacher engages the children in developing a web of ideas surrounding the topic (see Chapter 2), the children give teachers their thoughts to record on the web, and many strive to read what has been written. As they create child-size versions of adult environments for dramatic play (such as a hospital), they also role-play the reading and writing. Young investigators often copy and save words about things in which they are interested. Even for preschool children, the posting of lists of project words encourages the child to learn the words and to use reading and writing as tools. In a study of first-grade children doing projects and units, the children were more involved in reading and research in the project than in the teacher-directed unit (Bryson, 1994). Teachers whose projects are described in this book have made similar reports.

FIGURE 1.3 • Jordan (3 years old) observes Ashley (4 years old) drawing. Encouraged by her modeling, he then requests a clipboard to do his own drawing. Learning from peers is characteristic of project work.

Projects provide a purpose for representation. Pam Scranton describes the experience of one 3-year-old who was drawn into representation through interest in a project:

> For example, Jordan had no interest in the Fire Truck project, but on the Vet Project he became involved. I have a picture [see Figure 1.3] of Jordan bending down to talk to Ashley. Ashley is describing what she is doing. Jordan marched over to me and said, "Can I have a clipboard, teacher?" Then he drew a horse. He had never written or drawn anything before. That would never have happened if I told him to do it. I just love to see children do that, to be motivated and to learn from each other. He was so proud of it. It wasn't a wonderful drawing; but it was a wonderful drawing by a 3-year-old. It was the first time Jordan had ever even wanted to pick up a pencil.

This is what project work often does. It causes many children to want to represent their ideas and observations by putting them down on paper in writing and through drawing.

Projects and Problem Solving

Most projects involve a wide variety of types of problem solving. In teacher-directed instruction, opportunities to solve problems are often limited. When the problems to be solved are set mainly by the teacher, the children are not necessarily motivated to search for solutions. However, problem solving develops naturally in the project process. Young children are consistently challenged in project work to solve mathematical problems and to do scientific thinking. They become aware of the function of number and quantity concepts. Projects create a reason to quantify information as they gather it and to represent quantities with numerals. Projects also provide reasons to classify and sort, to develop categories for things so that they can think about them. Children learn to use tools for investigation, to experiment and observe the results, and to make comparisons among objects. Projects provide a natural provocation for learning and using mathematical and scientific thinking.

In the first phase of a project, the children generate a list of questions. They then discuss possible strategies by which to seek answers to those questions. This generation of a list of questions to focus the project is a key indicator that the learning experience is a project and not a thematic unit. Even figuring out how to find the answers to these questions becomes a problem as they search for resources and experts. Teachers encourage children's problem solving by asking additional questions such as "Who could answer that question for you?" and "Where could you find out about that?" Sometimes young investigators solve problems by direct, first-hand investigation. For example, question "What's inside a radio?" led to the problem of how to get the radio open so that the children could see inside it.

Project work with young children often results in constructing models, drawing diagrams and charts, and creating playing environments. These activities are often rich with opportunity for young children to solve problems by using measurement, counting, and graphing. In the course of this problem solving, children become aware of many mathematical concepts, such as shapes, area, distance, and volume. For example, designing a model hospital with a limited number of blocks or building a grocery store in the classroom while still leaving space for other activities are problems that require serious group consideration and consultation. Individual young investigators may also have their own problem-solving experiences within a project. For example, a child may investigate many ways to make a cardboard tree stand up in a display before finding the best way. Problem solving changes as a project progresses and new problems arise.

GUIDING PROJECTS WITH YOUNG CHILDREN

Structure of the Project Approach

Teachers of young children who have not had an opportunity to observe others guide project work are often at a loss as to how to get a project started and then follow it through. The structure of the project approach, however, provides guidelines for the process. It may be helpful for teachers who have not observed a project in action to read the summary of the Vet Project, a project by 3-, 4-, and 5-year-old chil-

FIGURE 1.4 • The Vet Project

<table>
<tr>
<td colspan="2" align="center">

A Project by 3-, 4-, and 5-Year-Old Children

Bright Beginnings, Woodford County Special Education Association, Eureka, Illinois

Length of Project: 8 weeks　　　　　　　　　　　　　　*Teachers:* Pam Scranton, Brenda Wiles
</td>
</tr>
<tr>
<td>Phase I</td>
<td>

Beginning the Project

The Vet Project began when one of the children, during morning group time, cried because he had to leave his kitty at the vet's office to be neutered. After talking through the experience as a group, the rest of the children couldn't not let go of the subject and continued to talk about David's kitty the rest of the morning. The next day we talked about the possibility of going to a vet clinic, and the children began asking questions and predicting what we would see. Kati shouted: "You better start writing, Teacher!" We started making a list of what they knew about a vet clinic. I discovered that they the children had a limited "vet vocabulary." We decided to go to the library to choose some research materials.
</td>
</tr>
<tr>
<td>Phase II</td>
<td>

Developing the Project

After the trip to the library, the children began reading the vet books and had some discussions about what kinds of animals we would see at the vet's office. Some of the children thought that we would see monkeys, zebras, cows, and pigs. We made our beginning web and prepared interview questions for the vet. On During the actual field experience, the children were divided into two groups. Those children most interested and involved in the project were responsible for graphing certain aspects of the clinic, recording answers to their questions, and sketching parts of the clinic. The expert, Dr. Marge, took the children through a typical exam and the children manipulated lots many of the vet tools. After we returned to the classroom, the children began to make plans to construct their own vet clinic. They used their field sketches and photographs taken on the field experience to construct it, using boxes and the various scrounge items that parents brought into the classroom. The small group of children building the clinic were very concerned with making the clinic look as close to the one they had visited as possible, and they had to solve problems in the construction of key pieces of the clinic. This same group also visited the high school art class, where the art students encouraged them to model with clay and represent the animals they saw at the vet clinic.
</td>
</tr>
<tr>
<td>Phase III</td>
<td>

Concluding the Project

As the month of May approached, the dramatic play that had been so intense a few weeks earlier began to wane. I gathered the project group together, and they decided to take down the vet clinic. We made another web and found that they knew a lot more "vet words" now and could tell anyone the important parts in a vet clinic and why they were needed. We made a list of their ideas about sharing their learning with their parents and the ECE class next door. The group decided to make a book,. They and then made a list of important things they wanted included in the book. They collected the displayed drawings and graphs from the walls for processing into the vet book.
</td>
</tr>
</table>

dren conducted with Pam Scranton (see Figure 1.4). This summary provides an overview of one project's progress.

Teachers are frequently awed and incredulous at the stories of problem solving and the examples of observational drawing and early literacy skills that are collected by teachers who document the progress of a project. They are afraid that they will not know how to recognize and take advantage of the opportunities for problem solving, literacy development, and social–emotional experiences that are so beneficial to the young child's development. Some teachers also fear that doing projects with children means relinquishing control of the educational program to the children or that their classrooms will become chaotic.

The structure of the project approach, as defined by Katz and Chard (2000), can be used to guide the process and to reduce many of these teacher concerns. The structure consists of three distinct phases (see Figure 1.5). During these phases the teacher evaluates the suitability of a topic, anticipates needed resources, plans field experiences, and identifies experts who can be brought into the classroom for interviews and demonstrations. Documentation throughout the project helps the teacher recognize opportunities for problem solving and the application of concepts and skills so that good learning opportunities are not missed.

The project approach provides a structure but not a prescription for learning experiences. There is a fine line

FIGURE 1.5 • Phases of a project

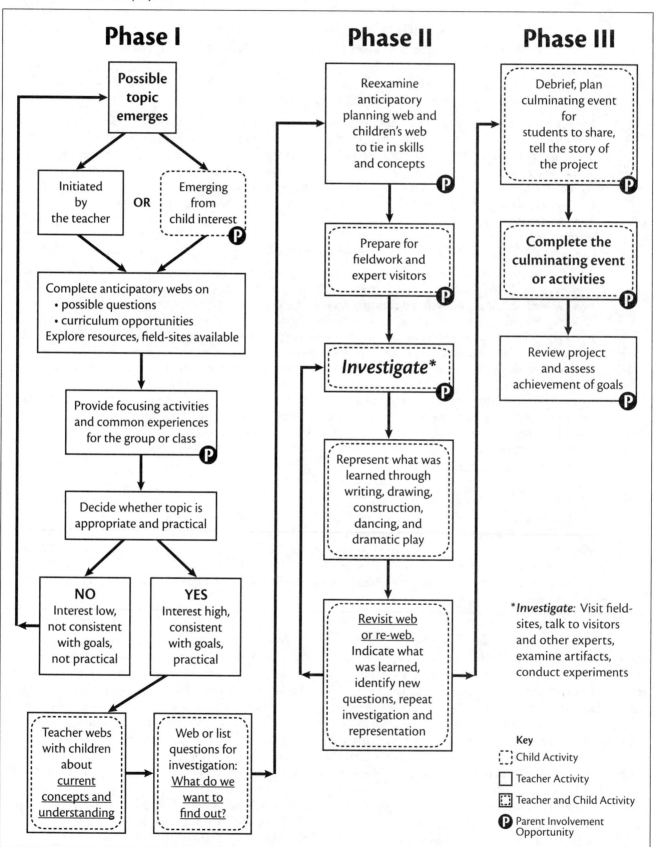

between supporting children's investigation and teacher-directed inquiry—between supporting children's learning and taking over the learning experience. One of the most challenging tasks in teaching young children is to learn how to recognize that line and avoid crossing it. The structure of the project approach can help teachers learn to do this. In learning how to implement the project approach, the teacher learns how to support and not crush children's curiosity and natural dispositions to learn, and yet still achieve curriculum goals. "Approach" can be defined as "a way or means of reaching something," "an entry" (*The American Heritage Dictionary*, 1992). The project approach can be an entry, a way for teachers to reach their goal of supporting active, engaged, meaningful learning and intellectual development. For some teachers, it can be an entrance into teaching in a more effective, child-responsive way. It is important to remember, however, that an entryway is never the end destination and that the structure of the project approach is a guide to supporting children's learning, not the end result.

Organization of This Book

As the structure of the project approach provides a guide for supporting children's projects, this book provides a guide for teachers to learn how to do projects. Chapters 2 through 5 explain the phases of the project approach in detail, focusing particularly on how these phases look in childcare and education programs for young children from toddlers through first-graders. Step-by-step explanations of the phases are accompanied by illustrations and children's work from actual projects. Chapter 5 also presents a variety of methods of documentation and a framework for evaluating the project and extending and expanding the approach in future projects.

Chapter 6 is a detailed description of the Camera Project, which was carried out in a prekindergarten classroom, and Chapter 7 presents the Fire Hydrant Project from a toddler classroom.

Chapter 8 addresses the issue of using the project approach to meet required curriculum goals or academic standards. It also addresses how early literacy experiences and other academic skills can be strengthened during project work. A number of other issues that teachers often want to discuss are also presented. These include involving parents, employing technology, and using the project approach with specific populations, including children with special needs and second-language learners. The chapter also presents ways in which administrators can support project work.

At the end of the book is the Project Planning Journal, which teachers may copy and use in guiding young investigators. Originally designed to support teachers doing their first project with young children, the journal became a preferred way to plan and organize for project work by many experienced teachers. It became, in subsequent projects, a journal in which the teachers could record the progress of the project and their thoughts, as well as note documentation that had been collected. This journal was used by teachers in a number of the projects described in this book. Readers will find references to specific parts of the journal as they read about the project approach in Chapters 2 through 7.

Using the journal, however, is not a requirement for undertaking the project approach. There is no workbook for doing a project with young children. The journal and the projects described in this book are offered to support teachers as they learn to follow the interests of their children in implementing the project approach. Although different groups of young children may be interested in similar topics and may engage in similar project activities, the course of projects is never the same. Authentic projects such as these cannot and should not be duplicated.

Learning to do projects is a journey, one that we have been privileged to share with the teachers represented in this book. The journey appears to be never-ending, and teachers of young investigators appear never to stop learning from children how they can do it better. The sharing of the journey begins in Chapter 2: Getting Started.

CHAPTER 2

· · ·

Getting Started

LAUNCHING THE PROJECT is referred to as Phase I, Getting Started. During this phase the topic of the investigation is selected through a process of discussion with the children and the teacher's provocations concerning possible subtopics. The teacher also evaluates the feasibility of the topic in terms of local resources and opportunities for the children to have first-hand experiences related to the topic. During Phase I, the teacher creates a topic web that helps to anticipate possible directions the investigation can take and ways it can relate to the local curriculum requirements and district standards. The teacher also assesses the availability of resources, potential expert visitors, and field-sites to be visited.

Once the teacher and children are clear about the topic of the project, the teacher involves the children in discussion concerning their own experiences and understandings related to the topic. With the teacher's support, the children generate their own topic web to be used as a basis for the investigation. Based on these discussions and the children's topic web, the young investigators, with guidance of their teacher, generate a list of questions their investigations will try to answer. As the development of the questions for investigation comes to a close, the project moves into Phase II, Investigation. The flowchart of Phase I is a graphic representation of the progress of the project during the beginning phase (see Figure 2.1).

ISSUES IN SELECTING TOPICS
FOR PROJECTS

One of the most important features of Phase I of project development is the process of selecting the topic to be investigated. There are a number of issues that deserve consideration in the processes of topic selection.

Common Experiences

The nature of the topic young children investigate influences substantially what can be accomplished in the proj-

ect. Compared with older, primary school children, preschoolers and kindergarteners have as yet a small range of experiences on which to base a project. Very often, younger children are less likely to have common experiences to which all members within a class can relate. In general, teachers implementing the project approach with young children spend more time and effort providing a basis of common experiences and eliciting their interest and curiosity than is required of teachers of older children.

When a group of young children is new to project work, having common experiences related to the topic increases the chances that each of them can contribute questions, suggestions, and ideas for how the investigation might proceed and what it should include. By way of example, we have worked with several kindergarten teachers who started project work with a study of the children's school bus, primarily because in their particular schools every child traveled on one, and thus could readily suggest many features of it to raise questions about and to examine more closely.

For some topics, the teacher can help to get a project launched by providing common experiences for the class. However, in such cases, because the teacher is making decisions about the first steps, there is a risk of making a project into another teacher-telling or teacher-directed experience. The central feature of a project, as we use the term, is that the children, in discussion and consultation with their teacher, take initiative, make decisions, and take major responsibility for what is accomplished. If the teacher overstructures the children's experiences, the project does not provide opportunities for the kinds of development and learning that come from child-initiated activities.

Determining Children's Interests

Project topics are most likely to elicit good responses from young children when the topics are either already among their interests or something that can engage their interests fairly readily. Thus, one of the teacher's tasks early in a project is to identify the young investigators' current and

FIGURE 2.1 • Flowchart of Phase I

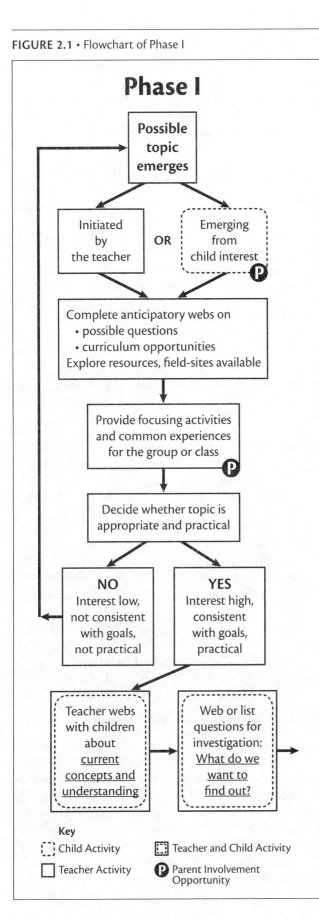

Phase I

Possible topic emerges

Initiated by the teacher **OR** Emerging from child interest ℗

Complete anticipatory webs on
• possible questions
• curriculum opportunities
Explore resources, field-sites available

Provide focusing activities and common experiences for the group or class ℗

Decide whether topic is appropriate and practical

NO
Interest low, not consistent with goals, not practical

YES
Interest high, consistent with goals, practical

Teacher webs with children about <u>current concepts and understanding</u>

Web or list questions for investigation: <u>What do we want to find out?</u>

Key
⌞⌝ Child Activity ⌞⌝ Teacher and Child Activity
☐ Teacher Activity ℗ Parent Involvement Opportunity

emerging interests as well as to consider what new interests they might just be ready to acquire. Teachers should not hesitate to encourage children to acquire new interests.

A few children may spontaneously express interest in a particular object (e.g., a backhoe being used outside the school for road repairs), an event (e.g., a classmate goes to the hospital), a particular place (e.g., a nearby restaurant), or a story or book about a topic. Young investigators may demonstrate this interest for the teacher by asking questions or requesting more information on the topic.

With the youngest children, many with limited verbal skills and vocabulary related to a topic, it helps if the teacher looks for expressions of interest through their behavior, perhaps by observing their spontaneous play. Three-year-olds often push forward for a closer look at an item that interests them. They often pick up items or hoard "souvenirs" of experiences such as objects collected on a class walk around the school. The very young child also signals interest by extending the typical length of time focusing on objects or listening to conversations. Young investigators who are interested in a particular topic, even though very young, often attend closely to what other children say on the subject as well as listen intently to the teacher reading a book about the topic or telling a story of a related event or phenomenon.

Child-Initiated Topics

Children often initiate their own projects. Sometimes the topic emerges out of an event that provokes their curiosity. Something happens and suddenly the class becomes immersed in a topic with intense interest and raises many questions for investigation. The event or experience that sparked the interest in a particular topic is called a *catalytic event*, something that causes a series of processes to begin. For example, construction of buildings commonly becomes the focus of a new project when such a construction begins near the school or childcare center and children can easily observe it from their playground or as they travel to and from school. One characteristic of a project that comes from a catalytic event is that it often moves into the investigation phase relatively quickly because the young investigators all have a common experience. An example of this is a Fire Truck Project, which began with the catalytic event of the children seeing a fire truck during a walk. Because the firefighters stopped and showed them the truck, all the children developed background knowledge. Progression to the investigation phase happened quickly.

In another school, a group of 4-year-olds became intensely interested in the experiences of a classmate who was anticipating a tonsillectomy. On learning of this impending event, the teacher made arrangements with the hospital for the class to have a guided tour especially designed for young children. The children's interest in the hospital grew and deepened into an extensive project that included exploring an ambulance brought to the school site. The children documented this experience by preparing drawings to use as a basis for building an ambulance of their own in the class. They examined the emergency equipment, interviewed the drivers, and conducted an intensive investigation of many more subtopics related to hospitals.

Teacher-Initiated Topics

A teacher may also choose a topic because it has the potential to provide beneficial experiences. For example, in the Car Project, which was documented by Sallee Beneke (director of the Illinois Valley Early Childhood Education Center) in *Rearview Mirror* (1998, 2004), the car was considered as a topic because one child, Taylor, showed an interest in machines. Up to that time, he had not engaged in a variety of classroom activities or participated in previous projects. Teacher-initiated topics work best with young children if they are broad enough to allow for a wide range of possible interests among all the children in the class. On the basis of her examination of the curriculum goals and what she had learned from her extensive previous teaching experience, Ms. Beneke decided that cars was a broad enough topic to be able to provide subtopics of potential interest to all of the children in her group. However, she also knew that it is difficult to predict with certainty whether children will respond with interest and enthusiasm to a given topic and thus wait to commit to the topic until she had observed the children's response to focusing activities.

Another example of a teacher-initiated project is the Real Estate Project that was conducted in Judy Cagle's multiage classroom. She initiated an investigation of the topic of houses when she discovered that a subdivision was under construction across the street from the school. She realized that the young investigators would have many opportunities to observe the development of the subdivision from the initial digging to the actual sale of the houses over a period of the entire school year. As the first phase of the project developed, she listened and watched for the young investigators' expressions of interest. Although the children began with drawing the site and the earth-moving equipment, they became very interested in the real estate signs and the process of selling the houses. Gradually the project came to focus on the buying and selling aspects of the subdivision's development, and it became an investigation into the development of a nearby real estate office.

Sometimes a project arises from a teacher-initiated unit or theme. An example of this was the Apple Project at the Hong Kong International School. The teacher, Mary Jane Elliott, typically begins school with a unit on apples. This unit led to further investigation of apples and the Apple Project. Although Ms. Elliott had initiated the topic, the in-depth investigation of apples was the children's idea. Projects often grow out of planned units or themes in this way. The Art Museum, another project in Judy Cagle's classroom of 3- and 4-year-olds, grew from a unit on Eric Carle, the author of several favorite children's books.

General Guidelines for Selecting Topics

Even with extensive experience in implementing project work, teachers are often surprised by how young investigators respond to a topic. Some projects that they expect to work well actually fail to engage the children, and others they were skeptical about seem to take off. Furthermore, teachers have reported that topics that are embraced enthusiastically by a group of preschoolers one year have been rejected by those in the class another year.

Although it is clear that topics of interest to the children should be the main focus of a project, it is also important to note that not all interests of children are equally worthy of the kind of time and effort involved in good project work. Katz and Chard (2000) provided the following topic-selection guidelines for planning projects for children of any age:

1. The investigation should help children understand their own experience and environment more fully and accurately. However, not all phenomena in children's experiences and environments are equally worthy of their attention and energy.
2. The topic should strengthen children's disposition to look closely at phenomena in their environments worthy of appreciation.
3. The topic should provide ample opportunity to employ a wide variety of interactive skills and dispositions during the investigation.
4. The topic should provide opportunity to develop insight into the functions and limitations of a variety of different media and to develop skillfulness in applying the various media to their work.

Practical Considerations in Topic Selection

Along with the guidelines for topic selection for children of all ages, there are practical considerations for topic selection for projects with young children. These considerations respond to the nature of how young children learn and the fact that generally young children have not yet mastered reading and writing. Because the success of a project with young children is so closely related to the appropriateness of the topic, the following additional topic criteria can be useful, especially for the first project undertakings:

1. *The topic should be more concrete than abstract and should involve an abundance of first-hand experiences with real objects that young investigators can interact with directly.* The ready availability of artifacts, objects, or items related to the project topic (e.g., a sling or stethoscope in a hospital project) enables young investigators to explore phenomena in ways that are most effective for them: touching, moving, carrying, modeling, hearing, tasting, manipulating, and looking at closely. When the topic itself is defined in concrete terms (such as "Fire Truck" rather than "Fire Fighting" or "Fire Safety"), young children can more easily generate specific questions for investigation.

2. *The topic should be easily related to young investigators' own prior experiences.* It is difficult for young investigators to think about topics for which they have little background experience or vocabulary. The topic "Boats" might be appropriate for young children who live around them and have some first-hand experience of them. Without such experience, the topic is unlikely to lead to the children taking initiative or to productive effort without substantial teacher direction.

3. *The topic should have related field-sites nearby that can be conveniently visited and revisited a number of times as the investigation proceeds.* Young children often have difficulty focusing on the topical issues when making a first site visit, and tend to benefit from returning to the site with new questions. As they progress in the project, they also develop a better understanding of how to use observational skills and of what they want to accomplish in the project. Studying the lawnmower that is used to mow the school lawn might be a better project than studying airplanes because the latter involves the complexities of a trip to the airport. When there is no possibility of revisiting a site, the teacher has to make plans to "capture the site" and bring it back for frequent revisiting— perhaps by means of videotaping the site visit and taking digital photos of important items observed.

4. *The topic should have aspects young children can investigate with minimal assistance from adults.* Investigations for young children consist of observing, manipulating, experimenting, asking questions, trying out ideas, and visiting sites. Young investigators are less likely to become deeply involved in the work when their role is passive and receptive rather than active, and when they have to rely on secondary sources such as books, videos, encyclopedias, or experiences of adults. Thus, historical topics are not likely to work well for projects for young children. Topics like "Pioneer Life" or "The Sinking of the Titanic" are not appropriate project topics for young children in that they necessarily depend upon secondary sources of information. The study of "Pioneers," however, might be an appropriate project topic for older children who can read, use encyclopedias and the Internet, and understand media presentations and extended timelines.

5. *The topic should allow young investigators to represent what they know and learn by using skills and techniques appropriate for their age.* In the process of selecting a topic, teachers may find it helpful to think about how information, concepts, and skills that have been learned can be represented in drawings, paintings, sculptures, or role-play events. It seems to be especially helpful for young investigators to become involved in creating large structures in which they can play. For example, a Fire Truck Project included building a fire truck out of a cardboard box. In principle, the younger the children involved in a project are, the more important it is that the topic has rich potential for dramatic play and construction. Mary Ann Gottlieb, kindergarten teacher, comments:

> I think the projects that allow us either to play in a dramatic sense, or create a functional object or place, such as the bakery, have more interest. This stands to reason because the children are actively involved on a daily basis. In the Hospital Project we made a hospital in the hallway, and it was a dramatic play situation for them. They were playing in that hospital. In the Bakery Project we actually made a bakery and sold baked goods, and in the Candle Project we actually made candles. This created a lot of interest.

6. *The topic should relate to the curriculum goals of the particular program or district, which leads to more support of the project by administrators and parents.* Many childcare centers and schools have specific curriculum guides that teachers are expected to follow. These guides designate objectives considered by the sponsoring agency to be worthy of learning. Curriculum guides can be a good source of broad topics for exploration. For example, a kindergarten teacher with the science objective "to understand what living things need to survive" might begin a search for a topic by exploring children's prior knowledge about plants or animals. Curriculum goals, especially those that relate to early literacy skills, emergent writing, number awareness, and scientific investigation, can be integrated into projects that are totally student-initiated. In fact, projects present many opportunities for young investigators to see the value of those skills and to apply and practice them in an authentic context. Mary Ann Gottlieb explains:

> Required curriculum fits naturally into projects. For example, take math, when you need to measure, you measure! In a previous project, the children

learned to measure. Today when we were reading a story about an elephant, it told how big the elephant was. I had a little girl jump up and get a ruler to measure how long an elephant's trunk would be. She learned to do that in projects. Depending on what your topic might be, you can use objects for sorting, classifying, and patterning. Any construction you make involves mathematics, and you as a teacher find that you can pull the math in when it is relevant—number recognition, one-to-one correspondence, measuring.

7. *The topic should be culturally relevant to the children and their families to encourage active engagement and in-depth learning.* The relatively restricted world of young children consists mainly of the family and their immediate environments—the home, the neighborhood, and the school or preschool center. Topics about these environments are more likely to capture children's interest because they have some prior knowledge of them. They are more likely to be interested in the pick-up truck that Daddy drives than the airplane they have never seen. If children are to become actively engaged, the topic must be one with which they have some familiarity.

For example, young children in Peoria, Illinois, seem particularly interested in construction equipment. One reason may be that many Peoria-area parents or neighbors are employed by Caterpillar, Inc., or Komatsu-Dresser, companies that build tractors, engines, trucks, and other products used in the heavy construction industry. As the children observe these massive machines in road building or on work sites, their parents point them out and discuss them. Interest in construction equipment is part of the culture of the central Illinois area and a popular project topic.

When the topic has local relevance, interactions between parents and children are more likely to occur. Parents then reinforce what is being learned in the center or school and can support children's dispositions to be curious and to find answers to their questions about the issues being investigated. In other words, parents can contribute significantly to a project if it is also relevant for them.

Reflecting on the practical considerations outlined above when selecting project topics increases the chances that teachers will identify topics that have the greatest probability of success with young children and, at the same time, contribute to meeting their curriculum requirements.

Reports of Successful Topics

Because the success of a project depends on the prior knowledge, environment, interest, and curiosity of the children, developing a list of recommended topics for young children is difficult. As discussed in the preceding sections, the issues in topic selection are so complex and the importance of children's interests and curiosity so vital that such a list might actually do more harm than good. Barb Gallick describes some of the projects that have been successful in her childcare program for a group of mixed age 3- through 5-year-olds.

During fall semester we did two projects: the Butterfly Garden and Building a Tree House. Both were based on events that occurred to the children in our center, and we scaffolded these into project topics.

We also began a project last spring on vehicles/forms of transportation, which the children turned into a project on a Monster Truck Parade. The children planned a parade from the beginning to completion, using monster truck toys they brought from home—other entries were allowed! This turned out quite well also.... So far this semester we have yet to find a common theme among our children's play or discussions. We are watching carefully, but two topic ideas that the teachers are tossing around are the pet store or pets and the post office.

It is just as difficult to identify inappropriate topics as appropriate ones. Although space travel might not at first seem like an appropriate topic, for a classroom near a shuttle launch area, it might be very appropriate, especially if many of the children's parents are employed in the space industry. In the process of selecting topics, it helps to be a good listener and to know your children, their families, their culture, and their interests.

Divergent Interests

In a class or group of children, the range of interests is likely to be very wide, adding one more challenge to the selection of project topics. Furthermore, the odds of all members of the group being equally interested in a given topic are very small. It is to be expected that some young investigators will participate and respond more eagerly to one topic than to another. Projects are occurring alongside many other activities in the classroom, such as block building, stories, dramatic play, and so forth. Young investigators will approach each project in different ways. Pam Scranton describes the approach of her 3-year-olds:

We may have some children who are not interested in a topic. I have learned that children, especially the 3-year-olds, might be drawn into the project later or they might not at all. They may be very involved, however, in the next project.

Even though some children may not contribute to the investigations, they are often interested in reports of the work others are doing and may learn much about the topic by observing their classmates as they build structures and discuss the progress of their project plans.

Teachers who are new to the project approach and who work with mixed-age groups sometimes think that the range of abilities and experiences of the children adds additional challenges to implementing project work. However, the combination of ages in the group enhances project work by providing contexts in which older children can initiate complex activities in which younger ones participate but could not have initiated by themselves. Older children can take the initiative in the investigation, and the teacher can encourage them to find appropriate roles for the younger ones and strengthen their own growing competencies by teaching their younger classmates what they are learning. Older children can provide many verbal and fine motor skills the younger ones are only just beginning to develop. In the case of mixed-age groups, the process of selecting project topics should include consideration of the different ways that children in the age range can become interested and involved in investigating the topic.

Some teachers are concerned that children with special needs or developmental delays may not be able to participate in projects. However, teachers of these children typically report that if they readily show marked interest in a particular topic, they can easily become engaged in project work. The teacher can make appropriate adaptations to ease their involvement in project work in the same way that he or she would for other classroom work for such children. This topic is discussed more fully in Chapter 8.

A special challenge for teachers of preschool and kindergarten children is that many are working in half-day or alternate-day class sessions. This can be particularly challenging if teachers have more than one class group in their classroom within a day. Teachers new to projects are often concerned that different topics would emerge from each group of children, putting the classroom and the teacher in the predicament of providing resources, work space, and

(text continues on page 22)

A CLOSER LOOK   • TOPICS THAT CONNECT CHILDREN WITH NATURE •

PROJECT TOPICS do not always have to be about nature or science; however, teachers may want to focus at least one project a year on a nature topic. If you have a classroom full of children who spend time outside with access to bugs and trees and other forms of nature, a topic will often emerge as children discover items and bring them in or tell stories about their experiences. By listening carefully to children's conversations, you can often detect a possible topic gaining momentum as a child shares something and interest grows among the other children. If you then spend some time building background knowledge about the topic with the children (see how in the Project Planning Journal at the end of the book), you can gauge the level of interest as they become engaged with the topic.

Some children, however, may have had few experiences with nature, may have spent little time outdoors, and may actually be fearful of the outside environment. In one classroom, the teacher reported that one of her prekindergarten boys was very afraid to step off the sidewalk onto the grass. Another child held his arms wrapped around his body the first few times the class walked in the woods. Fears may also emerge as children encounter such living things as insects, snakes, toads, or even some plants. If no project emerges through the life of the classroom and a child is unlikely to bring in something from home, the teacher may want to introduce a nature topic to the children.

Although many teachers believe that studying nature is an impossibility for their classroom because they are in a city location or have only blacktopped play spaces, there is almost always some nature in even the most urban environments. In our work training teachers in programs in downtown Chicago, we have become accustomed to teachers bringing in rich nature projects even from schools where field trips are limited. The teacher may find it helpful to survey the neighborhood around the school to look for possible topics. This is especially effective if other teachers also participate. Each teacher takes a notepad and walks in a different direction from the school or center. Ten minutes walking away from the school, then 10 minutes walking back, should yield a good list of possible nature topics. (Ten minutes represents the distance that the class can walk without losing too much time in travel, when investigating a topic.) If each teacher puts his or her list up and shares it with the group, everyone will benefit from the survey regardless of they direction they went.

The staff of one school in El Paso, Texas, did this walking survey, and a teacher discovered that just one block from the school, in a place where "gravel" yards were common, there was one lush and well-cared-for garden. She talked with the resident, who was an enthusiastic gardener and was interested in sharing his expertise with her children. Later she took the children on that same walk and let them "discover" the garden. Thus the Planting Project began.

Another technique for encouraging projects that connect children with nature is to increase opportunities for direct contact within the daily life of the classroom. A common method is to hang a bird-feeder near a window or to put out corn for squirrels. One classroom of 4-year-olds was having a grand time collecting nuts that fell from a tree overhanging their play area. They piled their "finds" into buckets and left them outside by a classroom window. They were shocked the next day to see that the squirrels were enjoying a work-free lunch. The children stretched out on their tummies and watched the squirrels through the low windows of the classroom. Seeing an opportunity to deepen observation, the teacher gave them clipboards, and they began to sketch. As they sketched the hungry visitors, they started to ask questions, and soon the teacher guided them into a discussion about what they knew. Before long the Squirrel Project was going strong.

When surveying an area for possible topics or taking a walk with children, be sure to look on the ground, even digging a little or turning over rocks, or give the children magnifying glasses to focus on the grass and the ground. Many successful projects have focused on earthworms and caterpillars as children discovered them in their natural habitat. Studying something much smaller than they are is a great way for young children to grow comfortable touching, looking closely, and thinking about animals.

Getting a classroom pet or adding an aquarium to your classroom is another way to increase interest in nature, especially if access to the out-of-doors is limited because of location or safety. The whole process of choosing a pet, getting ready for it to come, then caring for it can be an authentic project and very meaningful for children. Remember, however, that successful implementation of the project approach requires that children take the lead and that their questions determine the direction of the project. It is still important to provide those experiences that we classify as Direct Contact. Children need to do the mucking about, planning, digging in, and documenting what they have learned. Buying an aquarium and having the children watch as you assemble it might be a beneficial experience for them, but it would not be a project.

These are some especially successful nature topics that we have observed:

- *Toddler:* Leaves (in the fall), water, worms, mud and sand, planting a seed, flowers, rocks
- *Prekindergarten:* Cats, rabbits, gardening, birds, meadow, stream, woods
- *Kindergarten and first grade:* Meadow, gully, pond, llamas (near the school), chickens, the river, trees, birds, park, pets

As we have often found, a good project can emerge from a thematic unit. For example, one teacher anticipated a project on apples after visiting an apple orchard. Instead, the children were very interested in the bees they saw there. This led to a lengthy in-depth study of bees, including a visit from a local beekeeper.

When looking at nature topics, or any topics, teachers may find the circular diagram by Bess-Gene Holt (1989) on *distance from self* to be very helpful. The more the learning experience is connected to the child's own immediate daily reality, the more successful it will be. The topics Now, Space, Shelter, Care, Food, and Warmth form a circle around the Child's Self. These topics are the reality of life for the very youngest investigators. Projects for toddlers that relate to these topics about their world, such as the flowers in their yard or the food they eat, are usually successful. As preschoolers grow and develop, the topics that work well for them expand, as does their world. Good preschooler topics would be in the next tier of words, such as Garden, Local Wildlife, or Trees. Kindergarten and first-grade topics are more successful if limited to the next tier, extending as far as the rectangular labels. Those topics that are on the outer ends of the labels or beyond the rectangular labels are less likely to be meaningful for young investigators. Doing a project on topics that are distant from the "self" of the children will result in the teacher doing a lot of the research. This diagram is especially helpful in choosing project topics because projects require a high level of engagement and the ability of the children to take control of their learning. As the higher tiers are reached, the only way young children can learn about them is vicariously through the interpretation of others. For example, Costa Rican rain forests and endangered species require the understanding of both time (years and history) and distance (far away places, regions, exotic objects). A better topic for prekindergarten children would be related to what is in

Bess-Gene Holt (1989, p. 119) produced this circular graphic to predict the physical, cognitive, social, emotional, and cultural distance of educational experiences from the child's immediate daily reality. This can be helpful for project topic selection.

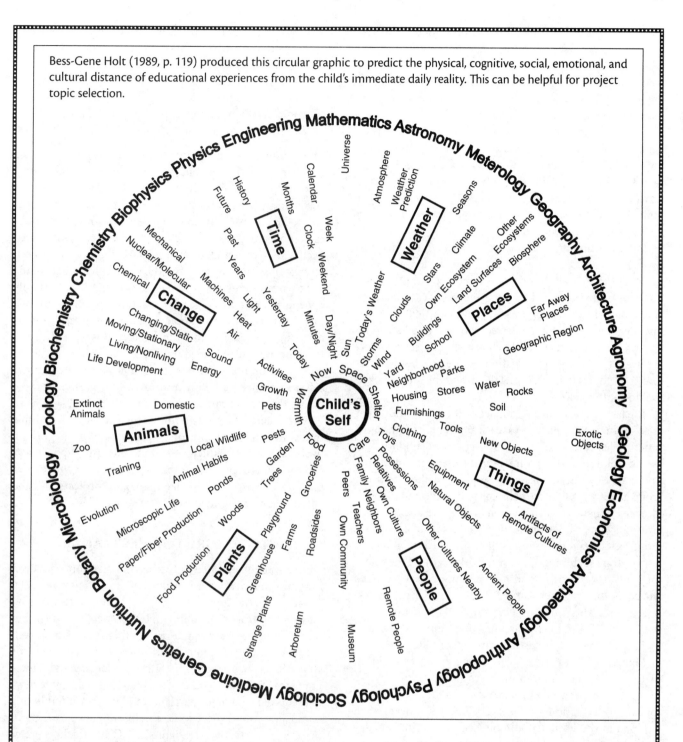

their yard or animals such as their pets. However, kindergarten and first-grade students would be more likely to be engaged in topics about parks, roadside habitats, local wildlife, and different animal habitats. There are, however, sometimes events or unique characteristics of a school or environment that make a particular topic closer to the self of the child than it might otherwise seem. An example is the Llama Project mentioned earlier. The llama farm was immediately adjacent to the children's playground, and the children were able to stand at the fence and interact with the llamas. This made a topic (exotic animals) relevant and meaningful for children. Likewise, teachers in a toddler program next to a wooded area should not hesitate to immerse the toddlers in that habitat on a frequent basis, creating an immediate relevancy for toddlers.

planning for two or more different project topics. Teachers who have two classes of children have found that projects can be successful by using a broad topic for all groups. By recording the young investigators' comments in developing the webs and lists of questions, the teacher looks for common interests and questions. The classes can share responsibility for conducting the investigations and finding the answers. When the projects move into construction, then the two classes can share responsibilities for particular parts of the construction. For example, in building a grocery store, one class constructed the checkout area and another built the meat department. Each group followed its own investigation of the subtopics.

Although finding a topic that would be meaningful to two separate classes seems like a difficult challenge, it often works out quite well. In one case, a morning kindergarten class was more interested than the afternoon class in a specific topic. The afternoon class agreed to participate in the investigation of the topic selected with the understanding that the next time they would choose the project topic. As it turned out, as the investigation progressed, both classes found subtopics that interested them, and the topic worked well for both sessions.

Teachers can also take advantage of the opportunity that arises from these challenges to teach and support communication skills. Several kinds of learning can be supported by asking children of one group, perhaps the morning group, to dictate or to draw messages or signs for the afternoon group about what they are planning to do next, and to solicit ideas from them. A teacher of a morning and an afternoon group of 4-year-olds found that when she debriefed the groups at the end of their sessions and asked them to dictate or draw such messages for the other group, they were thoughtful, respectful, and encouraging of each other's efforts. In this way they learned quickly to offer supportive suggestions. The young investigators had opportunities to use in a purposeful way the kinds of communicative and social skills that will serve them throughout life.

Many preschool teachers have one group of children three days a week and another group on the other two days. This creates an additional dilemma for selection of a topic or for even doing projects at all. Sallee Beneke, when working at the Early Childhood Center at Illinois Valley Community College, had children who attend part-time according to their parents' class schedules. Contrary to the expectation that project work would be more difficult or impossible in this kind of schedule, Ms. Beneke (1998) made the following comment:

> My view is that with this pattern of attendance, it is actually to the preschool teacher's advantage to engage in project work as opposed to short thematic units. Project work provides a tie that binds the group together. It provides continuity and coherence in a situation where children's experiences do not flow on a day-to-day basis as they might in a child care center setting where all attend full time. Children who had not been at our center for several days would arrive expecting to pitch right in on the continuing development of the car. (p. 19)

The consideration of a topic that would appeal to a large number of children would appear to be especially important in a program with this type of schedule.

There are two final cautions about topic selection. Teachers would be wise to avoid selecting a topic of intense interest to only one or two young investigators in a class. It often occurs that young children will have a particularly keen interest in something very specific with which others in the class have little or no experience. Although it is certainly appropriate to encourage some of those specific or unique interests in other ways, a topic should be of potential interest to a majority of children in a class if it is to be the basis for a meaningful extended project. However, the teacher of young children should not think that all children in the classroom must be highly motivated by a particular topic before the project can begin.

The final caution is to avoid being drawn into multiple topics in one classroom of children who are beginning projects. It is very difficult to simultaneously support several meaningful projects at this age level unless the teacher has had extensive experience managing projects and the children are accustomed to project work.

ANTICIPATORY TEACHER PLANNING

Once a student-initiated or teacher-initiated topic has been identified, teachers can continue the planning process by "trying out" the topic. One way to do this is to make an anticipatory teacher-planning web. This web helps a teacher think about the ways that a project might develop. A web may have a central topic focus and a variety of mini- or subtopics branching off of it. Some kindergarten and first-grade teachers like to do teacher-planning webs by reviewing required content or curriculum objectives and thinking about how the project topic might support growth and progress in each area (see Figure 2.2). Other teachers prefer to develop a teacher-planning web by focusing on the concepts inherent in the topic (see Figure 2.3). Still other teachers anticipate what questions the children might ask (see Figure 2.4). Some teachers put their thoughts on small Post-it® notes and arrange them several different ways, for example as a topic web, as a curriculum web, and as children's anticipated questions.

Inspecting these webs and reviewing the guidelines for selection of a topic discussed earlier in this chapter can help

FIGURE 2.2 • Teacher's anticipatory planning web with curriculum objectives (from Parker Early Education Center staff)

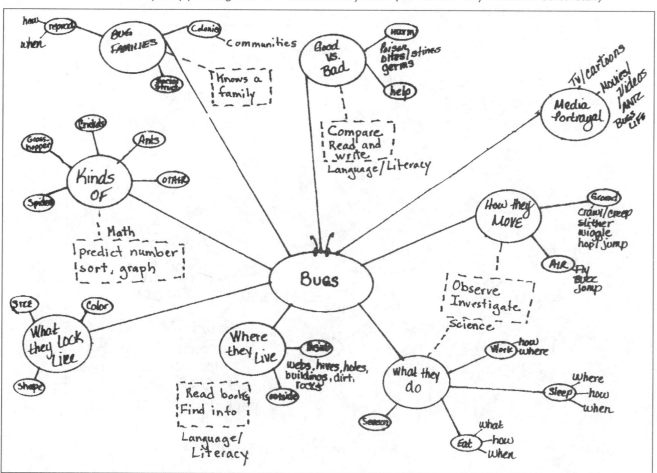

a teacher assess the potential benefits of a topic. Once a topic has been selected and the project moves into investigation, these webs can help a teacher predict directions in which the project might go and thus allow him or her prepare for lines of questioning and suggestions from the children. Ideas for possible integration and application of knowledge and skills also emerge from this anticipatory webbing. Although it is a lengthy process, "trying out the topic" and making anticipatory planning webs not only assist a teacher in evaluating the worthiness and practicality of a topic but also can help a teacher to integrate components of a curriculum.

During this anticipatory planning process of webbing and reflecting on required curriculum components, questions related to planning begin to emerge, for example:

- Are there experts that might be available to interact with the children?
- Are there relevant sites that might be visited?
- How might parents respond to the topic?
- How might parents participate in the project?

- How might young investigators represent the findings of their investigation and the learning that results from it?

The answers to these questions help the teacher assess the viability of the topic as a project. In addition, the teacher can use the planning web to help identify resources, such as books, that could be brought into the classroom to focus and enrich preliminary conversations and build common experiences.

BUILDING COMMON EXPERIENCES

If a topic is teacher-initiated, the teacher can use several strategies to provide a common background of experience for the young investigators to enrich their discussions and interactions before investigation begins. A teacher can tell a story of his or her own experiences related to the topic, and solicit similar stories from the children. An artifact, such as a piece of familiar equipment, might be shown to the children at group meeting time to provoke curiosity

FIGURE 2.3 • Teacher's anticipatory planning web with concepts about a topic
(from Little Friends Learning Center staff)

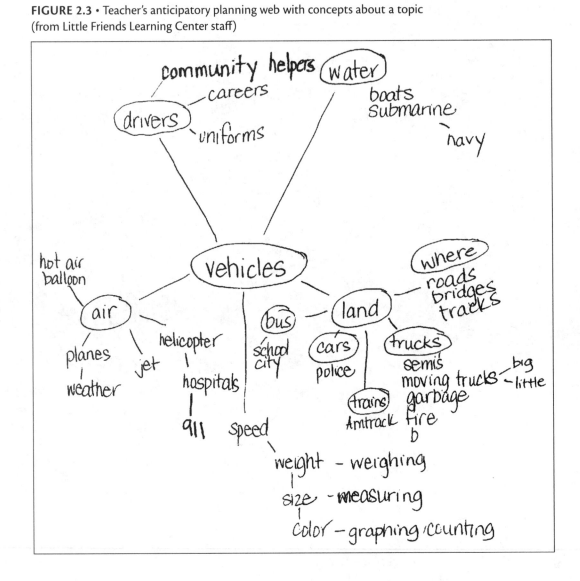

and discussion. A picture book can be read and discussed. Conversations between children about the topic can be encouraged.

Because young children can represent their experience and understanding through spontaneous play, teachers can begin a project by introducing props and costumes into a housekeeping or dramatic play area. As they use the artifacts in role-play, the young investigators represent and consolidate their understanding, and often exchange views related to the topic. Young investigators may also draw or paint what they know about a topic or build a block structure. It is important to build a shared perspective, a sense that a community is joined together to explore something of interest. Sharing and discussing these early explorations related to the topic help to build that shared perspective.

Pam Scranton describes her approach to the beginning of the Vet Project:

The Vet Project is a good example of a project in which children had a limited knowledge base. David came in upset because his kitty had to stay overnight at the vet's to get spayed. He was very interested in finding out about this, but other children didn't know what a veterinarian was. My children had limited experience with this topic, but I thought the topic had promise for being a good project. So we spent several days just getting to know about the topic. We went to the library and the librarian had a few books about vets. She also had a computer game, "I Want to be a Veterinarian," where they were able to see the animal

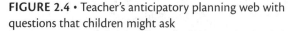

FIGURE 2.4 • Teacher's anticipatory planning web with questions that children might ask

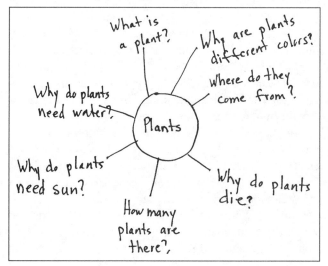

hospital on the screen. We just let them explore the library. Back in our classroom we started reading the vet books. There were books about large animal vets, small animal vets, terms, etc. We were just collecting information and building a knowledge base.

These types of activities are sometimes called "messing around with the topic." They build background knowledge, establish some basic vocabulary, and introduce some concepts about the topic. This provides a critical knowledge base for the young investigators to draw on and is most important for the very young child. This period also enables the teacher to observe the children's interest in the topic.

FINDING OUT WHAT CHILDREN ALREADY KNOW

Once the teacher determines that most of the children have developed some background on the topic, the teacher can find out about the experiences the children might have already had related to the topic, and what the children already know about it, in a more formal way. The teacher talks with the children and makes a graphic representation, such as a web, of what the children know. Graphic representations also contribute to the common knowledge base, enabling discussion and assisting young investigators in developing familiarity with the vocabulary of the topic. Everyone involved—the teacher, the children, and even their parents—becomes aware of the children's beginning knowledge of the topic.

Lists

There are many ways the young investigators' knowledge can be recorded or represented. The simplest way is to make a list of what the children know about the topic based on their comments in a class discussion. Even this level of response requires considerable help from the teacher for most 3-year-olds. When the teacher writes the comments that children make on chart paper, they see the written representation of their words and concepts.

Webs

Webs are graphic representations of the relationships between the children's comments or questions. Webs are similar to lists except that the items are represented as radiating from a central concept or idea. Sometimes teachers who are new to projects are hesitant to use webs because they think that young children cannot read words and do not understand the relationships represented by the connecting lines. However, experienced project teachers report that most young children seem to understand and respond to webs more readily than to lists. The process of having their words written down appears to be understandable to many 3-year-olds. Adding drawings or photos to the web assists the youngest children in connecting the written representation with their words and the words of the other children. Many 4-year-olds are actually able to explain the relationships between words when the teacher connects them on the web and often are also able to recognize the words. The key to success in making webs with young investigators is in the preparation and support given to the children during the first webbing experience and the care taken to be sure that children have enough prior knowledge of the topic to relate to the web in meaningful ways. Pam Scranton describes how she approaches webbing and listing with her mixed-age 3- and 4-year-old class in which children with special needs are included.

I feel that they have to be thinking about the topic quite a bit before we stare at that big blank piece of paper and start to web. Before we web, we always discuss the topic at least a couple of times. I will talk with children individually. I will even have a group discussion and ask questions such as "Where do you think we might want to go?" or "What might you want to see?"

I web with a small group of about 8 of those children most interested in the topic. I have never been able to web effectively with the whole class together. . . . I just use a big piece of paper, clip it to the easel and they just take off. Children grow in their ability to web. On the Fire Truck Project we had arrows going everywhere. With the same group in the Vet Project

FIGURE 2.5 • When the children in Pam Scranton's classroom were working on the Vet Project, they decided that their list of questions should be divided into large and small animals.

Small Animals
- "How come kitties got to get spaded?"
- "Do doggies got to get shots like kids do?"
- "Do they cry when they get a shot?"
- "Do you take care of squirrels? They're little."
- "How do you give medicine to doggies?"

Large Animals
- "How do you reach a horse to give it shots?"
- "How come horseys got to stand up all day?"
- "Can you give sheep their haircut? You know, take their wool off?"
- "How come cows go to the vet? Do they get sick too?"

that followed the Fire Truck Project, they classified the web according to large and small animals. They initiated it and told me where to write. They listed the large and small animals on the two sides of the list. "Well you better put that on the large animal side," said one of them! [See Figure 2.5.]

If they are younger or have never done projects before, you have to lead them a little bit—model for them. It is very easy for them to get off track telling stories. That is one reason that we have lots of discussions to provide opportunities to enjoy these earlier before we web. I ask them things like "What do you want to know about the vet?" "What's the thing you want to know about the most?"

In the Vet Project, I pulled out the books, and we looked at them again. That jogs their memory and reminds them of vocabulary. When looking at a picture of the operating room, one might ask "What do you want to know about in there?" Sometimes they just give me lists. Then they will get into questions. This is where I want them to go—to formulate questions for investigation. Sometimes the questions will just flow from the web, and I will put up another paper for listing questions, or I may do another web of what we want to know about. In the Vet Project, the questions flowed right from the web of what we wanted to know. "Will there be pills there?" "Why do the dogs have to be in cages?" "What happens if a squirrel gets sick?"

Most of the teachers with considerable project experience report a significant difference between the first webs of children and their subsequent webs on later projects. Where

young investigators are in a mixed-age group, the younger children appear to grasp the skill quickly from the more experienced children. It also appears that 3-year-olds who do not actually contribute to building a web also learn how to web. Teachers report that these same children may spontaneously contribute to webbing on the next project, sometimes even taking the lead. The key to webbing with young children appears to be spending enough time in advance accessing prior knowledge and helping children build a vocabulary for thinking about and interacting about the topic.

Sometimes teachers have difficulty keeping children's attention during a webbing process. This is especially a challenge when children are not yet reading. It is important to remember that the primary purpose of webbing is to get children's ideas and questions into writing. Although it is helpful for children to sound out their own words and watch the teacher model the writing process, this can be done at many other times during the day. During webbing for projects, the teacher wants to keep the pace brisk and keep children's ideas coming quickly. If they have to wait too long to offer their contribution, they sometimes forget. It is also helpful to do a web on an overhead projector. The smaller space enables the teacher to write quickly and children can still see the writing process and follow it. Children can also point on the screen where they want the word to appear as the teacher writes it. Young children also enjoy the use of Post-it® notes for webbing if they get to place their own notes on the web.

Webbing with kindergarten and first-grade children is easier than with prekindergarten children, especially if they have had prior experience doing projects. These older children are more able to focus on questions and to see relationships between concepts. Many of them enjoy thinking about how parts of topics are connected. The accessing of prior knowledge and extensive discussion before beginning webbing is not as vital to the outcome of the webbing as it is with the younger, less experienced children. For many kindergarten and first-grade children, putting a paper on the easel and asking for a list of questions will result in a good list of questions if the topic is appropriate and familiar to that group of children. The teacher can stretch the children's understanding of the topic and relationships between the subtopics in the way the webbing event is organized. Mary Ann Gottlieb reports how she experimented with her mixed-age 4- and 5-year-old class:

I tried something different this year. In the past I would web by putting the ideas up, and I would do the organizing—deciding where to write or how to connect the ideas, myself. Now I want them to see the connections between things on their own. As children gave me their ideas, I put one idea each on a Post-it® note. We then came back later, sometimes the next day, and the children organized these notes into a web. I also am trying webbing by writing the ideas radiating like sun rays around a circle containing the topic. Then I have the children come back at a later time and organize them. I am seeing that they can do it. They find the commonalities between the ideas, and group these together. Then they figure out what we can call that. We just have to work at it piece by piece.

Ms. Gottlieb also has found it helpful to collect these webs. She copies them onto 12" × 18" pages, which she keeps in spiral binder. This book of webs forms a history of the class's explorations over the year. The children can go back to, add to, or revise, recall, and discuss what they knew and how much they learned.

Dramatic Play

As we have already suggested, young investigators often show what they know through their play. A teacher may provide props that relate to a topic in a family living or play area. As children represent roles using the props, they show the depth of their knowledge of the topic as well as their understanding of the roles of adults regarding the topic. Often teachers of young children use props in a play area as a focusing device, and then watch to see what is revealed about children's prior knowledge.

An example of this strategy is the introduction of menus, order pads, napkins, placemats, and aprons into the housekeeping area in anticipation of a project on restaurants. As children choose to use the items, they show not only what they know about restaurants but also their interest in the topic. This is an especially effective technique to use with children who are not yet very verbal or who are learning a second language or for children with special needs who have language delays. The teacher can extend the opportunity for children to show what they know by participating in the play group. In this way, objects can be requested by name, and the teacher can give specific items to children to see how they are used and to take note of the vocabulary they have already mastered. This can all be done as part of the role-play activities.

Drawings

Asking children to draw what they remember about an event or a favorite part of their experiences related to a topic is often used with older children at this stage of project work and can work quite well with most kindergarteners and first-graders. Most children of preschool age are only just beginning to make sketches from observation. Young investigators who have been involved in multiple projects, however, are more likely to be able to do this, and their drawings will help focus their thoughts and provide the teacher with insight into their concepts about the topic. For example, a drawing of a turtle may consist of a circle with a small circle for a head and a smile on the face. The teacher can see that the child has very little understanding of what a real turtle's face might look like, how the mouth would function, or where the eyes and limbs are located.

Constructions

Young investigators also represent what they know through constructions. Often children will show their interest and also their beginning knowledge through spontaneously built block structures. For example, a small group of children consistently created construction sites in the block area and made blocks function as ground-moving equipment. These explorations can be encouraged by adding props related to the topic to the block area and also to the table toy area, where Legos or other construction materials are available. The art area is another area where structures may develop that provide insight into the children's knowledge of a topic.

Preserving First Representations

The first representations constitute the beginning items from which to build full documentation of a project. As young investigators explore a topic, they produce evidence of their knowledge, understandings, skills, and dispositions related to the topic. These should be carefully preserved because they can become excellent sources of documentation of the children's experiences from which their growth can be inferred. All of the webs, structures, drawings, and play experiences at this preliminary stage of the project will provide vital sources of evidence of the growth that has occurred over the course of the project, as later webs, structures, drawings, and play experiences are collected. For these reasons it is important for teachers to label and date the products of children's work. Documentation is discussed in greater detail in Chapter 5.

DEVELOPING QUESTIONS FOR INVESTIGATION

As the teacher documents beginning knowledge about the topic, he or she will also begin to get an idea of what the young investigators do not know and what they would like to know. With older 4-year-olds and 5- to 6-year-olds, questions often come quickly and naturally, and the teacher begins a list of questions that serves as the basis of the investigation. With younger children, however, asking what the child would want to know often results in the telling of a story instead. As Pam Scranton described above, the

FIGURE 2.6 • A teacher can provide more focus to the study of a topic and challenge children's thinking by asking them not only to come up with questions but also to predict answers.

Questions	Predictions	Findings
How many kinds of cereal are in the supermarket?	10 30 100	126
How many different magazines are in the supermarket?	25 100	142

teacher can help the youngest investigators develop questions by carefully tuning in to a child's interest and framing some of the children's thoughts into questions.

• "Is that something you would like to know about?"
• "Would you like to know how to use that?"
• "I am wondering about . . . ? What do you think?"

Sometimes the teacher may deliberately provoke thought by introducing an artifact and discussing it with the children.

• "What do you suppose this is for?"
• "How do you think this might fit with this?"

As suggested earlier, it is usually easier to stimulate the formulation of the research questions by asking the young investigators what they would like to know more about, or find out about. For example, in anticipation of the visit of an expert, the teacher can more easily get the children to generate a list of questions by asking them what they would like the visitor to talk about, tell them about, say more about, or show them. This way children might state what they want to know, and the teacher can convert their responses into a list of questions.

One way to strengthen the focus of a project is for the teacher to help the children generate a question table such as the one illustrated in Figure 2.6. When individual children offer their predictions, and if the prediction seems reasonable, it is a good idea to ask the child, "What makes you think so?" Some children will respond by saying, "I don't know." Some might say, "My Dad told me." But one or two might come up with a reasonable basis for their predictions. With this follow-up question, the teacher supports the development of the disposition to be aware and to examine the basis for their opinions.

When conducting projects with preschool children, it does not usually work well to ask them "What are your questions?" However, teachers are more likely to get them by asking "What would you like to find out?" (e.g., about the supermarket), or perhaps a question like "When the manager comes to visit us, what do you want him (or her) to tell you about?" This way children might state what they want to know, and the teacher can convert their responses into a list of questions.

It is important to view the first list of questions as a beginning for the investigation process. The list may be replaced with an entirely new list as new facets of the topic capture interest and arouse questions, and the questions expressed earlier in the discussion may dwindle as answers are found.

SETTING UP THE CLASSROOM FOR INVESTIGATION

Most prekindergarten and kindergarten classrooms have a block area, an art area with easels, a family living or dramatic play corner, a meeting area, and equipment for sensory and science exploration such as sand, water, or light tables. All of these are natural locations for project work. First-grade classrooms vary greatly in the amount of available space. For all age levels, a table or several shelves can be set aside to display artifacts, books, and other resources about the topic. Bulletin board space can be used to display webs, ongoing project word lists, photographs, and children's work. Because projects at the preschool and kindergarten level often result in some type of construction, it is helpful to have a large space where the project can be left undisturbed when other activities are occurring in the classroom. This encourages young investigators to come back and reflect on their work and add more detail.

Sometimes teachers replace an established area of the room with the project construction. For example, the block area can be used to build the farm, and the family living area can be transformed into the restaurant. Deciding where to place a construction and how best to make room for it in the classroom are part of the problem-solving process, and children can participate by contributing ideas and arriving at a solution. Sometimes a hallway or common space such as a multipurpose room can be used for projects. Some projects result in a number of smaller constructions such as clay sculptures. These can be stored in large plastic boxes with lids. These boxes for temporary storage are also helpful when there are two groups of children sharing the same classroom.

Gathering Equipment and Supplies

Some materials and equipment are especially useful when doing projects with young children regardless of the particular topic selected. These include construction materials, art materials, and literacy-related materials. Even though most preschool children are not yet reading, books can be an important resource for projects. Picture books related to the topics are helpful, but books for older school-age children can also be informative if they have photos, drawings, or diagrams. Realistic books are better than fantasy books for projects with young investigators. Fantasy books (such as *The Very Hungry Caterpillar,* Carle, 1984) can provide misinformation and are better saved for enjoyment at the end of the project.

In addition, there are some materials that all children in the group should have when they work on projects. Clipboards with pencils attached often become prized possessions of young investigators. Because clipboards are normally used by adults rather than by children, they signal to the children the importance of the project work. For young investigators, pencils are often attached by string and then placed under the clip when carrying the board. A laundry basket or other large tote with handles is convenient for stacking clipboards and transporting them to the field-site. Individual journals are also helpful for writing and sketching about a project topic or classroom experiences. As constructions develop, individual children may become "experts" or "researchers" on a particular aspect of the project. For example, during the Fire Truck Project, Jordan became the "ladder person" and spent several days studying and constructing ladders. Individual storage space for a child's particular exploration of a topic encourages the child to come back to the project the next day and perfect his or her work.

Projects and the Daily Schedule

There are several approaches to including project work in early childhood classrooms. Young children seem to benefit most from a schedule that is not segmented into short, discrete content areas, such as math time or reading time. Most early childhood teachers try to organize their day so that events flow smoothly without requiring abrupt shifts from one activity to another. A common way to arrange the schedule is to divide the day into blocks of time. It is important that children have at least 45–60 minutes for investigation and discovery. This time may be called choice time, free playtime, work time, or center time. Many early childhood classrooms use time blocks similar to the ones listed in Figure 2.7. This chart shows time blocks throughout the day, typical activities that occur within those time blocks, and how the project can be integrated into the class day without changing the schedule. Project activities may occur in only one or two of these time blocks or in many time blocks on any particular day.

Children Take Charge

Sometimes during the exploration of a topic, the project will take on a life of its own. Sometimes a topic is of high interest to the children, and unanticipated events occur that enable children to take charge and move the project. Here we recount the story of Natalya Fehr and her first project with 4- and 5-year-olds at Little Friends Learning Center. The class had been exploring the topic of vehicles. They explored transportation vehicles (cars, buses) and emergency vehicles, and then began to focus on heavy equipment such as trucks, combines, backhoe loaders, bulldozers, and cranes.

I tried to focus their minds towards a choice for a topic. They turned me a different way. One of the children said, "My dad works at Caterpillar so why don't we make his big machines?" Another child said, "I have special tools and my dad has a special T-shirt with the symbol of the company on it. What if I give this T-shirt to you and you will be our boss?" I realized that the children were leading me to a topic. I stopped talking, and they started talking about people who worked at Caterpillar. While I was talking, I could see the children fidgeting with excitement and their eyes sparkling. They agreed together that they would like to be workers and I could be their boss. Then one child said, "We have to have special rules for our work!" Then it was time for recess.

While we were outdoors, we saw construction going on a short distance away, and the children asked me if we could go closer. They were paying close attention to the tracks that the machine made in the dirt. They also pointed out the waist belts for tools that the workers wore and how they worked using their tools.

All of a sudden a big heavy machine came from behind a building and stopped between two houses. Right away he [the driver] proceeded to use the machine and dig. This was a perfect demonstration for the children. The children exclaimed, "It's a backhoe loader, a backhoe loader!" We watched this machine for about 20 minutes. . . . The children noticed a lot of details about this piece of equipment. The one child said, "What if we make this backhoe loader?" Another child said, "Let's draw a picture of it!"

Suddenly everything was out of my control, and the children were motivated as a team to start this project. I quickly went inside, and the children followed. They directed me to bring out paper and markers. I thought to myself, this is how a project starts. We went outside again. They worked on their drawings. One of the children said, "Can we draw a plan of who will do which things?"

FIGURE 2.7 • Scheduled time blocks and project activities

Typical Time Block	Project Activities That May Occur During the Time Block
Greetings Gathering Time	Viewing of displays on tables regarding topic Browsing of books or resources on rug Review and discussion of photos of previous work
Circle or Meeting Time	Exploration and discussion of new topics Sharing of group investigations Review of work Introduction of resources such as books or new artifacts Presentations by visiting experts
Work (or Center) Time (not less than 45 minutes)	Investigations by individuals or groups Meetings of small groups Opportunities for representation such as drawing, painting, or working with clay Creating play environments Construction and building of models
Review Time	Progress reports by groups Introduction of new ideas Sharing of representations Development of questions for further investigation
Outdoor Time	Project investigations and observations if relevant to topic Role-play related to project
Small-Group Activities	Focusing of small groups on project work Demonstration or practice of related content or skills Continuation of work begun in work time Adults sharing resources in small groups Presentations or demonstrations by experts Project activities needing more teacher guidance (detailed construction, modeling, review, and discussion with groups)
Story or Book Time	Sharing of expository books on project topic Sharing of project history books Sharing of storybooks that relate to the topic and are realistic Journal writing
Music Time	Sharing of music related to the topic
Language/Literacy or Math Workshop Time (first grade)	Introduction of content skills useful for project work such as graphing, charting, counting, measuring, problem-solving, reviewing and adding to the word wall, making items for communication needs of project (signs, invitations, brochures, thank you notes), writing in journals, writing narratives for displays and project history books

Each child was suggesting something, and I didn't have time to write all their words exactly. But I tried to get down on paper everything they said! One child said, "What will we name our team?" Another child said, "Yellow, Yellow" because this was the color of the backhoe loader. Another child said, "Well, the machine has symbols on it, and what if we use these also to name our team?" They decided between each other who would write the name. I helped David to spell the first part of *yellow* and then he had some problems, so Jessica helped to finish it. Then a third child wrote down the word *team* while the others helped him. Everyone on the team was excited to start on the project. I told them, "Tomorrow is another day." And that is how the project started.

Plate 1 shows Ms. Fehr working with the children on their plans for the project. The finished backhoe loader is shown in Plate 2.

THE NEXT PHASE

Once the topic for the project has been identified, the young investigators know what they want to know, and the room is prepared with materials and equipment, then the class is ready to move into the investigation phase, Phase II.

CHAPTER 3

. . .

Developing the Project

WITH THE FORMULATION of a set of initial questions to be answered by the investigation, the project moves into Phase II, which is discussed in this chapter and in Chapter 4. The main features of this phase are the young investigators' in-depth study of the topic, their efforts to seek answers to their questions, and identifying new questions.

BEGINNING PHASE II

As shown in Figure 3.1, the first part of Phase II begins with the teacher's review of the anticipatory planning webs and the children's web. Next, preparations are made for the investigative experiences and for collection of all kinds of data. A field-site is selected. The teacher shares with field-site personnel and expert visitors how children are learning through the project approach and the particular questions the young investigators are asking. Specific investigative skills such as asking questions, using construction tools such as staplers and tape, and observational drawing are introduced to the children, and they are given opportunities to practice these skills, if necessary.

Reviewing the Children's Web

Many teachers revisit the web or list of initial questions with the children a day or two after its completion. If the web and the list of questions are displayed in the classroom, they may spark additional thoughts as the children go about daily tasks. This happens frequently if the teacher occasionally reminds beginning readers as well as nonreaders of the content of the questions. For example, the teacher might draw a tire next to the question "How many tires are there?" Teachers also make webs more useful for young investigators by attaching photographs or photocopies of drawings to a question (see Figure 3.2). These graphic representations enable nonreaders and younger children to keep the topic in mind in the same way that readers use lists without graphics to recall information. A teacher may add graphic representations of the questions during preparation time,

and they are either discovered by the children or presented to the group by the teacher. Children 3 and 4 years old have been observed looking at the list of questions, adding clarification and details to graphics, and even adding more questions. For example, in a project on the school bus, the young investigators were interested in how the door opens when the driver pulls a lever next to his steering wheel. When the teachers sketched the door with the opening mechanism on the question list, one child went up to a drawing, took the marker, and then circled the lever by the steering wheel to show what interested him.

One purpose of revisiting and expanding questions is to encourage children to think in greater depth about the topic. Frequent revisiting of the list of questions throughout Phase II enables young investigators to ask more complex questions as their knowledge grows. However, teachers should not be surprised to find that young children often feel that the questions generated during Phase I are perfectly adequate for the progress of the project. When 3- and 4-year-olds revisit original questions at the beginning of Phase II, often there is no greater clarification or development of complexity of the questions. Revisiting the list of questions with these youngest investigators may still be valuable, however, if the discussion includes new information as the children discover it. Adding to the web helps young investigators understand that their knowledge about the topic is growing. This often brings new enthusiasm to the project topic. However, like everything else, revisiting the original questions can be overdone.

Revisiting the Anticipatory Planning Web

In addition to revisiting the children's web and list of questions at the beginning of Phase II, the teacher can revisit his or her own teacher instructional planning web, which was completed in Phase I. Once the teacher is satisfied that there is a good list of questions from the children and that the topic has adequate focus, planning can become more concrete. Some content and questions that the teacher predicted

FIGURE 3.1 • Flowchart of the first part of Phase II

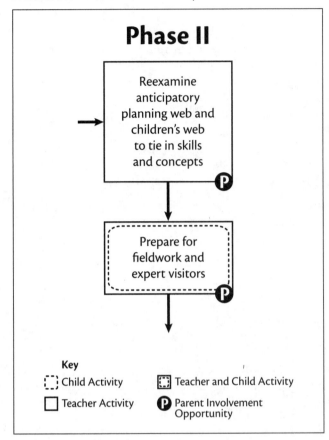

Phase II

Reexamine anticipatory planning web and children's web to tie in skills and concepts Ⓟ

↓

Prepare for fieldwork and expert visitors Ⓟ

↓

Key
⬚ Child Activity
☐ Teacher Activity
⬚ Teacher and Child Activity
Ⓟ Parent Involvement Opportunity

ful to take photos of the aisles, checkout areas, and aisle signs for later reference by the young investigators. As expected, creating a discount store in the classroom and playing in the store the children had created became a major part of the project.

Involving Parents

Although some parents may be involved in the project during Phase I, it is at the beginning of Phase II that parent involvement is best solicited. This is a good time to send a letter to parents announcing the project topic and describing the plans, including the list of questions that the young investigators are going to try to answer. The letter can also explain the source of interest in the topic and provide background information regarding the relationship of the topic to curriculum goals for the year. This is another benefit of the teacher anticipatory planning web. The teacher can share some of the content knowledge, skills, and dispositions that he or she now confidently anticipates will emerge from the project experience. When they begin their first project of the year, many of the teachers whose projects are described in this book share with parents the handout "How We Are Learning: An Introduction to the Project Approach," shown in Figure 3.4. It provides parents with a clear explanation of the project approach and will be meaningful to them at this time because their child is embarking on a project.

the children might want to know when the anticipatory web was created may now have become the focus of the project. Other concepts on the planning web may have become less important. Sometimes the children focus on a subtopic that the teacher had not anticipated at all. For example, one project began as an investigation of an ice cream store, but children's interests led them into an exploration of milk and where milk comes from. At this point, some teachers rework the anticipatory planning web either by circling the main focus on the web and using that as the center of planning or by redoing the web altogether if there has been a major unanticipated shift in the project. This process of movement of a topic from the center of the web, as shown in Figure 3.3, is often the turning point from thematic teaching to true project work.

As the teacher reviews the instructional planning web, it is also helpful to think about possible representations of the findings of the research. He or she might try anticipating whether the children might choose to make a play environment, a model, or a mural. In a project on a discount store, the Super Wal-Mart Project, the teacher anticipated that the young investigators might want to create a discount store in their classroom. To prepare for this possibility, she was care-

FIGURE 3.2 • List with graphic representation for nonreaders

Nathan
Do all sheep have tags?

Tyra
What do the sheep eat?

Bianca
Where do they live? Do they have a little house or something?

Ryan
Does it hurt to cut the wool?

FIGURE 3.3 • A teacher can maximize engagement by adjusting the topic focus to the aspect of the topic the children find most interesting.

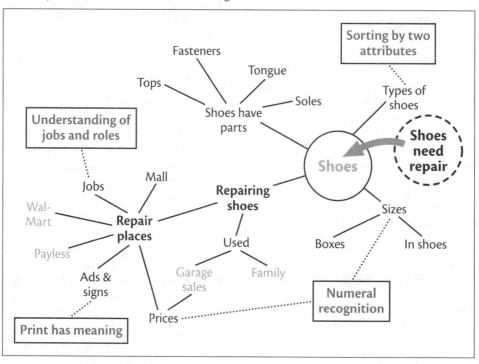

Source: J. H. Helm, "Got Standards? Don't Give Up on Engaged Learning!" *Young Children,* 63(July 2008), 18.

The beginning of Phase II is also a good time for the teacher to ask parents and others to contribute artifacts and resources for the children to study. Parents frequently will suggest experts or field-sites. Because questions have been clarified and the focus of the project is clear, communication to others at this time in the project can be productive. For example, parents who know that children are asking questions about what a turtle eats, where a turtle sleeps, and if a turtle has toys are unlikely to nominate a visiting expert on turtles whose focus might be beyond the young investigators' current understanding. They are more likely to think of the neighbor who has had a box turtle living in his garden for 25 years than of the college professor who studies extinct turtles. Parents can also more easily identify appropriate items or artifacts that would be most beneficial to share with the class. For instance, a parent may have a photo of a pet turtle she had as a child that she can share. Knowing what kinds of information the children are seeking, she might see that her knowledge could make a valuable contribution to the project.

It is also in Phase II that many opportunities arise to extend the learning about the topic at home. Communicating with parents about specific aspects of the project (e.g., the young investigators' questions and current understandings) encourages interactions about the topic between parents and children at home. New concepts about the turtle can become the topic of discussion at the dinner table. Through the discussion parents are then able to reinforce what is being learned and model their own dispositions to be curious and to find answers and solutions to problems.

The effect that knowledge of the project can have on family dynamics when a family is aware of and included in a project is clear in a story from a project about potatoes. Participating in that project was a preschool child who rarely contributed significantly to dinnertime conversations, which were dominated by her older siblings. One evening, however, as the older siblings reported on what they were learning at school, this child launched into a detailed discussion about what her class was learning in the All About Potatoes Project at Bing Nursery School, Stanford University, with teachers Jane Farish and Mark Mabry. Much to the amazement of the older siblings and the parents, the child had acquired substantial knowledge of types of potatoes—even beyond that of the adults at the table. The mother reported to the teacher that the dynamics of the family changed forever at that moment, and the young child, instead of being viewed as merely the baby of the family, was now listened to with respect. Many subsequent conversations about potatoes occurred, and the family actually experimented with eating different kinds of potatoes.

FIGURE 3.4 • This handout can be distributed to parents when the project begins and can also be used to inform experts and field- site personnel about project work.

How We Are Learning:
An Introduction to the Project Approach

What is the project approach?

The project approach is a method of teaching in which an in-depth study of a particular topic is conducted by a child or a group of children.

How is it different from others ways of learning?

Our children study one topic for a long time period. The topic is selected partly because they were interested in it and it is meaningful to them and their lives. The children will go into great depth and often at a level higher than many adults would expect for this. The teacher integrates content knowledge like math, reading, and science into the project.

How is a project planned?

The children make many of their own plans with the teacher's help. Plans usually include an on- site visit and/or inter-views with experts. An expert is anyone who knows a great deal about the topic of study.

How will children learn?

Children use a variety of resources to find answers to their questions. These include traditional resources like books. They also conduct in-depth investigations on site visits. The children plan questions for interviews and have assigned tasks for trips or for interviewing experts. They make field notes and draw or write on site. They make plans for building structures and play environments that will help them sort out what they are learning about the topic.
Children do their own problem solving with the teacher structuring problems and assisting in finding solutions and resources. Children will redraw and rewrite as their knowledge grows. Some of the ways that they will record their learning are project books, posters, murals, artwork, graphs, charts, constructions, and journals.

How does the teacher know if children are learning?

The teacher collects children's work, observes what they do, and analyzes their work. This is called documentation. The curriculum goals of the school or center are reviewed and documentation is planned to be sure that children are learning concepts and skills specified in the goals. Often a display will be prepared that shows what students are learning.
Is this the only way these children are learning?
   The project approach is one way among a variety of ways that children learn. The project integrates much of the same knowledge and skills presented in more formal ways in the classroom. Projects have the added advantage of providing an opportunity for children to apply and use what they are learning as they solve problems and share what they know. It provides opportunities for developing group skills such as working with others and challenges children to think, which supports brain development.

How can others help with projects?

Realize that children have their own questions and are learning to use you and many resources to find answers. Take their questions seriously, and listen to what they have to say. Provide space and opportunities for them to draw or pho-tograph what they are studying. Children learn best when many senses are involved, so anything that they can touch, see up close, or hear is helpful. Things that can be borrowed for study in the classroom are valued and appreciated, especially parts of machines, tools, samples of products, and so forth. We hope you will follow up, view our documenta-tion, and find out how children have processed what they have learned.

A CLOSER LOOK   • BUILDING YOUR CONFIDENCE ABOUT NATURE TOPICS •

SOMETIMES TEACHERS HESITATE to do a project on nature because they may not have had many experiences with nature as they were growing up. In the process of training and coaching on the project approach, we have often heard teachers bemoan interest of their children in such topics as worms or snakes. Young children are highly motivated to learn science concepts in the early years and have the foundational skills (observing, questioning, and experimenting) for science study. Teachers of early years, especially those in preschool, are not as prepared to teach science as they are literacy, according to a briefing report of National Institute for Early Education Research (Brenneman, Stevenson-Boyd, & Frede, 2009).

> Despite the existence of learning standards and increased curricular attention to mathematics and science, they tend not to be emphasized by teacher preparation or in-service professional development programs and evidence suggests that preschool educators tend not to support mathematics and science learning. (p. 1)

Think about this example: A teacher who was enthusiastically implementing the project approach for the first time followed a child's interest in the different kinds of pets of children in the classroom. The children then did some interviews of adults about their pets. As the project proceeded, the children eventually determined that what they wanted to really know about was a pet snake. Suddenly her enthusiasm dropped, and she wailed to her colleagues, "I can't do snakes! I know absolutely nothing about snakes! I am just going to tell them they are not allowed to study snakes!" Fortunately her colleagues discouraged that and supported her project work. Soon the Herpetological Association was bringing a variety of snakes into her classroom. The children had many questions and became not only appreciative of these animals but also quite knowledgeable. The teacher, as a co-learner with her children, not only learned from their questions and explorations but also asked her own questions, and her enthusiasm for project work returned. A few months after the project had ended, the teacher surprised the students by adding something special to their classroom—a pet snake!

Teachers are beginning to understand that connection with nature is important for children. Most teachers already understand that they are role models for intellectual curiosity, values, and attitudes. If we want our children to be adventurous learners, we will need to be adventurous also. There are some things that may be helpful when you encounter a topic that you feel that you know little about.

This kindergarten teacher has worked hard to become comfortable with a variety of animals in her classroom and share the interest and joy in connecting with nature with her children.

1. *Do your research.* Even just an hour on the Internet researching an animal or plant will provide an enormous amount of background knowledge for your preplanning.
2. *Hit the bookstore or library!* Instead of just looking for children's books on the topic, browse coffee table books, and look in the adult informational book section. You don't have to spend an extensive amount of time studying

advanced books, but simply flipping through a book and looking at the index and photos will give you an idea of the structure of content about the topic and still enable you to be a co-learner with your students.

3. *Be very conscientious about doing your teacher's anticipatory planning web, and revisit it frequently during the project process.* This will enable you to incorporate more curriculum goals as your understanding of the topic grows.

4. *Bring in lots of experts.* Work hard to find good experts for the topic, and rely on their knowledge. Follow the guidelines in the Project Planning Journal for preparing experts, but also give them an opportunity to tell you what they think the children should know or what they think would be a good activity or experience.

5. *Don't hesitate to directly teach more difficult concepts.* As rich science and nature topics become part of your classroom, you will find there are concepts and ideas that benefit from direct instruction. For example, it is very helpful in studying insects or certain animals to talk about the concept of life cycles.

6. *Emphasize vocabulary and classification.* Learning the names of living things and items in nature enhances interest and builds confidence not only for you as a teacher but for your children. For example, children will take pride in learning the names of birds or the parts of an insect. Understanding how attributes enable classification builds a strong foundation for later study.

7. *Don't miss the awe and beauty.* Take time for appreciation. One of the benefits of nature topics is an increase in appreciation of the beauty and order of the natural world. This is what will lead to stewardship of our natural environment. There are many things that can be learned when you suspend other activities in the classroom and sit quietly together to watch a chick hatch. Sitting in the woods, absolutely still, lets you hear the birds, the wind, the chirping of squirrels. There is more than a lot to be learned from that experience. There is also a lot of joy, especially when you share it with children.

PREPARING FOR INVESTIGATION

Selecting a Field-Site

Phase II is also the time for the teacher to begin the process of carefully evaluating possible field-sites. *Field-site visits* for projects differ from typical or traditional field trips in certain ways. Traditional *field trips* are usually taken at the end of a thematic unit, enabling children to see first-hand what they have studied. Traditional field trips also tend to have a broader focus than project fieldwork does. Children may visit the zoo, seeing as much of it as possible in the amount of time available. The agenda for many traditional field trips is planned by the hosts of the facilities visited. For example, a fast-food restaurant might have a standard field trip agenda that they offer to early childhood programs or school groups. The term *field trip* can also refer to simpler, less-focused experiences such as taking a walk around the block. All of these types of excursions outside the classroom can be valuable experiences for young children. However, they differ from the field-site visits that are part of the project approach.

Experiences in the field during project work—*field-site visits*—are specifically designed for the conduct of fieldwork. It is the part of a project that provides children with an opportunity to investigate the field-site and to become engaged in thinking in real depth about the topic. During fieldwork, young investigators attempt to find answers to their own specific questions. They closely examine the field-site and the equipment and materials they find there. They interview people at the site. Young investigators play an active role in capturing the experience through sketching, photographing, or videotaping, so that they may examine and reexamine these records later. They also borrow artifacts to take back to the classroom for further investigation (see Figure 3.5). This kind of field experience requires careful preparation by the teacher. The preparation for the field experience is so important that the success of the venture is often determined before the young investigators take the first step out of the classroom. In addition to the teacher's preparation for the experience, children also are included in the planning.

Before the field experience is launched, the teacher helps the children to become clear about which of them will take responsibility for which questions to ask at the site, and who will be responsible for sketching which items, collecting which artifacts, and so forth. One of the teacher's roles during fieldwork is to remind the children of their responsibilities and then to support the young investigators' efforts fully.

With very young investigators it is most helpful to select a field-site that will be easy to visit and that will enable multiple visits. That is why field-site possibilities should be considered in the process of selecting the project topic, as explained in Chapter 2. Because young children are often awed by the experience of going as a group to a different location, they may have difficulty focusing on the project topic. Many teachers have had the experience of planning a field trip with young children only to find on return that

FIGURE 3.5 • This is a loom that was borrowed by Jolyn Blank's class at University Primary School as part of the Clothing Project. Complex items that encourage discussion and investigation are often loaned to classrooms by visiting experts and field-site personnel.

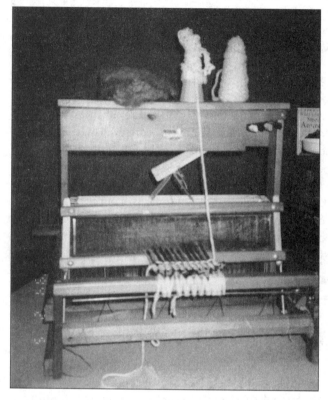

the most memorable part of the experience for the child was the bus ride. Field-sites that are close enough to the school or center to enable multiple visits have many advantages for projects for young children. If multiple visits are not possible, the teacher will find it helpful to consider seriously how he or she might capture the field-site to bring it back to the classroom with photographs (both digital and print) and through video- or audiotape recordings. We observed the use of photographic slides for this purpose during visits to the schools of Reggio Emilia.

Some teachers who have successfully used the project approach with young children believe that it is essential to make a preliminary first visit to the field-site without the children. One teacher planned a trip to a radio station without a preliminary visit. When she arrived with her class, she discovered that the studio was not large enough for more than a few children at a time, making it extremely difficult for the children to explore, sketch, or spend adequate time looking at the equipment. If a preliminary visit is not possible, the teacher will find it very beneficial to set aside time for an extensive phone conversation with site personnel. An advance visit to the site or extended phone inquiries should

provide the teacher with a realistic sense of the potential benefits of the children's visit to the site. In evaluating the site, the teacher should consider the following questions:

Safety

- Is the site safe for young children to visit?
- Will it be difficult to monitor the children as they explore the site?
- Will it be possible to shelter children from traffic, machinery, open water, or other dangers?

Investigation

- Are there areas, processes, or equipment that children can investigate on their own, instead of just hearing someone talk about them?
- Can they climb on, get in, look through, pull, push, lift, press buttons, or make noise at the site?
- Are there any tools, machinery, vehicles, or processes that might capture children's interest and stimulate their curiosity?

Concrete Objects

- Does this site have concrete objects with which children can interact? Are there things that can be touched, moved, tasted, smelled, or heard?
- Are there objects that can be sketched or studied closely by a small group of children?

Experts

- Will there be a host or hostess who can serve as an expert and answer children's questions?
- Is there someone on the staff who has children or grandchildren of a similar age or who has experience with young children to be that expert?

Artifacts

- Are there any artifacts (tools, equipment, products, and so forth) that can be borrowed and brought back to the classroom for further investigation?

By asking these questions in the preliminary phone call or visit, the teacher begins to form an understanding of the value of the field-site for the children's project.

Preparing Site Personnel

If the teacher has sufficient reason to believe that the field-site visit will be beneficial, he or she can then proceed with specific plans for the visit. This may occur in follow-up phone calls. A checklist for teachers to use as an outline for these phone calls or visits is provided in the Project Planning Journal found at the end of the book.

It is important to communicate with site personnel about how young children learn. The teacher will want to share the importance of child investigation and discuss how questions will come from the children. Teachers of young children find it helpful to provide an overview of what the children currently know and what they are interested in learning. Site personnel who are not accustomed to having visits from young children may have unrealistic ideas about what questions might be asked. Sometimes it is helpful if the expert who will be working with the children on site knows in advance the questions children will be asking, although this is not always necessary. Some experts are more comfortable responding naturally to children's questions. In this case, giving a few questions as examples can inform the site staff of what to expect, yet preserve the spontaneity of the answers to most of the children's questions.

It is also important in this discussion to share the importance of child investigation and the spirit of inquiry. One teacher has found the following phrases helpful:

Our children are learning how to
- Ask their own questions
- Use experts for resources
- Find out answers for themselves

The teacher will also want to share his or her belief in the importance of children's capturing the site and bringing it back to the classroom to study, especially if a return visit to the site is not possible. It is helpful for the site hosts to know how children will be recording what they learn. It is a good idea to tell the site host if you will be using audio or video recording or photographs and why they might be necessary. Some sites such as banks do not allow videotaping. It is also helpful if the site personnel know in advance that young investigators will be bringing clipboards and writing notes and sketching.

Many teachers find that asking on-site personnel about possible items or equipment that children might sketch is helpful. For example, a manager at a McDonald's restaurant suggested bringing out a French-fry basket and placing it on a table for the young investigators to examine and sketch. Another fast-food restaurant manager took the cover off the soda-dispensing machine so children could see the tubing inside the machine. A manager of a bank anticipated correctly that the young investigators would be very interested in the vacuum tubes for the drive-up teller. He made arrangements to have safety cones to close the lane so children could each experience using the tube and sitting in the lane to do field sketches. Once adults understand the level of the young investigators' knowledge and questions, they often begin to join in the spirit of inquiry and provide experiences for children that teachers are unlikely to think of on their own.

Brainstorming with the site host about artifacts to bring back to the classroom is also helpful. The teacher can ask advice about artifacts (tools, equipment, products) that

FIGURE 3.6 • When magazines, journals, and catalogs designed for adults and related to the topic are made available to young children, they often become the children's favorite reading materials. They are used for research and copying words.

might be borrowed and taken back to the classroom for further investigation. It is advisable to make a clear distinction between borrowing and giving the artifact to the class. Objects that a field-site host is willing to give to a group of young children are usually small and inexpensive and are not very complex or interesting to them. However, a field-site host will often loan expensive and complex equipment when they know it will be returned. Some artifacts loaned to classrooms for projects include

- A complete set of firefighter's protective clothing
- A bicycle (which the shop owner disassembled in the classroom with the children's help)
- The flashing warning light from the top of a school bus
- A mechanic's scooter used to work under cars
- Animals and their habitats (e.g., birds and snakes in cages)
- Publications unique to the topic (e.g., school bus magazines) (see Figure 3.6)

Another reason why it is a good idea to borrow items at the sites rather than receive them as gifts or donations is that many such items could present disposal problems for teachers once the project is over.

Preparing Visiting Experts

Phase II usually includes visits to the classroom by experts on aspects of the topic. These classroom visits may precede or follow the field-site visit. Often field-site visits result in additional questions for investigation. An expert can be invited to the class to answer these new questions. The same questioning and brainstorming process that is used to communicate with hosts of field-sites can be used with the visiting experts. Safety issues must also be considered with respect to any items experts might bring with them into the classroom. Such visitors will benefit from the same preliminary information concerning what children already know and what they want to know about a topic. A checklist of items for discussion for visiting experts is also included in the Project Planning Journal.

In Phase II of projects, support from a librarian becomes even more useful than earlier in the project. Even if the librarian had been contacted in Phase I while children were building background knowledge about the topic, he or she can be contacted for additional or more specific books again after the questions for investigation have been formulated. It is helpful to take the time to share with the librarian the list of questions that the young investigators have generated for investigation, as well as the class webs. In addition to the information that is shared with field-site hosts and expert visitors, librarians also find the instructional planning webs of the teacher informative.

For some teachers, taking the time to share this information with a librarian has resulted in locating books very specific to the focus of the project and even additional resources such as Internet sites and videos. It is important that the librarian also understand the importance of children's being able to actively seek answers to questions and to use books as resources independently. Because young investigators gain much information from studying books with photographs, drawings, and diagrams, books that have these are extremely valuable for projects. Unless teachers share how young investigators can use books as resources, some librarians may not realize that books designed for older children or adults can be just what a 3-, 4-, 5-, or 6-year-old investigating a project will need. A frequent comment from teachers who have used the project approach with young children is how surprised they were to find their young children spending significant amounts of time studying adult materials such as professional magazines that have photos on their topic. During one project, a building contractor's magazine was the most popular choice in the book area.

Introducing Skills to Young Investigators

There are many skills that children will use in Phase II of a project. Some of these can be introduced and practiced before they are needed for investigation. One skill that young investigators often need is how to pose a question to an adult, especially an adult who is not well known to them. Most young children in an environment in which they are listened to and encouraged to explore will naturally ask questions. However, young children do not usually know that what they are doing is asking questions. They are often confused when someone asks them, "Do you have any questions?" Teaching what a question is can be accomplished informally as children use questions:

Jason: Where is the red dinosaur book?
Teacher: That's a good question. Let's see if we can find an answer for you. Let's ask Matt that question. I saw him looking at it earlier this morning. Matt, Jason has a question for you.

The first time a group of young investigators conducts a field-site visit, some teachers have found it beneficial to practice asking specific questions planned in advance. On field-site visits, teachers usually put questions, or drawings that represent questions, on file cards or papers that are attached to clipboards to remind children what they are to ask (see Figure 3.7). In a simple role-play, the teacher or another child pretends to be the adult, and the child asks his or her question by "reading" it from the clipboard. Through this process children begin to see how speaking loud enough to be heard is important and how they can use their clipboards to remind them of what they want to say. It is important not to overdo this rehearsal and not to communicate to young investigators that the only questions that can be asked are those that were thought of in advance and put on their clipboards. Children should also be encouraged to ask questions spontaneously. It is also helpful if teachers remind children of the role-playing experience just before they make the field-site visit. The younger the child, the more beneficial this rehearsal can be.

On field-site visits, young investigators often want to obtain information that deals with quantity. The young investigator is especially interested in how many objects there are of a given kind or in a particular place. Many of the questions that are generated by children about a project topic include "how many" questions. For example, in the Fire Truck Project the young investigators wanted to know how many ladders there were on the fire truck. Many young children can learn to use simple tallying or graphing, even at age 3. This can be practiced in the classroom, where young investigators might indicate tally information about their classmates or their preferences. For example, children may tally the number of tennis shoes in the classroom, or survey the class to determine favorite kinds of ice cream. Four-year-olds frequently begin to write numerals with the tally marks. Simple, quick graphing and charting activities can be added to the classroom on a routine basis so that children are able to practice them and become skillful.

Another skill that young investigators use is observation. Young children are natural observers. However, looking at a particular object for a specific purpose at a specific time

FIGURE 3.7 • These clipboard sheets show how teacher Linda Lundberg wrote the children's questions and how the children recorded their answers at the field-site. One child recorded the answer by writing, the other by drawing. Recording answers benefits from practice.

may require some preparation. Teachers often provide practice in this skill by taking the class on a walk around the school or center, encouraging the children to talk about what they see as they see it, and then, when they return to the classroom, talking in a group about what they saw. One teacher has found that taking a small group on a walk to the school office where the secretary shows them how the photocopying machine works and answers their questions is excellent preparation for field-site visits.

Field sketching and observational drawing are also skills that can be introduced and practiced before a field-site visit. If children make observational drawings of objects on a daily basis in their classroom, then observational drawing and field sketching become productive ways to record observations rather than one of many novel experiences on a field-site.

Observational drawing may be added to the classroom by placing an object and paper, with clipboards or without clipboards, in the art area. Teachers can also model drawing by sitting down and doing their own drawing. The purpose of teacher modeling is not to show children how to draw but to demonstrate the act of looking, drawing, and redrawing. Taking small groups with their clipboards to other locations in the school to make field sketches is also good practice. For example, children can sketch the office or the office equipment. Smith and the Drawing Study Group (1998) provide additional ideas for how observational drawing can be introduced to children.

Another skill that young investigators use in Phase II is taking photographs. Children as young as 3 have taken photographs at a field-site. Each photograph was the responsibility of a specific child. When the children are as young as 3 years old or have coordination problems, adults carry the camera and give it to the child when it is time to take the photograph. Photography is also a skill that can be practiced. It is worth the price of a roll of film, or the time to print a set of digital photos, to give children a chance to practice taking pictures. A teacher might provide this experience by taking the class around the school and letting each child take an assigned photo. Sometimes teachers put these practice photographs into a book on "our school." Children's dictation can be added as captions to the photos. A discussion can take place about which photos show the objects in the best way, whether they are blurred or clear, and whether the photographer was close enough to the object. The result of this experience is project photos that are meaningful to the children. Taking photographs also enables the young investigators to keep their focus on the topic during the field experience.

Another useful skill for young investigators is construction and the use of materials such as tape and glue, and tools such as staplers. Although much will be learned about these materials and tools during project construction, prior experience is helpful. Materials and tools enable children to depict their thoughts about the topic and represent their knowledge by constructing play environments, models, and displays. Again, experience before project work will result in easier and more complex representations. Teachers can provide this experience by placing cardboard, tape, and tools in the art area or construction area and encouraging children to create something of interest such as a house or a car. Children can also be encouraged to collect and add scrap materials to the art area for this purpose.

Clay is a wonderful medium for children to use during projects. Children can make sculptures of artifacts and animals, and even buildings and more complex scenes. However, the young investigators' ability to use clay during projects depends on their familiarity with clay. Teachers will want to take time to introduce clay into the classroom. It takes considerable free exploration with clay before children are ready to use it as a representation medium. Teachers of young children who intend to implement projects with children will also benefit from taking a class on how to use clay. Teachers can learn how to select clay and keep it workable, how to wedge it, and some basic construction techniques such as using slip to join pieces, making and using coils, and making pinchpots. There are some excellent books on using clay with young children that will also provide the teacher with the background knowledge needed to help children succeed with clay (Herberholz & Hanson, 1994; Pelo, 2007; Smilansky, Hagan, & Lewis, 1988; Topal, 1983). Children will also benefit from watching others such as a potter or clay artist use clay. All of these experiences will build children's confidence in using clay so that when they want to use it in projects the skill will be there.

MOVING INTO INVESTIGATION

All of these project skills will continue to develop and grow as the project progresses. Teachers should not feel that most or even many of these preproject experiences are required for a project to proceed. It is important to keep the project moving at a good pace so that young children's interest will be maintained. As soon as a field-site visit can be arranged or an expert visitor can come in, the young investigators can begin their serious investigation.

CHAPTER 4

• • •

Investigation

CHAPTER 3 OUTLINED the beginning of Phase II, during which preparations for conducting the investigation are begun: Field-sites are selected, expert visitors are arranged, and special resources are placed in the classroom to help with the investigation. The main components of Phase II, however, are the actual processes of investigation that are conducted by the children. During Phase II, the young investigators engage in a variety of activities that will help them find the answers to the questions they generated during Phase I.

Investigation activities during Phase II include visiting related field-sites, interviewing experts, examining artifacts first-hand, and exploring a variety of additional resources such as books. As these experiences occur, the young investigators make drawings of what they are observing, try to write down what they are thinking and learning, build relevant objects, and role-play much of what they have learned.

As the children find the answers to their questions and use a variety of media to express their knowledge and understandings, interest may decline, and it may be time to move to Phase III, the culmination of the project. However, frequently new questions for investigation are generated during Phase II, and interest is often renewed. This sequence of events—investigation, representation, and discussions of what was learned—may be repeated several times (see Figure 4.1). In some projects with young children, the new questions that are generated move into different but related subtopics and concepts. Additional site visits and interviews of experts, followed by various kinds of representation, may occur several times before the young investigators' interest begins to subside and the project moves into Phase III.

FIELD-SITE VISITS

Organization of Fieldwork

During site visits with young children, it is essential to have several adults—parents or other volunteers—to help the teaching staff (see Figure 4.2). These accompanying adults will benefit from being fully informed about what is planned and expected, the main purposes of the site visit, and the children's on-site responsibilities. Adults can be assigned to specific groups of children for some of the activities and given information about the questions young investigators in their groups will be asking, the drawings that might be made, and the experiences that are likely to occur. The children's clipboards, with paper and a note or reminder of any assigned tasks, may be carried by the adult group leaders in tote bags, or placed together in a large container to be transported to the field-site. Pencils can be tied to the clipboard or placed under the clip of the clipboard to prevent their loss.

One teacher or other adult may have responsibility for the camera and a list of photos that the young investigators decided to take. Other adults can carry additional cameras, camcorders, or tape recorders to use in documenting the site-visit experience. A large shopping bag or box can be used to bring back to the classroom any artifacts borrowed from the site.

With children 3–6 years old, the field trip is often taken at the beginning of the project. Most teachers of young investigators think that making the field-site visit early in the development of a project is extremely important for their young children. Mary Ann Gottlieb emphasizes:

> Field trips are a very important part of projects. Children need to get to the site. I have concluded that the field trip is better at the beginning than at the end, especially for young children who have not had many or varied experiences. Going first is better than building expectations and ideas and then getting there and finding out it is not quite what you thought it was. It makes the topic and the investigation authentic right away.

Asking Questions and Preserving Spontaneity

As we suggested in Chapter 3, for young children multiple field-site visits can increase the depth of their learning, and more can be accomplished than with only a single visit. If

FIGURE 4.1 • Flowchart of the second part of Phase II

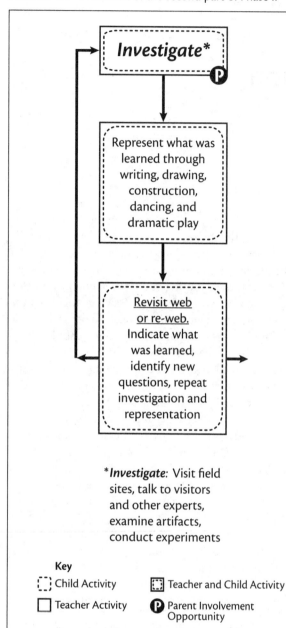

Investigate: Visit field sites, talk to visitors and other experts, examine artifacts, conduct experiments

Key
- ⬜ (dotted) Child Activity
- ⬛ (dotted) Teacher and Child Activity
- ⬜ Teacher Activity
- Ⓟ Parent Involvement Opportunity

FIGURE 4.2 • Parent Kristie Laurie assisted with the activities of the Farm Project. Here she heads for the bus with the children in her charge.

there are to be multiple site visits, the teacher plans which experiences to focus on or to provide on the first visit and which to postpone until subsequent visits. Teachers, however, are cautioned to resist the temptation to overprogram the visits. If there is to be only one site visit, teachers have to be especially careful that young investigators will feel free to ask their spontaneous questions as well as those that were prepared in advance and listed on a special piece of paper attached to their clipboards. It is also important that the children be able to take the time to focus on what interests them at the site that might not have been anticipated in the

planning before the visit. For example, an early childhood special education class visited a bowling alley as part of a project about balls. While at the bowling alley, several children became fascinated with the ball return and how it worked. They were especially interested in how the ball came up an incline into the rack near them, how it went over a lever that the ball pushed down while passing over it, and then how it was prevented from running back down the incline by the same lever, which had popped back up after the ball had passed. The teacher encouraged them to explore this unanticipated phenomenon as much as they wished.

It is easy to miss these kinds of opportunities for in-depth investigation if the focus of the field experience is restricted to only the predetermined questions and activities. With very young children, it is also important that adults realize that the children may not be able to generate questions about new things that interest them while on the site. For example, asking the question: "Does anyone have any more questions that they would like to ask?" is unlikely to elicit many questions from very young investigators, especially on their first project. Teachers and other adults

FIGURE 4.3 • Observational drawing requires intense concentration and careful study. Focusing on one part of an object, such as the tire on this large tractor, is often simpler for young investigators than trying to draw the whole tractor.

will have to be good observers of children's behavior, watching for signs of interest. Some nonverbal signs of interest are stopping and staring at something, reaching out to an object, and lagging behind the group to spend more time observing or manipulating a particular object. Very young investigators and children who are not yet verbally fluent may also indicate interest with the generic question "What's that?" or even simply point to an object.

In the experience with the bowling ball return mechanism described above, when the child pointed to the lever and asked "What's that?" the teacher concluded that this was probably a verbal expression of a number of other questions that the child could not verbalize, such as "What is the name of that? Why does it go up and down when the ball comes over it? What makes it go up and down? Can I push it down? Can I push the ball back over it if I push hard? What if I push it really hard? If I push the ball up the incline and make it roll over it, will it still go down?" When the child was allowed to explore the mechanism physically later, the things that he did with the mechanism implied he might be thinking such questions. The teacher recognized the child's interest on the basis of his simple question and his behavior. She then drew the host's attention to it by saying, "I think Michael is very interested in this and how it works." Her sensitivity to the child's behavior and her interpretation of it to the host enabled greater in-depth exploration.

Sketching on the Site

Ideally the children will have had many opportunities to do observational sketching and drawing in the classroom and around their school or center before they arrive at a field-site with clipboards in hand. Drawing and sketching as part of project work, and especially drawing on site, serve a specific purpose for investigation.

> Field sketches involve looking closely at the objects and people studied and making judgments about the parts of an object, the stages in a process, or the sequence of actions taken by a person. Sketches focus children's attention at the field-site, which enriches and facilitates later discussion on return to the classroom. (Chard, 1998a, p. 1:11)

Figure 4.3 provides an illustration of this point. It shows a child carefully studying the wheel of a tractor before beginning to make her field sketch.

Children often surprise adults with their ability to do observational drawing. Figure 4.4 is a 5-year-old's field sketch of a telephone at the bus barn in Linda Lundberg's School Bus Project. Notice the detailed drawing of the telephone, the careful attention to shape and size. On the same page, at the same time, the child also drew a person. The person is a memory drawing, drawn from the child's memory. The telephone is an observational drawing. At first glance, one might think that these were drawn by two different children, each at a different stage in their development of drawing skills. However, the picture reveals a difference not in developmental level but in the purpose of the child's work. Many teachers report being surprised by children's field sketches and the observational drawings they do

FIGURE 4.4 • When drawing plans for the construction of the dispatch office for the School Bus Project, this kindergartener created a detailed and accurate drawing of the telephone. The person in the same drawing, however, was drawn from memory and is less detailed.

in the classroom. Observational drawing is also assumed by some teachers to be outside of the range of abilities of 3-year-olds. However, the project work we have observed and that is described in this book provides convincing evidence to the contrary. Jolyn Blank had guided several highly successful projects with a class of 6-year-olds. When she subsequently began teaching 3- and 4-year-olds, she wondered what she could expect of these young investigators.

Because teachers know what a typical 3- or 4- or 5-year-old can do does not mean that children of this age should not have opportunities to exceed those limits if they have the desire and have the ability. They might tell you through their work, "See, I'm 4 and even though I might not be able to do this until I'm 5, I just did!" Projects allow for individualization and heterogeneous work. The children can participate on many levels, and on all levels their intellect can be respected.

Figure 4.5 is an example of 3-year-olds' drawings. Some teachers also question whether young children of 3 and 4 are actually representing something symbolically when they draw or sketch as part of their project work. Sylvia Chard has studied drawing in young children extensively and

FIGURE 4.5 • Three-year-olds' observational drawings

describes drawing as skill that is learned through modeling, being supported, and practicing, similar to how writing is learned.

> There was a time when people thought young children had to learn to write before they could express any of their own ideas in writing; i.e., master the skills of writing before they could use them. Now we know that children can learn to write through writing. The same seems to apply to drawing in our center with the three- and four-year-olds. Drawing skills and purposeful representation in drawing can develop hand in hand. The double and interdependent satisfactions of improving in both the use of the medium and representation can encourage the child to persist and make rewarding progress in both areas. (Chard, 1998b)

Most of the drawings that young investigators make during field-site visits are observational sketches. However, teachers are often surprised to see that they include details that are not actually there. For example, one child at a farm drew a horse and then put a rider on the horse's back even though there was no rider on the horse he was drawing. The child was drawing not only what he saw but also what he knew about horses from other experiences.

Choosing appropriate objects for field sketching is especially important for young children just learning to draw. Teachers who have conducted numerous site visits with young investigators report that it is more difficult for the children to draw large scenes and large objects than smaller ones. They seem to have difficulty moving overwhelmingly large images onto the small paper. For example, it is easier for them to draw a tractor than a barn when they are just beginners at sketching. For 3-year-olds, it is often easier to draw just a small part of a tractor, such as a wheel, than the whole tractor. It is also easier for adults and children to communicate about drawing if the object to be drawn is close to them, and in some cases is one that can be touched and examined in detail.

According to Nancy Smith and the Drawing Study Group (1998), it is important not to tell children steps to follow but rather to enable them to construct their own individual drawing strategies. Instead of specific steps, these researchers suggest a sequence of events to follow in a drawing lesson. This sequence has been helpful to many teachers when they are assisting children in drawing, especially during a site visit. The following motivational dialogue is suggested.

- Ask a question that focuses the children on the topic: *Do you know what this is called?*
- Ask a question that uncovers what they know: *Do you know what it is used for?*

- Ask questions to help the child make associations, to clarify ideas and create enthusiasm for the task: *Do you see how the wheels are the same but also different?*
- Ask questions that help identify the uses of various parts observed: *Which part do you think helps you steer?*
- Ask questions that help the child visualize a phenomenon: *How do you think the tire looks when you turn this wheel?*
- Ask a question that can help them figure out how to transform their responses into marks and lines on paper (not the teacher's solutions; they can be peers' ideas): *Can you see which parts are connected to the big wheel? How can you draw their shapes?*
- Ask questions that can help children make the transition from observing to starting to draw: *Which part will you draw first? How will you connect this part?*

In addition to these kinds of questions, Pam Scranton suggests that it is helpful to draw the child's attention to the paper and get started on drawing by asking "Where will you draw [whatever it is the child has selected to draw]?" "Can you put your pencil where you are going to start drawing that?"

At the beginning, when teachers are new to project work with young children, they are reluctant to assist or coach them in drawing during the project. They hesitate to provide guidance, especially if in their previous backgrounds drawing and painting were viewed as strictly expressive creative media. Using drawing, and later painting, for in-depth study and recording of observations should not be confused with children's spontaneous exploration and free artistic expression. Both the representational and the expressive aspects of using graphic media provide valuable experiences and should be encouraged and valued by the teachers of young investigators. Three- and 4-year-olds are more likely to make nonrepresentational drawings and paintings when they are not involved in a project and when their drawing is not intended for a particular purpose, such as observing or recording information. If children understand that all types of expression are valued, they can go back and forth between observational drawing, free exploration, drawing and painting from memory, and so forth, with little difficulty. They appear to take as much pleasure and pride in their experimentation in colors and shapes as they do in their representational work.

Drawing and painting are media that children can use to develop a better and deeper understanding of their world and their experiences. They can use them to sort out relationships, experiment with concepts, and communicate their ideas and thoughts. An example of a child using drawing to sort out relationships is 4-year-old Sarah's work on shelves for the Apple Store in Jolyn Blank's classroom.

FIGURE 4.6 • Sara, 4 years old, takes two pieces of cardboard and attempts to get them to stand up to make a shelf.

FIGURE 4.7 • This is Sara's second attempt at making the shelf. She has added more cardboard and a top piece to add rigidity.

FIGURE 4.8 • This is Sarah's drawing and her explanation of her thinking process as she made the shelves.

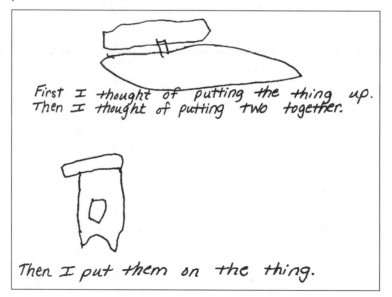

First I thought of putting the thing up.
Then I thought of putting two together.

Then I put them on the thing.

Sarah watches the other children trying to make shelves. She experiments with a piece of cardboard, then finally she settles on a construction (see Figures 4.6 and 4.7). Figure 4.8 is Sarah's drawing of her thinking process as she worked out this problem. The first drawing on her page is a top view, and the second is a side view of her final solution. Drawing helped Sarah to think.

Measurement

Young investigators also represent and gather information by measurement and counting. Younger children will more than likely use tally marks to gather data, as shown in Figure 4.9. The teacher may simplify the tallying and graphing processes by creating a way for children to record data and graph them at the same time. This is especially helpful for young children gathering data on site. A simple way to do this is to make a grid of boxes of equal size. Children can make one mark in the box or color in the box to represent an observation of the objects they are counting, thus using simple one-to-one correspondence to gather and represent quantities. The advantage of using a grid is that the boxes

FIGURE 4.9 • This tally chart shows how an adult can take children's questions about a car and provide a way for children to tally the data and to be able to make meaningful comparisons by the number of squares marked.

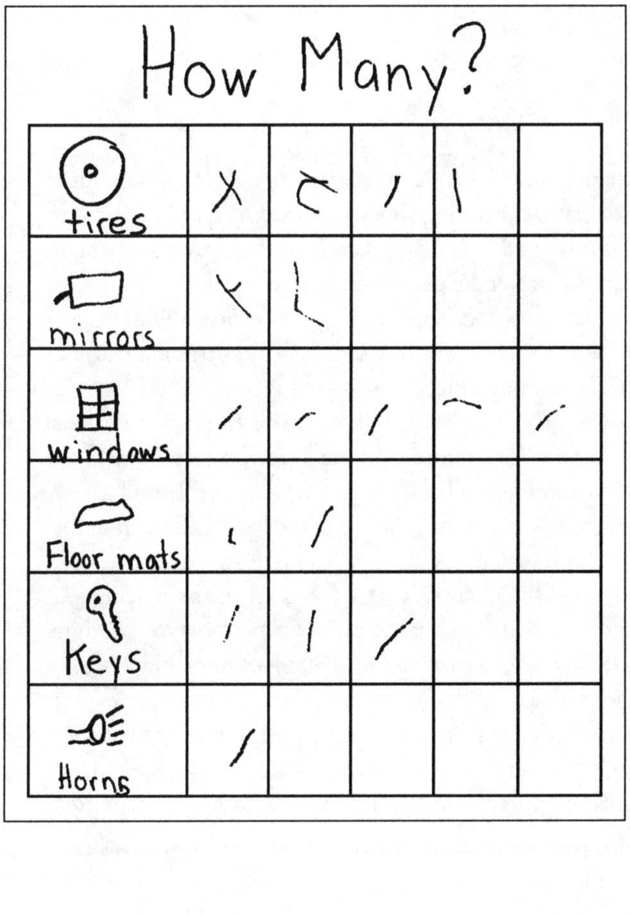

are of equal size, from which children can get a realistic sense of quantitative data by comparing the length of the columns or rows of boxes with marks. If there are older 4-year-olds or 5-year-olds in the group, these tally sheets can also provide a place for written numerals. The blank tally or graphing sheets are usually prepared in advance and placed on individual children's clipboards.

Writing

Young investigators are beginning the journey toward literacy and often have a strong interest in letters on signs and on objects. For example, they often ask, "What does that say?" Field-sites usually provide multiple opportunities to gather printed matter. Most sites have several kinds of signs: Directional, informational, invitational, and warning signs are likely to be readily available. Many objects may have labels on them. Signs can be drawn and letters copied, and children can also photograph signs to be copied in the classroom. If a videographer is documenting the children's experiences, it is helpful to alert him or her to the importance of capturing the use of letters and words on the site. The videographer can zoom in close enough for children to distinguish letters when they view the videotape on return to their classroom. Adult photographers can also help by observing the same guidelines.

Young investigators also often want to write words right on their observational drawings. If it has been decided in advance that young investigators are going to draw specific items, a word sheet can be placed on the clipboard to enable the children to copy words to label or accompany their field sketches.

DEBRIEFING

Reviewing Experiences and Fieldwork

Usually young investigators share what they have learned when they return from a site visit. Teachers report that it is helpful to have a general discussion about the trip so that the children can share what they remembered, what they liked, what surprised them, and what was of real interest. Often this general discussion flows into a focused discussion about the investigation. The young investigators talk about what they found out that related to their list of questions or to their web, and to what they wanted to know. Children share the answers they received to their questions, and the teacher adds these answers to their list of questions table or to their web.

Young investigators sometimes share other forms of representation during these discussions. These might be tally sheets they completed during the visits, or sketches they made at the time. Teachers often reserve a bulletin board for these sheets and information to be displayed in the

(text continues on page 52)

A CLOSER LOOK   • INVESTIGATING NATURE •

WHEN YOU BEGIN doing projects on nature topics, especially if you have a classroom full of children with limited experiences with nature, you will want to have particular tools and techniques to engage children. Young children in a woods environment for the first time are often overwhelmed with the enormity of the outdoors and have difficulty focusing on a project topic. One kindergarten teacher started an outdoor field-site visit with high hopes for engagement only to find that her children looked around the space but did not seem to find anything interesting. Even armed with magnifying glasses, young children do not always know how or what to look at. If you anticipate the need for skills and equipment to maximize engagement and guide your children to develop investigative skills, these will serve as a foundation for science study and provide enjoyment over the children's lifetime. A place to start planning for nature projects is to examine science standards (or in the case of kindergarten and primary teachers, standards and required curriculum goals). For example, the Illinois Early Learning Standards (Illinois State Board of Education, 2002) include the following:

- Use senses to explore and observe materials and natural phenomena.
- Collect, describe and record information.
- Use scientific tools such as thermometers, balance scales and magnifying glasses for investigation.
- Become familiar with the use of devices incorporating technology.
- Investigate and categorize living things in the environment.
- Show an awareness of changes that occur in themselves and their environment.
- Describe and compare basic needs of living things.
- Make comparisons among objects that have been observed.
- Describe the effects of forces in nature (e.g. wind, gravity and magnetism).
- Use common weather-related vocabulary (e.g. rainy, snowy, sunny, windy).
- Participate in recycling in their environment.
- Identify basic concepts associated with night/day and seasons.
- Begin to understand basic safety practices.
- Express wonder and ask questions about their world.
- Begin to be aware of technology and how it affects their lives. (pp. 17–20)

Once you have a firm grasp of the standards or required curriculum goals related to your specific program, these can then be placed on your anticipatory planning web. The anticipatory planning web was introduced in Chapter 2 to test the worthiness of a project topic. Additional information is provided in Chapter 8 on how the anticipatory planning web can become a vehicle for integrating of standards into the project experience.

To incorporate these goals or standards into planning, you web the concepts about the topic (the first step of making the web), then place the standards or required curriculum goals near the concepts that are likely opportunities for that standard or goal to be learned in the project (the second step of the web). Once those have been identified, you can then make a list of the activities or experiences (third step of the teacher's webbing process). This can be very helpful in anticipating what inquiry and investigative skills children will need. For example, during a tree project, Lora Taylor provided containers to collect leaves and magnifying glasses to examine the bark of trees when she planned a walk into the woods. In making her anticipatory planning web, Lora had anticipated that the standard "Collect, describe, and record information" could be authentically integrated into this project, and she prepared materials and introduced those skills. Carrying baskets and collecting leaves and nuts provided the children with a focus for the experience, yet still enabled direct contact and free exploration of the environment. There are many resources available for planning investigations of nature that are helpful for this anticipatory planning. *Early Learning Guidelines for Connecting Children with Nature* (Nebraska Department of Education, 2008) provides ideas for integrating standards into nature experiences for mathematics, language and literacy, science, and other areas. Each area in this resource also includes toddlers.

There are specific science and inquiry skills that enable investigation in nature projects. These include hands-on exploration of artifacts, collections of specific items, categorizing and grouping items, and recording information.

Comparing and categorizing objects, plants, or animals is engaging and fosters deep thought by children. For example, learning the names of birds expands vocabulary, but when the teacher encourages grouping those birds into larger categories (such as woodpeckers and songbirds, or birds that feed at the hanging feeder and those that eat off the ground), she is challenging them to establish and use criteria to think at a higher level.

Opportunities to learn how to use tools such as thermometers, balance scales, and magnifying glasses abound in projects on nature. Each tool needs to be introduced in advance so that children will understand the purpose and the information it provides. The use of observational drawing is a powerful way to encourage children to slow down, look carefully, and notice details in nature. Photos can be used to revisit details observed. A camera can be a wonderful tool placed in the hands of children outdoors. Even very young children can be taught to take photos. If a digital camera is used, many photos can be taken without being costly, and they can easily be printed out, manipulated, and shared using projectors and interactive whiteboards or in creating books and posters. Neumann-Hinds (2007) in her book *Picture Science* provides a wealth of ideas for using a digital camera. Some of these are:

Young children will observe more closely and become more involved with nature when they have a task. Just providing baskets for children to put their treasures in can focus an experience.

- Using photos to collect details
- Using photos to analyze data such as categorizing and grouping
- Capturing change (for example, plant growth over a long period of time or an event that happens quickly such as a chick hatching)
- Capturing the sequence of events
- Creating matching games (for example, beaks to birds)
- Making a story
- Making charts (flow charts of events, pie charts of data, growth charts) (p. 6)

Anticipating how these experiences might be integrated into project work will maximize the learning and engagement of children during an investigation. You need to be careful, however, that integration into the project does not turn that project into a teacher-led unit of instruction. Children must have a sense of ownership and engagement to reap the benefits of project work. The key is to keep the skills and experiences in mind and watch to see what content is most interesting to children, then introduce those skills and experiences in response to that interest. For example, there is a strong possibility that categorization will be part of a project on birds, but will the children be interested in categorizing types of birds, parts of birds, kinds of bird feeders, or the locations where birds were spotted? If they choose to focus mainly on numbers of different birds, categorization may not occur in that project but instead the opportunity to teach tallying might. You can be ready with the materials and tools to introduce and support work as the opportunities emerge. By reflecting on the project progress and the overall goals for the year, you can be intentional about introducing and providing practice for all these goals either in project work or during the more direct teaching sections of the day.

classroom. Often additional questions that emerged from these discussions are added to the list in a new color, or a separate list of new questions is started.

Photographs taken during a site visit can be shared as soon as they become available. One teacher of young investigators likes to let the children arrange the photographs on a poster board to tell the story of their investigation experiences as they perceived them. This kind of documentation creates much discussion and frequently provides a context for the use of new vocabulary. The children sometimes dictate accounts of what was happening in a photo. The ensuing discussion includes not only information about what they did during their site visit but frequently what they learned. These displays often remain visible for the whole period the children are working on the project, and are used to revisit their experiences from time to time. In Phase III, these same sketches and photos may be "published" in book format to share with parents and others.

Teachers of first-grade or kindergarten children, or even younger children who are interested in the conventions of writing, often take children's dictation about their experience and make an experience chart or a put it together in a large-size book. By watching the teacher write their words using punctuation and other conventions of print in their story, children begin to develop important understandings about the usefulness of reading and writing. During this process, some teachers also start a "wall of words," such as the one in Figure 4.10, that relates to the project. These words are sometimes written on a large sheet of paper. Some teachers prefer to put these words on index cards that

can be removed from the wall and taken to a table for the young investigators to copy when they want to. Children often nominate new words to be added to the wall.

Artifacts that have been collected during the field-site visit are put out on display tables or shelves in the classroom for close inspection. The placement in the room varies by the type of artifact. Some artifacts are placed in the sensory or science area, where they can be touched and manipulated. Empty water tables or sand tables can be used if there is are a large number of smaller objects such as car parts. Artifacts that are fragile and will not withstand handling by small children can be placed on pedestals in the art area, and children can be encouraged to observe them without touching and to draw what they see. Some teachers like to keep all project artifacts in one location and create a project table (see Figure 4.11).

Videotapes that are made during the site visit can be viewed by the children on their return. Some activities that accompany the viewing of videotapes include adding words or comments to their webs and adding words to the word wall. During this period of revisiting the field experience, the teachers also ask children to redraw the items they had sketched on the site. This is most beneficial when it is preceded by viewing of photos, artifacts, or portions of the video that might be relevant. Some young investigators, especially those in kindergarten or first grade, may want to use colored pencils to make these second or third drawings. Some younger children, however, may be confused by the addition of color at this time and are more comfortable using pencils or fine-line black markers.

This revisiting of artifacts and documentation, followed by drawing and redrawing, occurred a number of times in many of the projects we observed. Some teachers were at first hesitant to ask children to draw the same thing a second or third time. However, they discovered that each time the young investigators revisited and redrew something, they put more and more detail into their representations. Some teachers have found it helpful to have children prepare a drawing; revisit the video, photo, or artifact; and then go back and add more detail to the same drawing. This redrawing may occur the next day or even later. To document the process, a teacher often photocopies the first drawing and subsequent additions to the drawing. In this way, the teacher can capture the growth in understanding and complexity as the child extends his or her knowledge about the subject and grows in representational abilities. The successive drawings—whether photocopied or started fresh each time—are commonly called Time 1/Time 2 drawings, and they have become especially meaningful to teachers and parents.

Some children may also want to try the medium of paints and use their field sketches as a resource to plan and make their paintings or even to prepare to create a mural.

FIGURE 4.10 • This is a project word wall from the Garage Project in Rebecca Wilson's dual-language kindergarten classroom. This word wall was used by children to find out how to write words for their journals, and for other literacy activities related to the project.

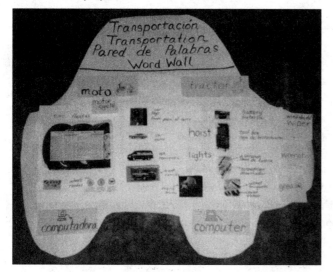

Plate 1. The children in Natalya Fehr's classroom decided that they needed a work team to construct their back hoe, just like at Caterpillar Tractor Company where many of the children's parents work. Here they are dictating team plans.

Plate 2. This is the yellow team's "backhoe loader," which they made. The process is described in Chapter 2.

Plate 3. This is the tiller that captured the children's interest in the Garden Project at Holy Trinity Lutheran Church Preschool. They were fascinated by how the tiller would "grind up the ground" to make it ready to plant seeds.

Plate 4. Kara, Rryley, Derek, Megan, and Michael use the photographs of the tiller, such as the one above, as a source for building their own garden tiller, which is located off in the lower right hand corner of the photo.

Plate 5. Michael, Megan, Brandon, Pam Podkanowicz (teacher aide), and Derek discuss the tiller, talking about what has to be added and how they might add it.

Plate 6. This constructed bulldozer, like many constructions for projects, becomes a focus for dramatic play.

Plate 7. Children at the Early Childhood Center at Illinois Valley Community College pose for a picture in the car they created during the Car Project. The car is on display in the central gathering place of the college and children serve as tour guides for the construction. Documentation of this project has been captured in *Rearview Mirror* (Beneke, 1998).

Plate 8. Kindergarten children in Linda Lundberg's classroom are finishing up the bus that the morning and afternoon class made during the School Bus Project.

Plate 9. Reviewing photos of field-site visits often helps teachers understand what children are trying to create with their constructions.

Plate 10. This child's cardboard shield and masking tape straps are a representation of the firefighter's equipment.

FIGURE 4.11 • This is the project table for the Garden Project at Holy Trinity Lutheran Church Preschool. Most of the items were supplied by a parent when she came to talk to the children and answer questions regarding her garden at home.

One teacher likes to use a photocopy machine to copy young investigators' drawings onto transparencies. These can be projected onto a wall for children to enjoy. The projected images can also be traced onto a large sheet of paper or plastic, and children can then paint or color them to make a very colorful and satisfying mural. The documentation of these and many other uses of media in the schools of Reggio Emilia (Cadwell, 1997; Edwards et al., 1998; Gandini et al., 2005; Hendricks, 1997) has provided inspiration to teachers to introduce children to new materials and new uses of familiar materials. Teachers should not underestimate children's willingness to explore and experiment with new media.

Introduction of Secondary Sources for Additional Research

During this revisiting of the field experience and beginning of representation, teachers often introduce additional resources. In many classrooms parents bring in materials for study. For example, parents can contribute new books related to the topic of investigation, documentation that they made during a field experience, or artifacts from sources other than the field-site. These can be shared with the children and added to the classroom materials. If new questions emerge as a result of exposure to these additional resources, they can become the focus of further investigation, and plans can be made to find the answers to these new questions. This process might lead to additional site visits or might result in asking specific additional experts to visit the classroom. Some teachers have been able to take a small group of the children in the class back to a site for more in-depth exploration. Parents have also responded to their own children's interest in the topic and taken them to other sites independently. These children then reported back to the class about what they learned at those additional sites.

Using New Knowledge in Play

Young investigators often process what they have learned and extend their learning through play. Children can be encouraged to play by adding props to the existing play environments. For example, adding hospital items to a housekeeping area can help transform the play into events related to a visit to a hospital. Play can also be encouraged by making an "instant" environment by projecting digital photos of the field-site onto a wall and enabling children to "get into" the experience through pretending. The same effect can be created with a colored transparency made from a photograph, placing it on an overhead projector on the floor and projecting it onto a wall. Young children enjoy changing these images and playing in the various backdrops that they can create with the transparencies.

The creation of play environments is often the focus for young children. Some play environments children have created in projects we have observed have included a fire truck, a store, a restaurant, a hospital room, and a veterinary clinic. When children of elementary school age engage in project work, they often create models or displays of what they have observed and learned about. With young investigators, however, the creation of a play environment often becomes the primary focus of the project during this phase. Field sketches, photographs, videos, and books can become resources for the accurate representation of the place or object they create. In the Garden Project at Holy Trinity Lutheran Church Preschool, the children were fascinated by the tiller (see Plate 3 in the center of the book) and decided to build one. In Plate 4, the children are studying their photographs. In Plate 5 they are discussing how to add details they noticed in the photographs. Notice the similarity of the children's construction to the real tiller.

Unlike the smaller models that older children make, young investigators often prefer to create large structures, especially structures large enough for them to get into, and to include items that they can use in dramatic play. Plates 6 through 8 show play structures of a variety of vehicles created by young investigators.

Young children who are new to project work or have no previous experience of creating a large play structure are unlikely to think of making a play structure on their own. Teachers are sometimes reluctant to give children ideas of what they might do, preferring to have children develop their own plans. Yet several teachers have supported children's thinking of creating a play environment by providing large scrap materials such as sheets of cardboard or boxes in the classroom and encouraging them to make something with these materials. Other teachers wait until spontaneous play that centers on the project topic emerges; then they encourage the young investigators to create props for the play. They may even suggest materials to use during children's first project experiences. Once children have experienced a project and have created a play environment, the idea of creating a new structure to use for their play, such as a delivery truck or a restaurant, comes to their minds readily.

Children, just like teachers, learn much about how to proceed in project work by seeing how other children do projects. Project history books and visits to other classrooms where projects are in progress help children build an understanding of the variety of ways they can represent their experiences and findings. Sharing projects within schools or early childhood programs provides not only a forum for the young investigators to report their work, but also a way for other young children to gain vicarious experience of a project. In this way children acquire some preliminary knowledge of how experiences can be represented. A child may suggest making "a big picture like Mrs. Johnson's class did," referring to a mural he had recently seen in her classroom.

It is in the building of the play environment that much problem solving occurs for young investigators. Older children's project work stimulates them to hypothesize about and experiment with relevant concepts. Younger children engage in problem solving as they figure out how to make a window for a bus, or how to make a horse's head stand up straight on their pretend horse, or how to represent accurately what they have observed during their fieldwork. Sallee Beneke (2004) talks about problem solving in Phase II:

Translating their perceptions into two or three dimensions requires children to consider and select from the media and materials available to them. Depending on her prior experience, a child may have many questions about how to work with these materials, so the product will look the way she envisions it: questions such as, "How do I make it bend? How do I stick it together? How big should this piece be compared to that one? What can I draw on it with? How do I write this word?" Many of these questions stem from problems that arise as the child meets with problems during the course of construction. Social problem-solving is also likely to occur in this phase, if children are working together in a small group to create a representation. They have to agree on what will be done, and they have to reach consensus about who will perform the tasks involved.

The Fire Truck Project in Pam Scranton's class provides an example of social problem solving. Two young investigators struggled with making lights for the fire truck that looked both colored and shiny. Two other children who were working on another section of the fire truck critiqued and made suggestions about construction of the lights. Considerable discussion among the children, and their willingness to listen to each other's ideas, led to the final solution.

Teachers who are new to project work often have difficulty knowing when they should intervene in this problem-solving process. Sallee Beneke (2004) offers this advice:

As long as children are still trying various means of solving the problem themselves, there is no reason to "step in." I think we are often in too big of a hurry to solve children's problems. If it seems as if they are giving up, then it is probably time to step in. When children are accustomed to using the teacher as a resource, they will often ask for assistance when they really need it.

Sometimes you can tell a young child is getting frustrated and needs help. The child gives up, sulks, walks away, or damages his work (for example, he knocks down his block construction).

Sometimes when I offer help I am pretty direct: "It looks like you're having some trouble getting this to work. Let me show you how to do something that might help you." I try not to give solutions. I try to offer just enough assistance so that the child or children can operate without my assistance again. I try to be honest, respectful, and direct. I try to help the child enough that he can proceed, but not so much that the project becomes mine rather than his. For example, if a child is having trouble connecting two pieces of cardboard with tape, I might say something like, "It looks like the tape isn't holding very well. Other things that we have that might work to hold cardboard are wire, string, or brads. Would you like to try one of those?" If the child asks how to do something, I can demonstrate and/or let him practice on a sample, and then encourage him to apply his new skill on his project work.

Another way that Ms. Beneke supports children's problem solving during construction is by making materials available, as she did in the car project. This sequence is documented in *Rearview Mirror* (Beneke, 1998):

As children began to construct the car, they tried out different types of steering wheels [see Figure 4.12]. Taylor had constructed a steering wheel from sticks and connectors and a circle was cut from tag board on these attempts. Even with tape the pieces would not stay attached to the dashboard and actually turning the wheel would cause the wheel to fall off the dashboard. It wasn't long before they brought a real steering wheel to the project area. Both children and

teachers began to wonder how we could attach the steering wheel to the car so that the children could turn it as they drove. . . .

The student teachers began to discuss among themselves how they might solve the problem. I advised them that if we found a pole or poles that might fit into the steering wheel, we would need to put the pole in with the project materials and give the children the opportunity to discover the solution for themselves.

At home in my basement, I found a pole that I knew would work. I placed the pole in the corner of the project area, and when the children were working on the car that morning I said something like, "You know, maybe one of our car books will show how the steering wheel is connected to the dashboard in a real car." In his typically efficient way, Taylor went to the book collection and found a book that showed the shaft that connects the steering wheel to the wheels [see Figure 4.13]. . . .

Once Taylor decided he needed a pole, he went to the corner and started examining the poles we had collected there. He said, "I think this one will fit," and began to try to separate the duster head from the pole [see Figure 4.14]. . . .

After Taylor had freed the pole, he inserted it into the steering wheel and discovered it was a great fit [see Figure 4.15]. I helped him to cut a hole through the dashboard with a knife. He found that the pole fit through the hole and down into the box next to the motor [see Figure 4.16]. (pp. 28–31)

In this problem-solving sequence, Ms. Beneke supported Taylor by providing resources that he could use to see how

---

FIGURE 4.12 • Taylor tries to make a steering wheel out of Tinkertoys.

FIGURE 4.13 • Taylor uses books as a resource to find out how the steering wheel works.

FIGURE 4.14 • Taylor takes apart the mop to be able to use the handle for the shaft of his steering wheel.

FIGURE 4.16 • Taylor tries out his steering wheel in the car and finds that it works to his satisfaction.

FIGURE 4.15 • Taylor puts the steering wheel onto the shaft without assistance.

others had solved the problem (car diagram in a book) and then by bringing materials (e.g., poles) to the classroom where children could access them. She was able to scaffold Taylor's problem solving.

Young investigators often solve problems in unique ways. Adults are often surprised at how young investigators sometimes mix a verbal representation into the structure. For example, a silver stripe was represented by sticking plastic knives, forks, and spoons along a line. The children's explanation was that it worked because the items were "silverware." Another young investigator, while constructing a pretend library with a check-out system, insisted that books that were brought back should have their cards marked with a red marker because the book had been "read."

Young investigators also often create representations as they play in the play environment. When children in Jodi Knapp's classroom visited the bus barn during the School Bus Project, the children were given the opportunity to see the underside of the school bus by lying down on the mechanic's scooter and being pushed under the bus. When they emerged, they did field sketches of the underside of the bus. On return to their classroom, they constructed a bus using a cardboard refrigerator box. One child spontaneously took a long cardboard gift-wrap tube and raised one end of the cardboard box and propped it up with the cardboard tube. He then lay on his back on the floor under the box in the exact position that he had observed the mechanic in when under the bus he was repairing, and the same position he had been in while observing the underside of the bus during the site visit (see Figure 4.17).

These play experiences are very valuable for young investigators. Through their play, they often consolidate and make deeper and more accurate sense of their experiences and related concepts. As they act out scenarios and roles they observed in their investigations, they make connections

FIGURE 4.17 • These photos show (*left*) the children in Jody Knapp's preschool observing the mechanic on the scooter at the bus barn and (*right*) the way the children raised their bus to work on it from the same position.

between their new knowledge and their own previous experiences and internalize the relevant concepts. Play also creates a purpose for using new words about the project topic so that they become part of the child's active vocabulary.

Projects create opportunities and encourage children to engage in increasingly advanced play. This is especially helpful for children who have not had extensive experience with dramatic play, or who have had a limited range of experiences. Heidemann and Hewitt (2009) present a framework for observing and supporting the development of play skills in children. The framework provides a list of play skills in developmental progression, with suggestions for supporting their development. Play skills that are often observed and that teachers can support during project-related play include the following:

- Pretending with objects (real, substitute objects, then imaginary objects)
- Role-playing (using a sequence of play, declaring the role "I am the doctor," imitating actions, including dress)
- Verbalizing about the play episode (using words to describe actions, then using words to create a play scenario)
- Persistence in play (staying in a play episode for an extended period—10 minutes or longer at age 5)
- Interactions (playing with other children, playing with different partners, playing with three or more children)
- Entrance into a play group (watching what the group is playing, imitating behavior of the group, and joining the play episode)
- Conflict management (using verbal solutions, accepting compromises)
- Supporting peers (offering help, taking suggestions from peers, and encouraging peers)

Many of the most complex play skills emerge naturally as children become involved in playing roles they have observed during site visits or from the visits of experts who came into their classrooms. Projects can motivate children to become involved in dramatic play and enable teachers to support and coach the development of play skills.

Creating a play structure such as a school bus, or a play environment such as a hospital room, and then playing in it may extend for some time as children make sense of the experience. Representation through play should not be rushed. This is especially true for the younger children, who use play as the primary method of representing their understandings. In many of the projects described in this book, 3-year-olds were often observed representing their understandings and knowledge through play and less often through construction, drawing, or story telling. In the Fire Truck Project in Pam Scranton's class, 4-year-olds did most of the planning and construction of the fire truck. Although Ms. Scranton anticipated extensive rich play by the construction group when the fire truck was finally completed, the 4-year-olds spent only one day playing in the structure they had built. However, 3-year-olds, who had mainly observed the construction of the fire truck, took over the structure and began to play in it, and continued to use the play environment for exploring and revisiting their experiences.

Sometimes problem-solving is an independent activity by an individual child. In Plate 9, two firefighters demonstrate the use of fire protective gear. In Plate 10, the 4-year-old—after trying several different approaches—decided that masking tape would work perfectly as straps to hold on the fire shield she had designed. The energy of a problem to solve will often bring children together, even if it is only to provide another pair of hands to hold materials or put on straps.

Discussions

Throughout all of these experiences of processing information, the ability of the teacher to respond to children during discussions becomes a critical determinant of how much children gain from the project experience. This is how Barb Gallick, Head Teacher, experienced in guiding projects for young investigators at Illinois State University Child Care Center, thinks about discussions:

When facilitating discussions and participating in discussions with young children, I think I try to continually remind myself not to jump in with an "answer" or give a correct solution to the children. Often teachers hear a child misrepresenting information and feel they need to provide the "right" answer—sometimes they respond without thinking. I try to stop and think for a second before I respond. By doing that, I can make an effort to respond to a child's statement, comment, or question in a way that will extend their thought and encourage more discussion. I may respond with another question or make a comment suggesting ways we could find an answer to a child's question. Sometimes, I might propose a question to the other children, such as "What do you all think about Joe's idea that a greenhouse is a house painted green?" Hopefully, other children will respond with ideas that might be different—thus encouraging more discussion and sometimes exchanging conflicting ideas. If I can draw out conflicting ideas, the group would want to find ways to determine which ideas are accurate, thus setting the stage for further investigations and group work.

My main goal in facilitating discussion would be to draw out the children's thoughts, ideas, and questions so that the children and the teachers could plan experiences that would help us find out more. Early in a project, this goal translates into finding inconsistencies in the children's knowledge of our topic. That's where those conflicting ideas help. We try to ask a lot of "Why do you think . . . ?" or "What do you think about . . . ?" questions. This leads to "How and where can we find out . . . ?" questions.

Later in a project, the goal of drawing out thoughts and ideas becomes more focused on finding out what the children have learned; how their thoughts and ideas have changed; what new questions they might have; and what else they have become interested in about a topic. This type of facilitating is not necessarily new to teachers, but I think in a traditional classroom, it gets lost in the routine of sharing our knowledge with children. I think teachers just beginning to use the project approach really need to look at how they respond to children's statements and questions. They need to focus on improving their technique of asking open-ended questions and making open-ended comments. It is a constant learning experience. I feel I am continually working on my ability to respond in such a way that it extends the children's thinking rather than providing an answer.

Here Ms. Gallick describes an example of a discussion that took place in the center. Lisa Lee and Scott Brouette, additional Head Teachers, are the other adults involved in the discussion.

During the web experience the children made a category of kinds of insects: fly, butterfly, bee, etc., including frog, alligator, and a few other non-insects. We, of course, wrote them down and moved on. Today, the children found a dragonfly in the play yard. We put it in the aquarium. As I carried the aquarium around for all to see, Georgia made an interesting observation.

Georgia (4.8 yr): The dragonfly and the grasshopper must be related. They both have four wings and probably they both have six legs. Also, my daddy told me that the little things on the front of the spider were part of his mouth.

Breanna (4.3 yr): They are part of its jaws.

Dylan (5 yr): They look like snitchers.

Charlie (4.1 yr): When me and Mikey were climbing the tree we saw this dead cicada shell. We were up in Michigan.

Lucas: We heard cicadas up in the tree at the farm. They were very loud.

Charlie: I saw a Monarch butterfly. I think my white caterpillar turned into it.

Breanna: Really caterpillars don't have wings.

Lucas: Yes, they do. They turn into moths.

Barb: Let's talk some more about what Georgia said about the dragonfly and the grasshopper being related. Can you think of other things that might be related to them?

Emily (3.4 yr): Spiders.

Breanna: The spider had eight legs.

Barb: How many legs did the praying mantis have?

Kayla: Three on each side.

Lisa: How many does that make all together?

Class: Six.

Scott: Did the praying mantis have wings?

Class: Yes.

Scott: Did the katydid have wings?

Georgia: Yes, it flew.

Scott: How many legs did the katydid have?

Allison (4.11 yr): Six.

Brandon (3.4 yr): Ladybugs have wings.

Scott: What about a butterfly?

(We got the dead Monarch off the science table to look at.)

Brelynn (3.11 yr): It has two wings on each side.
Georgia: That makes four.

(In looking closely at the butterfly the children counted six legs.)

Katie D. (5.3 yr): I think ladybugs have six legs.

(Brandon got the ladybug model off the science table and Lisa helped him count the legs.)

Brandon: There are six legs.
Lucas: How many legs does a spider have?

(Lucas got some spider models off the science table.)

Lucas: One, two, three, four, five, six, seven, eight.
Lisa: So, do spiders have the same number of legs as the other things we have looked at?
Katie H. (3.10 yr): No. There are two more legs.
Kayla: Two of them had wings.
Barb: What do we call those things with six legs?
Lucas: Bugs.
Barb: What's that other word?
Georgia: Insects.

After that morning meeting, some children drew the dragonfly while others began to chart out the differences and similarities that had been discussed. We were thrilled that the realization of just what an insect is came from the children themselves. We had hoped to make a chart comparing some of the insects and other animals that had been listed on the original web, but [it] never had the interest of the children when it was offered as an activity choice. Today, though, on their own, they began to categorize and classify, see similarities and differences.

It is important to remember that an alternative choice that these teachers might have made was to simply begin the exploration of insects by telling the children how adults defined insects. This example shows not only how the teachers facilitate the conversation but also how children, even at this age, do not always need to be told information, but— given the appropriate experiences, time to investigate and process information, and an effective teacher facilitator— can develop some very complex concepts on their own.

Project work provides frequent occasions for whole-group and small-group discussions on all aspects of the work. Discussions are contexts in which young children also can sharpen their expressive, listening, arguing, and other communicative skills. Teachers can support and strengthen all aspects of these skills by encouraging children to respond to each other during these discussions. Often teachers of young children inadvertently teach children to speak directly to them, from which the youngsters learn that discussion is just taking turns to have your say to the teacher. For example, one of us observed a teacher of a group of 21 4-year-olds in the early stages of planning a project related to fishing. The children were seated around her in horseshoe formation, and the teacher began, clipboard on her lap, to collect answers to the following question put to each child in turn: "What's your favorite fish?" The first child hesitated a bit and finally offered "goldfish." The teacher responded, "That's one of my favorites too," and moved to the next child, who in turn hesitated a while and came up with, "I like tuna sometimes," and so on. By the time the teacher reached the tenth child in the semicircle, the first nine had tuned out, having no investment in what their peers offered. However, the teacher could have encouraged the children to respond to each other, to make suggestions to or ask questions of each other—encouraging cross-child communication.

The capacity of young children to respond to each other is often underestimated. But such communication skills can be learned. For example, the teacher might be informed by a small group that they cannot figure out how to represent what they just found out about how many baskets of mail the mail truck delivers each day. The teacher can then encourage a member of that group to raise that question with the whole class and solicit their advice. We have observed children even at the preschool level willing and able to engage in this kind of joint problem solving and taking considerable satisfaction in being able to help others with their questions.

Taking time to talk one-on-one with children during the project is also important. Scott Brouette shares his thoughts about talking with a child during a project (see Figure 4.18):

Some children are less likely to answer questions or give observations as quickly as others. This is a great

FIGURE 4.18 • Scott Brouette shows how listening to children involves patience and attention. He patiently waits for the idea of what to do next with their bug sprayer to come from the child.

opportunity for a one-to-one interaction. In this instance silent thinking is a large part of the interaction. We are both contemplating what to do next with our "Bug Sprayer." With a one-to-one interaction as in this case, it is a lot easier to wait for an answer than with a group of children. Sometimes to help the children that are less verbal it helps to make some suggestions and let them decide from there.

However, it is also important for the teacher to realize that there are times not to keep quiet. One of these times is when children need to be encouraged to be accurate, to develop conceptual clarity. Several teachers reported to us a real reluctance to "tell" children anything about a topic. This could result in missing opportunities to open up the topic in a discussion. For example, in a kindergarten project on vehicles, the children revealed that they considered only trucks and vans vehicles. In a situation like this, a teacher could ask the children if they would add bikes to the list, and if not, why not. If the children said yes, the teacher could add something like, "Well, what about skate boards or roller blades . . . etc.?" and further discussion could be encouraged. The project provides a context for just this kind of dispositional development—the disposition to reflect on one's own assumptions about everyday things, and thereby be motivated to look up information and try to find experts who could clarify things.

MOVING INTO PHASE III

At some point, young investigators begin to run out of questions, and the class and the teacher begin to tire of the topic. Children choose to do project activities less frequently, they look at the project table less, and the project discussions provoke less interest and participation. These are all signs that the project is ready to move into Phase III.

CHAPTER 5

. . .

Concluding the Project

THERE COMES A TIME in the life of the project when children are ready to move on to other things. This can happen for several reasons. Children may simply no longer have questions; their curiosity may be satisfied. Children may also have reached a point at which further investigation requires skills such as reading and writing beyond their current abilities. The topic of the project and the previous experiences of the young investigators can also affect the duration of their enthusiasm for the project. The project may simply have run its course. Sometimes teachers who are new to projects assume that waning interest indicates that the topic was wrong and that the project has failed. They express disappointment as children lose interest and become interested in other topics. However, any topic can be run into the ground! Waning interest is part of the natural progress of a project and indicates that it is time to move into Phase III.

There are three main components in Phase III (see Figure 5.1). For young investigators, the main task is to decide what has been learned and how to share it and then to go about sharing it. The teacher's role includes debriefing the children, reviewing the project through documentation, and assessing the achievement of goals.

CULMINATING THE PROJECT

One of the many benefits of project work comes from the carefully planned, purposeful, and definite culmination of the work. In culminating activities, children begin to see themselves as learners and gain confidence in their ability to undertake investigations and solve problems. Teachers are able to see the results of the project and evaluate its effectiveness with respect to their goals for individual children and the whole group. Good culminating activities also help the parents to see and reinforce the knowledge, skills, and dispositions that were strengthened by the project. The community, if invited to participate in culminating activities, develops a better understanding of how young children learn and a greater appreciation for their intellectual abilities.

Focusing on What Was Learned

In the culmination process, the young investigators summarize what has been learned. It is important for children to have the opportunity to "elaborate what they have learned so that its meaning is enhanced and made personal" (Katz & Chard, 2000, p. 84). Articulating what they have learned helps children consolidate and integrate information from different experiences in the project. In Phase III, it is just as important to involve the children in decision making as it is in the first two phases. With older children, this is fairly easy because they have usually had experience with the options of giving a report, making a book, or preparing a display. With young investigators, these processes and products take time and patience.

The process usually begins with the teacher's asking the children how they might share what they have learned about the topic with others. With young investigators it is helpful to start this discussion by focusing on the web. The teacher may start a new web entitled "What We Now Know." Or the teacher may choose to use the web that children made at the beginning of the project. If during Phase II the teacher added answers to questions and additional concepts to that initial web, he or she may want to simply review the web with the children and ask for further additions. If the original web has not been changed since Phase I, the teacher may use another color of marker to show what has been learned. It is especially important to record additions to webs or comments during Phase III in a way that they can be distinguished from webs or comments made in Phase I and Phase II so children and adults can easily tell which words and pictures on the web are new.

Talking about what they have learned is easier for young investigators if they can look at their work and other forms of documentation such as photographs and constructions during the discussion. For children from 4 to 6 years old, reviewing the documentation and asking them what they found out and what they now know usually starts a productive discussion. However, children who are new to projects, or children who are not yet very verbal, may be at a loss

FIGURE 5.1 • Flowchart of Phase III

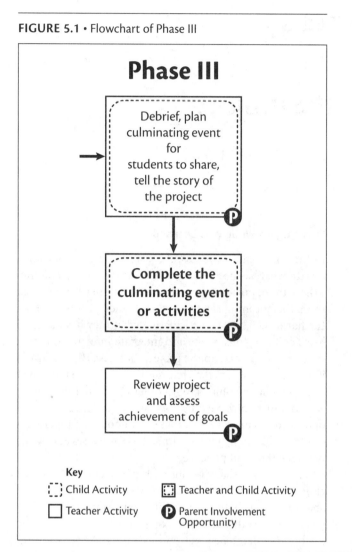

Teacher: These are things you learned then? Fire truck ladders are big and heavy. Firefighters climb them to get people out. They hang on those hooks.

Another way to elicit what the children have learned is to use some of the same techniques used in Phase I to generate questions. For example, if a book or a large photograph was used as a focus to generate questions in Phase I, the same book or photo can be used as a focus for children to discuss what they now know. If there is a wall display of documentation, then conducting a discussion while seated in front of it can also provide a focus for talking about what the investigation uncovered.

Young investigators can be encouraged to represent what they have learned through sketching and drawing. Sylvia Chard (1998a) talks about how drawing can be used in Phase III:

> Drawings, especially for the younger children, can be very helpful in enabling them to tell what they have learned. In one kindergarten class the children paired up with their fifth-grade buddies and shared three pictures they had selected from their project folders to explain what they had learned through their project work. The older children were to write what the young children told them about the items in the pictures. (p. 1:12)

Children can be encouraged to prepare a new drawing and put in it everything they have learned about the topic. These pictures can be reviewed and discussed with the teacher and the other children involved in the project. Children can critique each other's work and remind their classmates of details to put in. It is helpful to do this over several days, saving the drawings and adding more details to them each day.

The review and discussion activities are probably the most beneficial parts of the culmination process. As children see more and more words being written on the web, they develop a sense of the learning process. As one kindergartener said, "Wow! We know more now!" As they review their work, they see changes in Time 1 and Time 2 drawings and appreciate their own developing skillfulness. Among the feelings teachers of young children want to engender are feelings of self-esteem and self-confidence. In the course of examining their own growing skillfulness in drawing, for example, children's feelings of esteem and confidence are strengthened in genuine ways. In projects, the children's work, in the form of repeated drawings or attempts to write, is not for "show off." The drawing and writing are purposeful efforts to represent the children's experiences and ideas, in the process of which teachers can encourage them to evaluate their own accomplishments.

At this point, the teacher may want to talk with the children about what they might do to remember this project and what they learned. If they do not have any ideas, the

when asked the question "What did you learn?" They may respond more fully to a question like "What did you find out?" or "What did X tell you when you asked questions about Y?" Starting with a review of the documentation is also a good way for the teachers to support these children. In the process of reviewing documentation, the teacher can help children verbalize what they know about the topic. A conversation with a 3-year-old might go like this:

Child: There's Ashley and the ladders.
Teacher: You learned a lot about the ladders. Let's say some things you know about ladders. Fire truck ladders are . . .
Child: Big.
Child: Heavy.
Teacher: Do you remember what the ladders are used for? Fire truck ladders are used to . . .
Child: Climb.
Child: Get people out.
Child: They hang on those hooks.

teacher can suggest making a book that tells the story of the project. Sometimes teachers believe that to culminate a project, there must be a big event. With young investigators, however, activities in the classroom such as making a book about the project, or putting together a bulletin board or a display, may be the most meaningful way to draw the work to a close. The project book may be checked out to parents, who can share it with their children at home. Parents can be invited to view the displays. These provide a sense of closure and enable the children to experience satisfaction from their accomplishments.

If the children have created a role-play environment such as a Pizza Hut restaurant, role-playing in that environment can be a meaningful culminating activity. For example, a group of classrooms at Valeska Hinton Early Childhood Education Center in Peoria, Illinois, studied the local hospital. Each class created a part of the hospital in the hallway outside their room (e.g., the x-ray room, the gift shop, and a hospital room). The culmination of the project consisted of providing each group of children with assigned uninterrupted playtimes in which they could role-play and enjoy the use of the props in the hospital that they had jointly created.

Sharing with Others

Some projects, however, lend themselves to a more elaborate culmination process. As young investigators become more experienced with projects, they can be encouraged to share what they have learned in a variety of ways. After discussing and documenting what has been learned in the project, the children may be asked what they would like to share with others.

With young investigators, it usually helps to identify a target audience. For example, "What would you like to show your parents about how we learned about the fire truck?" or "Now that you know so much about fire trucks, how about telling Mrs. Brown's class what you did, where you went, and what you found out?" Young investigators who are doing their first project are unlikely to come up with many ideas on their own. The teacher may have to present clear alternatives. Some culminating activities that have worked well with young children include exhibits, pictorial histories of the project, reports, plays, dramas, music, scrapbooks, and school presentations.

In the Fire Truck Project in Pam Scranton's class, the children decided to make a movie (video) about the process of constructing their fire truck and to invite another classroom to come to a "movie party" and to see the video. This probably came about because the project had been documented by video, and the teacher had used video to review and extend the field-site visit. The children had become interested in the videotaping process.

FIGURE 5.2 • University Primary School apple store

In Jolyn Blank's 3- and 4-year-old class at the University Primary School at the University of Illinois, the Tree Project, which included the study of apple trees, culminated in the opening of the Apple Store the children had created (see Figure 5.2). In projects in which children create a store or a business, the children sometimes chose to actually conduct business on their open-house day. For example, they sell apples or bakery goods or whatever fits with the project topic.

Many projects with young investigators include in the final phase some type of construction that can be shared with others. For example, when a cardboard car was built by the 3- and 4-year-olds at Illinois Valley Early Childhood Education Center, the culminating event was to display the car in the student center (Beneke, 1998). However, projects for young children do not always result in construction. Judy Cagle, teacher of 3- to 5-year-olds at Valeska Hinton Early Childhood Education Center, has guided several projects with young children in which the culminating activity did not include any kind of construction.

The type of culminating activity really depends on the projects—most projects at this age level lend themselves to construction of something as a culminating activity but some do not. The ones that do not can be just as meaningful and valuable for the children as the ones that result in a construction as long as they have some things for the children to do—to sink their teeth into, so to speak. In my mixed-age classroom we've had a project end in a ballet performance, several end in play performances, and one in museum tours.

Ms. Cagle goes on to describe her favorite culminating event, which occurred when she had a classroom of 4- and 5-year-olds. In a teacher interview, Ms. Cagle told how the children came to create an art museum tour as their culminating event.

> The whole project developed from children's interest. We were doing a study (or a unit) on the author/ illustrator Eric Carle. We read his books and saw a film on how he makes his pictures. The children got interested in how he made collages. They then wanted to learn to make collages. They made a mural and several children made small individual collages.
>
> At the same time we were reading one of the books about the "box car children," which was about a mystery in a museum. That sparked interest in displaying their work. They started talking about what was in a museum, then they talked about different kinds of museums. The discussion turned to what other kinds of art they could put in the museum. That was the beginning of the Art Museum Project. This led to an investigation of what a museum is like, what things go into museums, and how objects are displayed in museums.
>
> They ended up with a museum in the hallway. It had their collages, the mural, some watercolors they did of peonies and irises. They made clay sculptures, which we fired in the kiln. One child made a watercolor painting of the *Titanic,* then a clay model of the *Titanic,* and then a Lego model of the *Titanic.* That was all displayed together in the museum. Then they decided to give tours of the museum and that became the culminating event.
>
> Everyone participated in the museum tours in one way or another—making tickets, giving out invitations, or giving tours. They discussed the schedule, how many tour guides were needed for each time slot. Children could sign up if they wanted to be a tour guide, but not everyone wanted to do that. The biggest discussion was on how to rotate the tour guides in the time slots so anyone who wanted to give tours would have a chance to do that. Each child could do as much as he or she wanted. No one was left out because there wasn't a job.
>
> We invited other classes. If a whole class decided to come, the children decided to divide them into two parts. Others who were invited and came were office staff and parents. Several times parents came into the school for some other purpose during that week, and the children would ask them if they wanted a tour and one or two children would give an unscheduled tour.

Ms. Cagle and her aide, Lynn Akers, agreed that the creation of the museum was one of the best culminating events of a project partly because it built on the children's interest in the topic. Ms. Cagle taught the same group of children the following year when some of them had turned 6. She noticed that they used the same planning processes for the culminating event for another project.

> They began a project on water. The children created a play about what they knew. It was very meaningful to them, and like the museum, the idea came up first in a discussion and then seemed to naturally evolve into a culminating event. Like the museum, I could see them incorporate all they had learned. I thought it was a great culminating event because the children felt that it was a great culminating event.

Ms. Cagle cautions, however, that culminating activities with an event require careful planning that includes documenting the event.

> One problem with culminating events that don't have a product is that they happen and then they are gone and over. We don't have a lot of documentation of the culmination of those projects, like we do the projects where children constructed something. But I know the experience was so meaningful for the children.

Ms. Cagle and Ms. Akers consider these kinds of culminating experiences to be the best culminating events because, as Ms. Cagle said, "I know the experience was so meaningful for the children." Teachers new to projects would be wise to keep meaningfulness to children as one of the major criteria in planning a culminating activity for a project.

Like the events that Judy Cagle describes, many culminating activities involve more than just the children in the classroom and their parents. Culminating activities can be shared with other classes of all grades in the school.

A benefit of culminating events as distinct from other types of culminating activities is that events provide motivation for teachers and children to review skills and consolidate knowledge. Having an event also provides a deadline and a purpose for the culminating work. Preparing and then participating in a culminating event can create enthusiasm in the children and parents. Indeed, one of the major benefits of good project work is the positive way most parents respond to their own children's enthusiasm, involvement, and motivation to work hard. It also provides a sense of teamwork and community as children and parents work together and celebrate together the accomplishments of the project.

Culminating events benefit the young investigators who worked on the project as well as the children who observe the results of their work. Learning to do project work involves complex processes. Children in other classes learn much about project work by looking at other children's projects, especially if they also have a chance to discuss the work with the investigators. They learn how young children can formulate questions for investigation, represent in constructions what they learned about a topic, and plan culminating activities for a project. They see children become more skillful, which increases their confidence that they too will be able to master difficult skills. Early childhood teachers who are learning to use the project approach can form a support network and share project books and

documentation of culminating events. This can enable children to see even more of the projects implemented in other classrooms.

Culminating activities can also be shared with the wider community, including those experts and field-site personnel who were involved in the project. Besides culminating

A CLOSER LOOK • SHARING NATURE PROJECTS EDUCATES OTHERS •

AS A PROJECT enters the culmination stage, opportunities arise for children to educate others about what they have learned about a nature topic. One of the goals of increasing children's connection with nature is the development of an attitude of stewardship toward the environment. As children use the project approach to study nature topics in depth, they often become protective of living things. One kindergarten class that was studying a wild area near a park by their school became quite concerned to discover trash littering the area. They worked hard to clean up the trash, and after much discussion, decided to make a poster telling others not to "throw your stuff here." This led to making more posters and putting them in other places throughout their community.

Posters are an excellent way for children to not only use what they learned in a meaningful way but also share with others. One class created posters of the different birds that frequented their bird feeder. These were used by other classes and adults to learn the names of the birds. Posters can also be made by the children to warn others that an area has been planted with seeds and should not be walked on. Other posters can serve as alerts for something happening in the natural world. For example, a poster might indicate the location of a bird's nest so others will not accidentally knock it down. A poster might alert walkers to the dangers of a patch of poison ivy. Still other posters may be used like labels to identify trees and plants. When these are created for the out-of-doors, they should be laminated so they will be more lasting.

Another way that children can educate others is to create books about their nature topic. These can be shared with other classes and even with interested adults. The creation of a field guide to a natural area at the school or nearby can be a major project that might take several classes or several years to be completed. In these handmade field guides, children capture with drawings or photos the living things in the area, look up the correct names, indicate the location, and write what they learned. This can be a very simple field guide on a narrow topic, such as "Field Guide to Our Bugs" created by prekindergarten students. Or it can be a sophisticated book assembled by primary-grade children using a computer to include photos, scientific names, and information gathered from Internet searches.

Through project work children at the kindergarten, first, and second grade level can deepen their knowledge base about the natural world. This may develop into a concern about such things as water or energy conservation or local pollution. The children can share their concerns in many ways, including the creation of PowerPoint presentations, letters to the editor, or meetings with government officials. These kinds of experiences can help children become not just stewards of the environment but also advocates for it.

These preschoolers are using their clipboards to draw something that captured their attention during their walk in the woods. Their drawings will be used in a book about the woods.

events, the community can also be included by having an opportunity to view the documentation of the project. For example, a documentation display on the Drive-Up Bank Project from Kay Hughes's first-grade classroom in the Harlem School District was put on display for several weeks in the bank the children had visited and investigated. The Peoria Zoo displayed the Zoo Project documentation panels made by Mary Ann Gottlieb. There are many advantages to broadening the audience for the project, including educating the community about the advantages of active, engaged, and meaningful learning experiences such as projects (see also Helm & Helm, 2006).

THE POWER OF DOCUMENTATION

When a teacher carefully collects, analyzes, interprets, and displays evidence of learning, it is called "documentation." Documentation of projects usually includes observations, collections of children's products, portfolios, self-reflections of individual children, and narratives or stories of the learning experience. Documentation may be collected in the form of anecdotal notes, children's work, photographs, and audio or video recordings. Children, teachers, parents, and the community can use documentation of projects for a variety of purposes.

There are many reasons that documentation is considered an integral part of the project approach. Comprehensive, good-quality documentation of a project can provide evidence of children's learning in all areas of development: physical, emotional, social, and cognitive. It provides a framework for organizing teachers' observations and recording each child's special interests and developmental progress. Good documentation makes it clear that learning through projects is an interactive process by capturing young investigators' active exploration and interaction with adults, other children, and materials. Documentation also can show how children learn from activities and materials that are concrete, real, and relevant to their lives. Documentation is especially helpful for looking at the kinds of complex integrated learning experiences that are part of good project work.

The most valuable feature of documentation in projects with young children, however, may be how it helps guide the teacher in the progress of the project. Gathering and analyzing documentation throughout the project enables the teacher to assess what each child knows or can do, and just what materials or activities he or she is most likely to benefit from next. The teacher can then increase the difficulty, complexity, and challenge of an activity as children are engaged in it and as their understanding and skills evolve. Teachers who conscientiously document the children's experiences during projects are more likely to make productive decisions when planning for the project. These

decisions include the classroom setup and schedule, what to do next, what questions to ask, what resources to provide, and how to stimulate the development of each child through the project process.

Lev Vygotsky's sociocultural theory explains the importance of teachers' decisions in maximizing learning (Bodrova & Leong, 2006). According to Vygotsky (1978), the teacher is most effective when teaching is directed toward a zone of proximal development for each child. Children learn most easily when the teacher provides experiences within that zone of development. To determine the zone of proximal development, the teacher assesses a child's development in particular skills or knowledge, probes the child's thinking on the topic, and then provides experiences that will build a bridge or a "scaffold" to higher-level thought processes (Berk & Winsler, 1995). Often the most helpful information for the teacher is that which reveals what the child understands only partially, or what the child is beginning to be able to do even if only inconsistently, or what the child is trying to integrate into his or her existing knowledge. In projects there are many opportunities for young children to reveal their understanding and misunderstanding to a teacher who is observant and vigilant about documenting the children's experiences.

Teachers report that children become aware of the documentation being conducted by their teachers, and it is taken by them to mean that their work is important, worthwhile, respected, and valued. Teachers who carefully document the children's activities have reported that as they increased the attention given to documentation, children became more careful about their work and more evaluative of their own efforts. When teachers document children's first, second, and even third attempts at a task, such as drawing and labeling a bicycle part, children begin to reflect on their own skill development. Children also understand the effect documentation of their work has on adults. Even quite young children are aware, perhaps not consciously, of the positive responses of their teacher and parents to their work.

Documentation of projects in a variety of ways also helps teachers respond to demands for accountability. A strong trend in education is an increase in the demand for accountability, meeting official performance standards, and participating in program evaluation. Schools and other early childhood programs are being required more and more to inform constituencies of the effectiveness of their programs. If the teacher is documenting for program evaluation or to demonstrate accountability, it is important to obtain a copy of the program's goals and objectives or any curriculum guides. Documentation for this purpose will be most effective if it is focused on the knowledge, skills, and dispositions that the school district or early childhood program wants children to develop. Documentation enables the teacher to provide evidence to decision makers and all other stakeholders that learning is occurring as a result of first-hand learning experiences like those afforded by the project approach.

TYPES OF DOCUMENTATION

Most teachers of young children have some familiarity with documenting children's experiences, from which inferences can be made about their learning. They may use a developmental checklist, take anecdotal notes, or systematically collect some children's work, such as self-portraits at the beginning and the end of the year. All of these are useful in documenting projects. There are, however, as many different ways to document experience and learning as there are ways that active, engaged children try to make sense of their world. The book *Windows on Learning: Documenting Young Children's Work* (Helm, Beneke, & Steinheimer, 2007) is recommended to help teachers learn how to document.

Teachers who are learning to use the project approach with young children may find it helpful to spend some time studying documentation and the many different ways to document. For example, in a project on the school bus, a teacher might ask a young child to explain a drawing she has made of the bus, but not think to record what the child says in the pretend bus barn. A teacher may record the whole group's questions and comments on the web but fail to record which child said what so that such information could be placed in a child's portfolio. Documenting in a variety of ways enables the teacher to do a better job of getting accurate information about each child. For example, a child who has not developed extensive language skills may be able to draw a picture or construct a block play environment that shows the depth of understanding the child has about the topic.

Figure 5.3 summarizes the types of documentation discussed in the following sections. Many teachers find it helpful to use this chart to incorporate ways for documenting into their written plans. Thinking in advance about what types of documentation can be collected for different project activities assures that a variety will be used. A fairly common mistake that teachers make in documenting their first project is trying to capture all learning in photographs or to photograph activities for which other documentation has already been gathered. Reviewing the list in Figure 5.3 when planning for documenting can help avoid this pitfall.

Observation

Because projects are largely child-directed and teacher-guided, they present wonderful opportunities for observing children. In project work, children pose and seek answers to their own questions. They solve problems on their own and with other children and sometimes in consultation with the teacher. As the young investigators are engaged in the learning experience, the teacher is able to observe the children's use of language and their interaction patterns, play levels, and dispositions. These are captured in a variety of ways. The teacher may make anecdotal notes on what he or she observes, noting knowledge, skills, or dispositions. Audio or video recordings may be used to document the exact words and actions in a dialogue or problem-solving sequence for later analysis. The teacher may also note what behavioral indicators of dispositions have been observed, such as verbal and nonverbal expressions of interest, choice of activities, and time spent on activities.

These observations can be used as evidence for developmental checklists or for documenting achievement of curriculum goals. Observations and checklists along with children's work products may become a part of children's individual portfolios.

An example of an observation in a project is this description by Sallee Beneke (1998) of 4-year-old Lisa's participation in the Car Project:

> Lisa began at mid-year to attend our center 2 days per week. She had been very quiet and reserved and had taken an onlooker role in classroom activities until we began the Car Project. Most of her participation up to that point had taken the form of vigorous nodding in answer to questions. Lisa volunteered to fill in the "yes" and "no" boxes in the chart to indicate which car parts were actually steel or iron, and which were not. I wrote a model of the two words "yes" and "no" for her and she copied them on the chart in the appropriate places. Completing the chart provided Lisa with a sense of the purpose of print, and she was highly motivated to learn to express herself in writing. Taking on these tasks helped her to find entry into the classroom community. The other children came to appreciate her abilities and her helpfulness. (pp. 36–37)

Projects provide contexts for in-depth learning experiences that extend over a period of time. For this reason, they provide opportunities to observe development in a way that captures growth and change.

Collections of Children's Products

Products are one of the most obvious ways to document children's learning in projects. Pictures, webs, musical expressions, constructions, collections of data, and samples of oral language and emergent writing all provide effective documentation of the knowledge, skills, and dispositions that develop in project work.

There are many written language products that young investigators produce in projects, even though most young

FIGURE 5.3 • How documentation is collected in classrooms for young children

Type of Documentation	How It Is Collected in Classrooms for Young Children
I. *Individual Portfolios*	Specific content area items collected at specific intervals, for example: • Writing samples • Record of problem solving using numbers Unique items that show • Learning style • Interests • Unique talents of individual
II. *Products* (Individual or Group)	Products that children make or produce, such as • Spoken language as collected in anecdotal notes or audio/visual tapes • Written language as collected in signs, captions to photos and drawings, letters, labels, or child-made books • Constructions such as play environments, Legos, or block structures • Drawn pictures or paintings • Records of data collection • Musical expressions, such as made-up songs or dances • Webs, lists of words, or other records of vocabulary or concepts learned
III. *Observations of Progress and Performance*	Observations made by the teacher and recorded as • Specific knowledge or skills on a developmental checklist or curriculum guide • Anecdotal notes on events indicating knowledge, skills, or dispositions • Behavioral indicators of dispositions (expression of interest, time spent on activities, self-selection of activities)
IV. *Child Self-Reflections*	Children's statements of understanding their own • Preferences of activity • Enjoyment or interest in content areas • Pride in accomplishment • Acceptance of need for persistence and hard work
V. *Narratives of Learning Experiences*	Stories of learning experiences of individuals, small groups, or the whole class in • Teacher journals • Displays on projects and units • Books or explanations for parents • Books or stories for children

Adapted from Documentation Web, Helm, J. H., Beneke, S., & Steinheimer, K. (2007). *Windows on learning: Documenting young children's work* (2nd ed., p. 21). New York: Teachers College Press.

investigators are not yet fluent writers. A 3-year-old may scribble and call it "the doctor's message about the baby being sick." This documents an understanding of how writing is used and the purpose of print. Four-year-olds will often use letter-like shapes for communication. Figure 5.4 shows a child's sign that was a product of a project. The children collected clothing and donated it to a charity as part of the Clothes Project at University Primary School. The children made the sign so that they could sort the clothes into categories to give to the charity.

Young investigators also write letters and other communications in the process of a project. For example, during a field-site visit, the clipboards used by young investigators have sheets of paper on which the questions they are to ask are written. These may be written by an adult with child or adult illustrations. They may be written by an adult and then copied by the child. If the child is beginning to sound out words, the clipboard notes may be written entirely by the child. When a child obtains the answer to the question, he or she writes or draws a representation of the answer. After returning to the classroom, the children read what is on their clipboards as they report back to the group on what they found out about their questions. These answers on clipboards document writing as well as reading. Other

FIGURE 5.4 • The children at University Primary School made signs so they could sort clothes they had collected and give them to a charity.

written products of projects include books written by children as individuals or in groups. Three- and 4-year-olds will dictate words to accompany photos or drawings. Five- and 6-year-olds will often write their own words.

Webs are good products to represent group discussions. When a teacher records children's ideas on a web at the beginning and at the end of projects, contrasting the two webs reveals the growth in the young investigators' vocabulary and the concepts of the topic. Figure 5.5 shows the contrast between what Linda Lundberg's kindergarten class knew about turtles in September and what they knew in October. If the process of making the webs is taped (auditory or visual), or if the names of children are recorded with their comments, the webs can serve as documents of the growth in understanding of individual children as well as the group.

FIGURE 5.5 • When first webs from a project are displayed next to webs completed after investigation, the growth in concepts is easily understood.

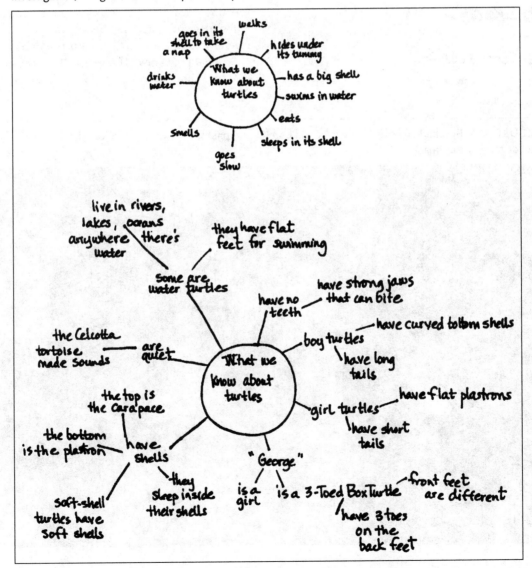

FIGURE 5.6 • Linda Lundberg prepared this sheet for her kindergarten children to record data during the field-site visit.

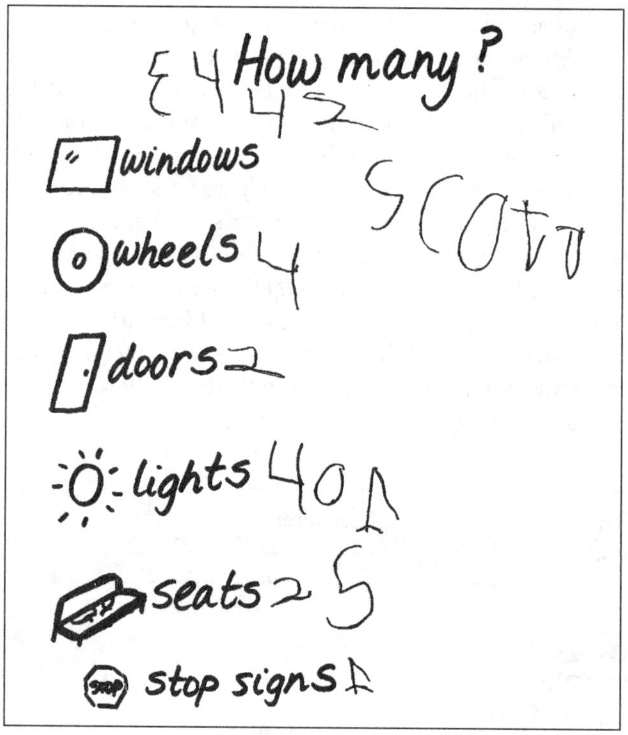

How many?

windows

wheels 4

doors 2

lights 4

seats 2

stop signs 1

Graphs, charts, tally sheets, and other mathematical representational products also often emerge from projects and can be used as documentation. Figure 5.6 is an example of data collection in a project that documents mathematical thinking. Here children are writing down numbers of items on a school bus.

These products can be produced either individually or by a group of children. Occasionally the product speaks for itself, but in general a product's usefulness as documentation can be increased by the thoughtful accompaniment of written narrative explaining the significance of the product. In displays of group work, a teacher may choose to select those products that are significant in telling the story of the project or in documenting the development of an individual child through participation in the project. It is not always necessary to display every picture made by every child.

Because the creation of play environments is one of the favorite ways that young investigators explore the project topic, group-constructed play environments are one of the most effective products to use to document children's knowledge and skills. Children build what they know, and careful examination of their constructions enables us to "see" what they know. Figure 5.7 shows the bulldozer created by 3- and 4-year-old children at Little Friends Learn-

FIGURE 5.7 • The children of Little Friends Child Care Center paid special attention to the detail of the bulldozer that they made.

FIGURE 5.8 • Real bulldozer that served as the model for the children at Little Friends

ing Center. One can see in the photo how much the children had learned about the bulldozer just by looking at the construction, how the children use the construction, and how the construction compares with the real bulldozer shown in Figure 5.8. It is also possible to see the children's skills in construction and how they solved construction problems.

The extended time and in-depth nature of projects enable rich documentation of children's growth and their development of skills. This is why it is important to make plans to capture children's knowledge and skills at the beginning of a project. This beginning documentation can then be compared with experiences that are documented later in the project. An example of this is the common documentation method of collecting Time 1, Time 2, and so forth, drawings of the same objects observed throughout the period of a project. This documentation is even more beneficial when it is collected from project to project so that it shows children's growth over a longer period of time. For example, Jolyn Blank collected Time 1 and Time 2 drawings by the same children over a period of 2 years in consecutive projects. Figures 5.9–5.13 show drawings by Edo, a second-language learner as a 3- and a 4-year-old. Figure 5.9 shows 3-year-old Edo's first drawing of a tree in the Tree Project. Figure 5.10 is Edo's drawing of a sheep at the sheep paddock. During his 4-year-old year, Edo did the Time 1/Time 2 drawings of a police car shown in Figures 5.11 and 5.12. In the first drawing Edo could not get all of the letters in the space so he wrote only the middle letters of "Champaign." In his second drawing he allowed enough room to get almost all of his letters in. The last drawing by Edo (still 4 years old) is an aerial view of a tricycle (see Figure 5.13). This sample of Edo's work shows how effective this type of documentation can be in understanding children's growth.

FIGURE 5.9 • This is Edo's first drawing at the preschool as a 3-year-old in the fall.

FIGURE 5.10 • The following spring Edo did this drawing of a sheep.

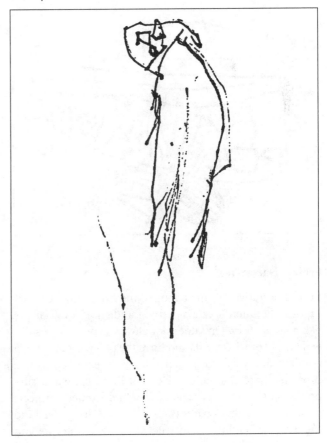

FIGURE 5.11 • As a 4-year-old, Edo became much more detailed in his drawings. On this drawing he attempts to put the letters "Champaign" on his police car.

FIGURE 5.12 • In Edo's second drawing of the police car, he made the area where the letters would go larger so they would almost all fit.

Project Narratives

Project narratives, or the telling of the story of the project, capture the interest of a variety of audiences. Projects are like a good story. One does not always know how a story will unfold or what twists and turns the plot will take. When children are involved in active learning experiences like projects, there is an added element of surprise and suspense. Stories are an excellent way to document projects because stories help parents and other adults understand the way that children construct their own concepts and build understanding through their experiences.

FIGURE 5.13 • This drawing in the spring of his 4-year-old year shows how Edo is beginning to understand the importance of perspective in drawing. This is a drawing looking down on a tricycle.

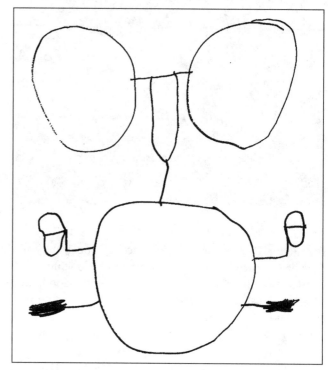

When stories are shared as they are evolving, the element of surprise increases the adults' interest in the project and encourages their participation and attention. Teachers who are new to project work have a tendency to gather documentation during a project but to wait until the project is over to analyze and share the documentation. Not only does this make it difficult for teachers to get the maximum benefit from documentation for guiding children's work during the project, but it also reduces the suspenseful impact the project story can have on others.

To capitalize on the evolving nature of the project, teachers sometimes write narratives to accompany wall displays in the classroom or in the hallway outside the classroom. They then continuously update the narrative as children's work proceeds. Photo captions are used frequently to tell the story on these displays. Teachers often share their reflections on the project experience and what they are learning about the children through the project. Children and adults are able to check the display to see the progress the class has made in investigating the topic.

These wall displays are easier to understand if the teacher also displays a project summary. Project summaries assist viewers in understanding more fully what they are seeing. The summary briefly tells the essential story elements of the project, similar to synopsis or a condensed version of a book. It lists the classrooms involved, the names of the teachers,

FIGURE 5.14 • Project summary of the Tree Project

Teachers: Jolyn Blank, Karla Lewis, Betty Liebovich
University Primary School, University of Illinois

Age Level: 3- and 4-year-olds

Time Span: September–October

Title or Focus of the Project

Trees: We investigated the trees in our playground and around our building. We observed and represented parts of trees, differences among trees and their parts such as shape of leaves, sizes, and changes that occur in the fall.

History of the Project

This project emerged from explorations of found artifacts and field experiences in our immediate surroundings. After creating an initial web of prior knowledge about trees, children began representing the trees around us. Interesting observations of squirrels drawn to a collection of acorns led to further dialogue about trees as homes for animals. Another question for investigation that emerged was, "What comes from trees?" A list was developed that included a variety of fruits that come from trees, and children visited an apple orchard.

What Did the Children Learn?

Through the investigation children learned to recognize differences among trees, names of various types of trees, and that it is possible to identify trees by examining the leaves. They identified parts of trees, including the veins in the leaves and the sap and roots of trees. They also thought about the changes that occur in trees in the fall. Some of the children engaged in first experiences with representation and explored a variety of media for representation. In addition, children identified some of the "gifts" of trees, recognizing some of the things that trees provide for people. They learned about a career in forestry and some of the jobs people do at an apple orchard and store. Some of the children looked at the process of growing apple trees, harvesting the apples, and creating products for sale in a store.

Plans for the Future

This project will continue as children complete construction of the apple store. We plan to sell goods from the store. From this experience, we might move into a project about grocery stores.

the ages of the children, and the time span of the project. Space is then provided for paragraphs under headings such as "Title" or "Focus of the Project," "History of the Project," "What the Children Learned," and "Plans for the Future." A project summary for the Tree Project in Jolyn Blank's classroom is shown in Figure 5.14. These displays, which share documentation as it occurs, are especially helpful for parents because they enable them to discuss the project with their children. While a project is in process, a summary and handwritten notes accompanying fresh documentation are sufficient to accomplish this goal.

Narratives can also be written for and by children. These narratives are often called "project history books." They usually include photos of the project and the children's words describing what happened. Children's work is also included in project history books. Project history books

sometimes focus on only one aspect of a project, such as the building of a structure or the field-site visit. Children enjoy these books, which are made available for them to read and reread and are checked out to parents. Project history books are also read in other classes where young children are learning to do project work.

Teachers who do projects with young investigators find it helpful to apply good storytelling principles when sharing narrative documentation about the project. An example of a good storytelling principle is tailoring the narrative to a particular audience. In narratives for parents, the teacher may want to share in-depth information about how the topic fits with curriculum goals. He or she may want to share expertise and tell what a particular observation or event indicates about a child's development. In narratives for children, the teacher may choose to focus more on the events of the project and what children saw and did. This enables the children to revisit and reprocess the experience and to see themselves as investigators.

Some teachers have managed to combine these purposes by making displays and books that provide in-depth, content-oriented information for parents at the same time they present the story of the project for children. One way to do this is to put additional information for parents on colored pages or in a smaller type font on the same page. The parent can read the story in the book to the child and read the parent text silently or at another time. Another approach is to put pages for adults on the left-hand side of the book and pages for children on the right-hand side. Parents can read the book to a child easily by focusing on the right-hand pages and come back at another time to study the left-hand pages.

When teachers are doing projects with young investigators, they may find that it is best to provide narratives in the children's own words. This is especially appropriate when children are beginning to understand the function of print or are attempting to figure out the reading process by matching letters with spoken words. It is respectful of the learning process to record in writing the child's comments or opinions exactly as spoken, instead of editing them for grammar.

USING MATERIALS AND EQUIPMENT FOR DOCUMENTATION

The teacher planning for collecting documentation should keep in mind the variety of ways to document. A simple planning sheet (see Figure 5.15) can be used to think about the activity of the project, the type of documentation that might be most appropriate for that activity (e.g., "observation"), and how it will be documented (e.g., "tape recorder in dramatic play area"). Most important, it is helpful to think about who will be responsible for doing the documenting. If the "documenter" normally has a task to do at the time of the activity, it is important to think about that task and who can do it so the documenter will be free to proceed with the documentation process. The planning sheet can be ongoing and completed from day to day as the project progresses.

There are many kinds of time-saving materials and equipment that can support documentation in an early childhood center. These include Post-it® notes for writing down observations and folders for collecting children's work and anecdotal notes. Some teachers place pens and notepads around the classroom so that notes can be jotted down quickly right in the area where children are working. Some teachers make sure there is a clipboard for each child, with the child's name on it, and paper. This not only encourages children to write and draw throughout the day but assures that these products can be easily collected by the teacher. A camera ready to use is essential. A tape recorder can be very helpful, and access to a video camera at certain times during a project can enrich the documentation. Teachers also use a photocopy machine for a variety of purposes. These include copying children's work that they wish to take home, reducing or enlarging samples of work so they can be more easily displayed, and making multiple copies of children's books or project history books for children to check out and share at home.

When documentation has to look professional, many teachers use a computer with a simple desktop publishing program to make displays and narratives. A scanner greatly simplifies the process of making books, displays, and newsletters. Teachers can scan children's work and copy photographs. Children's work can be scanned directly into the computer, reduced so that it is manageable, and shared in a variety of ways. Many teachers find a digital camera easy to use to record project events and to photographic work. Simple digital cameras are now available that can be used by very young children to document the project work. If a multimedia computer system is available, the teacher, older children, or a parent can produce a multimedia record of projects.

FIGURE 5.15 • Documentation planning sheet.

Anticipated Project Events	Possible Types of Documentation	Equipment or Materials Needed	Collection Task Assigned to	Coverage of Collector's Tasks

All of this material and equipment is helpful because it encourages documentation and enables the teacher to be more efficient, and it allows the documentation to look professional. However, many teachers begin documenting with just a spiral notebook, some note cards, an inexpensive camera, and an organized system for collecting children's work.

DISTILLING DOCUMENTATION

Display panels, transcripts of children's conversations, and project history books have opened teachers' eyes to the value of projects for young children. The polish and complexity of some documentation, however, intimidates some teachers, especially those who are new to the project approach. Much of the documentation that is shared with others is carefully prepared or distilled documentation. Project documentation is collected as the project unfolds and is discussed and shared with others who are working with the children on the project. Only the most informative documentation is "published." Preparing documentation for sharing with a larger audience or for display is referred to as "publishing documentation"—carefully mounting, typing, or displaying it. In *Windows on Learning* (Helm et al., 2007), this process is called "distilling." Sallee Beneke (1998) talks about the distilling process in her center:

> In a sense there are really four levels of editing or "distilling" to the documenting we do at our center. The first level takes place as the items are selected for the project board in the classroom. The second level takes place as items are selected and sometimes reformatted for our hallway display. The third level takes place when the documentation is removed from the hallway and panels or history boards are prepared as a final record of our project. This book [referring to the Car Project] in which I have described the project and included samples of the children's work along with my own reflections is perhaps a fourth level. (p. 69)

Detailed advice on publishing documentation and organizing displays is available in *Windows on Learning* (Helm et al., 2007).

Documentation enhances projects with young children, but extensive documentation displays are not necessary for children and teachers to have a successful project or for children to develop new knowledge, skills, and dispositions from the project. The skills of documenting children's work and sharing documentation take time to learn, and teachers are advised to set reasonable goals for documenting the first projects they do with young children.

Learning to document can be compared with learning to drive a car: The first attempts are slow, and each step has to be carefully considered and planned. Eventually a driver becomes so skilled and confident that he or she can drive without consciously thinking about most of the separate tasks, like starting the car. Integrating comprehensive documentation into a project is also a skill that takes time to learn. The teacher who works at improving documentation eventually finds that documentation is so helpful and so natural to the project process that it too becomes automatic.

EVALUATING THE PROJECT

Projects, like all educational experiences, benefit from reflection and evaluation. Guiding projects for young investigators and documenting children's work is sometimes described by teachers as "teaching on the fly." The teacher has to make many decisions during the teaching process in response to children's questions, interactions in the classroom, and children's work in process. The process is a dynamic one. Since *dynamic* is defined by the *American Heritage Dictionary* as "relating to energy or objects in motion," "characterized by continuous change, activity, or progress," and "marked by intensity and vigor," the term can be accurately applied to the teaching process when the project approach is used with young children.

Teaching on the fly, however, cannot and should not mean that teachers have no goals and objectives, that they have no plan of action, and that they are not well prepared for the activities of the day. It is important that teachers strive to improve their teaching skills and anticipate where children's interests might be going and how they can best support the investigative and representational processes in which young children engage.

Projects as Engaged Learning

One way to look at the success of a project is to consider whether the experiences it provided were engaging and absorbing, and from which much was learned. Did the learning experience engage children according to the definition of engaged learning described in Chapter 1 (Jones et al., 1994)?

In addition to defining engaged learning, Jones et al. also provided guidelines for examining various aspects of learning experiences—such as the type of tasks engaged learners do, how learning is assessed, and teacher and student roles—and determining how these would look in a classroom where engaged learning is occurring. The following evaluation questions are based on those guidelines adapted for early childhood programs. Following each question is an explanation of what teachers should look for in analyzing that aspect of project work. The questions are provided in checklist format in the Project Planning Journal at the end of the book.

1. *Do children take responsibility for their own work or activity?* Children demonstrate participation in the processes of the project by asking questions. They "take charge" of the experiences by explaining or showing the teacher what they want to do, and by soliciting the teacher's advice when necessary.

2. *Are children absorbed and engrossed in their work?* Children find satisfaction and pleasure in their work. They appear to be developing a taste for solving problems and deepening their understanding of ideas or concepts.

3. *Are children becoming strategic learners?* Children are developing and using problem-solving strategies and skills. They are applying what they learn in one experience to similar experiences.

4. *Are the children becoming increasingly collaborative?* Children work with other children. They talk about their ideas to others. They are fair-minded in dealing with those who disagree with them. Children offer each other support, suggestions, and encouragement. Children are beginning to recognize their strengths and the strengths of others.

5. *Are the tasks in the projects challenging and integrative?* The project is complex and requires sustained amounts of time and effort over days or even weeks. Tasks require children to stretch their thinking and social skills in order to be successful. Children are learning how components of literacy, math, science, and communication skills are helpful and useful. All children, not just a few, are encouraged to ask hard questions, to define problems, and to take part in conversations.

6. *Is children's work in the project used to assess their learning?* Documentation is collected on how children construct knowledge and create products to represent their learning. The documentation matches the goals of the curriculum. Documentation includes evidence of individual and group efforts. It makes visible children's dispositions such as the disposition to solve problems and to ask questions. Documentation includes drafts as well as final products. Children are involved in the documentation process and encouraged to reflect on the documentation. Children are encouraged to generate criteria, such as what makes a good observational drawing or a good question.

7. *Does the teacher facilitate and guide the children's work?* The teacher provides a rich environment, rich experiences, and activities. The teacher encourages sharing knowledge and responsibility. The level of information and support given by the teacher is adjusted based on children's needs. The teacher helps children link new information to prior knowledge and helps children develop strategies to find out what they want to know.

The teacher models and coaches. With the children, the teacher becomes a co-learner and co-investigator.

Variations in Engagement

It is doubtful that a teacher will see in one project all the indicators of engaged learning listed above, especially if this is the young investigators' first or even second project. It is also important to realize that all children will not be engaged in all projects all of the time or to the same degree.

One determinant of the degree of involvement may be age. Many 3-year-olds are observers of the project process and may float in and out of project activities. These children may experience a project in a way similar to how they experience a teacher-directed unit: enjoying activities, developing some background knowledge about the topic, and sharing some group experiences. They may not at first contribute significantly to generating questions, problem solving, or the kind of in-depth investigation that makes a project different from a unit. However, these children are still learning much about the topic through their classmates' work and often become more engaged in subsequent projects. Teachers report that children who participated very little in one project sometimes use skills that they observed other children use but had never themselves practiced, during the next project. Their ability to participate in webbing, to draw, or to ask questions shows that they had followed closely the progress of the project and their classmates' work.

With young children, the degree of engagement is also a function of the project topic. As the teacher is evaluating projects, it is helpful to look at the level at which each child in the classroom has experienced the project. This information can then be factored into consideration of topics for subsequent projects. By reviewing the evaluations of previous projects, the teacher can consider how appropriate topic selection can improve the probability that more of the criteria of engaged learning will be met in the classroom.

Besides engagement in learning, there are other factors—such as the achievement of required curriculum goals—that may have to be considered in project evaluation. These may differ from one teacher and from one program to another. Chapter 8 presents a discussion of required curriculum and other issues in implementing the project approach.

IN CHAPTERS 2–5 we have walked you, step by step, through the phases of a project and included examples from parts of many projects to illustrate our descriptions. Next, in Chapters 6 and 7, you can experience two complete projects from beginning to end. Chapter 6 is a preschool project, and Chapter 7 is a toddler project. Your guides are two experienced teachers of preschoolers and toddlers.

CHAPTER 6

• • •

The Camera Project
Preschoolers Engaged and Learning

THIS CHAPTER presents the Camera Project as described in the words of Lora Taylor, the teacher in whose classroom it occurred. Ms. Taylor has been teaching for 14 years, 8 of those at Northminster Learning Center in Peoria, Illinois. Northminster Learning Center is a Reggio-inspired, faith-based early childhood program that includes toddler, preschool, and kindergarten programs, as well as after-school care for approximately 250 children. The Center is funded by the Illinois State Board of Education to provide a Preschool for All program. Project work and documentation are core values at Northminster Learning Center. Ms. Taylor was assisted in the project by her associate teacher, Stephanie Martinek, and by a student teacher from Bradley University, Erika Goldstein. Ms. Taylor has two groups of children: morning and afternoon classes of mixed-age 3- and 4-year-olds. She usually works with the same topic for both morning and afternoon sessions and completes an average of two projects a year in her classroom.

PHASE I: GETTING STARTED

The Camera Project started when a couple of children became really involved with a camera I had placed in the house corner area as a play prop to stimulate creative play. I thought the children might want to pretend to go places and take pictures. They took the camera outside of the play area and began running around the classroom saying, "Cheese." I questioned them:

"What are you taking a picture of?"
"What are you going to do with that camera?"
"How are you going to get the film out of there?"
"How do you know that there are really pictures being taken?"

As this play persisted, we continued the questioning. Because the play was persistent, I decided to put some film in the camera one day. I told the boys and girls there was real film in the camera, and I just let them play around and snap pictures. Then the next day I brought in the developed pictures. It was fun for them to see how disorganized the

pictures were. There were pictures of the ceiling, the floor, and their fingertips. So we discussed how one can really take pictures. I asked them if they knew how to take a picture of a person. They wondered how that worked. That was the beginning of the Camera Project. It blossomed from there. The topic came from the children's play. Just adding a little play prop in our dramatic play area led to this engaging project.

Anticipatory Planning

When we decided that the camera was probably going to be the focus of our next project, we became serious about our planning. As this was not a topic I was familiar with, all three of us sat down together to write out everything we knew. Ms. Martinek, Ms. Goldstein, and I webbed the concepts that we expected the children would encounter. Here are some of the things the three of us talked about at our planning meeting and put on our web:

- Where you could take pictures
- Children's literature that we wanted to share
- Possibly some real pictures and fake pictures
- History of the camera
- Film and how it works
- Different kinds of cameras

As we talked more and more about cameras, I remembered that when I was young, we used Polaroid cameras, and now digital cameras are used more often. We thought perhaps the children would want to experience the different types of cameras and all the accessories that can go with them. We also talked about reasons why children might be involved in picture taking, for example, sending family pictures during the holidays to show the growth of their family over time. We talked about pictures being memories for people, for example, having photos of family members displayed throughout one's house

After we wrote on our web all the things that we thought we knew, we started to plug in different curriculum areas that are relevant (see Figure 6.1). We began to think of

FIGURE 6.1 • Ms. Taylor and her assistants developed this planning web to help them anticipate concepts children might learn and to integrate curriculum goals.

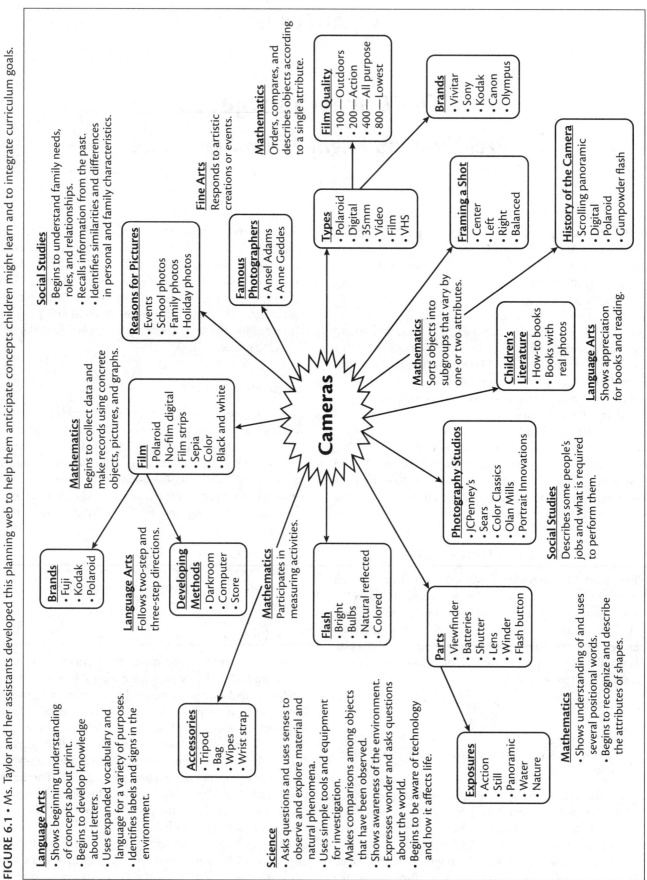

Language Arts
• Shows beginning understanding of concepts about print.
• Begins to develop knowledge about letters.
• Uses expanded vocabulary and language for a variety of purposes.
• Identifies labels and signs in the environment.

Social Studies
• Begins to understand family needs, roles, and relationships.
• Recalls information from the past.
• Identifies similarities and differences in personal and family characteristics.

Fine Arts
Responds to artistic creations or events.

Mathematics
Orders, compares, and describes objects according to a single attribute.

Reasons for Pictures
• Events
• School photos
• Family photos
• Holiday photos

Famous Photographers
• Ansel Adams
• Anne Geddes

Film Quality
• 100—Outdoors
• 200—Action
• 400—All purpose
• 800—Lowest

Brands
• Vivitar
• Sony
• Kodak
• Canon
• Olympus

Mathematics
Begins to collect data and make records using concrete objects, pictures, and graphs.

Film
• Polaroid
• No-film digital
• Film strips
• Sepia
• Color
• Black and white

Types
• Polaroid
• Digital
• 35mm
• Video
• Film
• VHS

Framing a Shot
• Center
• Left
• Right
• Balanced

History of the Camera
• Scrolling panoramic
• Digital
• Polaroid
• Gunpowder flash

Cameras

Brands
• Fuji
• Kodak
• Polaroid

Language Arts
Follows two-step and three-step directions.

Developing Methods
• Darkroom
• Computer
• Store

Mathematics
Participates in measuring activities.

Mathematics
Sorts objects into subgroups that vary by one or two attributes.

Children's Literature
• How-to books
• Books with real photos

Language Arts
Shows appreciation for books and reading.

Photography Studios
• JCPenney's
• Sears
• Color Classics
• Olan Mills
• Portrait Innovations

Social Studies
Describes some people's jobs and what is required to perform them.

Accessories
• Tripod
• Bag
• Wipes
• Wrist strap

Flash
• Bright
• Bulbs
• Natural reflected
• Colored

Parts
• Viewfinder
• Batteries
• Shutter
• Lens
• Winder
• Flash button

Exposures
• Action
• Still
• Panoramic
• Water
• Nature

Mathematics
• Shows understanding of and uses several positional words.
• Begins to recognize and describe the attributes of shapes.

Science
• Asks questions and uses senses to observe and explore material and natural phenomena.
• Uses simple tools and equipment for investigation.
• Makes comparisons among objects that have been observed.
• Shows awareness of the environment.
• Expresses wonder and asks questions about the world.
• Begins to be aware of technology and how it affects life.

activities children might be interested in doing. Then we thought about what we could do with those ideas. We discussed where we could go, what we could see, and what kind of activities we could do in the classroom. On the web we added the Illinois Early Learning Standards, which we use as curriculum goals, and noted how our activities would meet these goals. We recorded our brainstorming ideas about what we could do in the different domains: fine arts, science, social science, mathematics, and language arts. From our work on the anticipatory web, we decided that the topic was good and viable because it was something the children were aware of and that was part of their lives, but something they may not have thought a lot about before. The topic would be interesting to them. There would be many vocabulary words that they may not have been familiar with. Some knew a lot about digital cameras, others not so much, so there would be much that children could share with each other. As we did our anticipatory planning web, we could see that, obviously, the topic was going to meet a lot of our curriculum goals in many different areas. It is a rich topic that encompasses technology, math, and science.

As we were working on our own webbing, we started adding more cameras to the classroom because children were arguing over access to them (see Figure 6.2). We ended up with three different types of cameras: Polaroid, digital, and film. As each camera type was a little bit different, this raised more questions from the children. When the photos the children had taken came back from processing, they put them into a photo collage. We spent about a week on focusing activities to build interest and background knowledge. Our planning involved exploring with the children, observing and listening to them, then doing more anticipatory planning, then more exploring.

What They Knew

You can tell what the children knew before we started investigating by looking at their Time 1 web (see Figure 6.3). We created the children's web by meeting in small groups for about 20 minutes; there were about nine children in each group. These children had not had a lot of project experience, so we wanted to use smaller groups to give them more teacher attention and to talk webbing through a little bit more. Each teacher took a group, and then we combined the webs. We combined webs from the morning and the afternoon classes because they had similar ideas. I have kept morning and afternoon webs separate when the thoughts of the children were different, but on this particular project, the webs were pretty similar. On other projects webs may be very different and focus on different ideas about the same topic.

When we worked on this web, the children started talking about colors. What colors can a camera be (golden or black)? Then the list just blossomed into all the colors of

FIGURE 6.2 • Children's interest in the project grows when they have access to real artifacts.

the rainbow. As teachers, we doubted that there were that many colors of cameras, but we wrote them down because, really, how would we know that there aren't pink cameras or orange cameras? It is part of the learning process to record the children's basic knowledge so they can test it out. Then they started to talk about what they could take pictures of. They knew the names of some of the types of cameras: real, fake (toy), digital (they knew a lot about the digital), and someone knew about the Polaroid. The web was pretty basic, mainly naming objects that children at this age might know related to cameras.

We have learned a few tricks that we have found support such discussions. In this project I asked the children to remember when they were playing with the cameras. "Remember how you were taking pictures with the camera? Tell me about that; tell me what you already know about cameras." I might prompt them a little bit by focusing on a particular aspect of the topic, such as "Tell me what they look like." To encourage talk, I focus them on the sensory experience of the topic:

"What do the cameras look like?"
"What do they sound like?"
"How did the camera feel?"

FIGURE 6.3 • The children's web of their prior knowledge about cameras shows much of that knowledge consists of names of items.

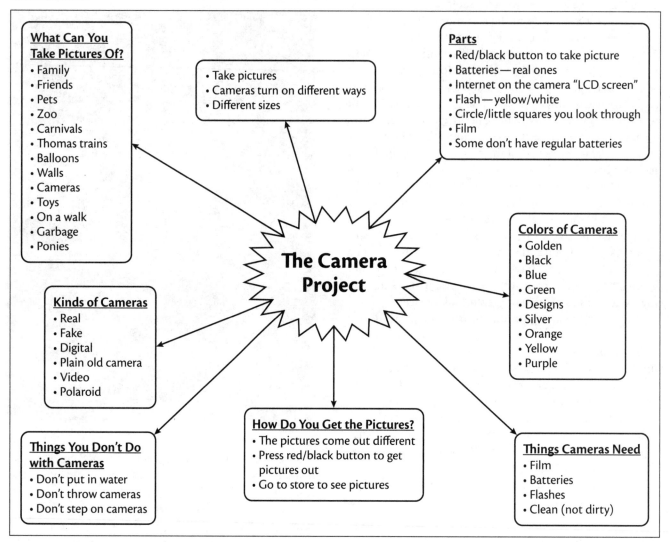

If the children have a little idea or what I think is the start of an idea, I might say, "Tell me a little more about that." I also try to get them to discuss together. Once someone has an idea, I might say, "You know, Johnny mentioned that he could take pictures of his family. What could you take pictures of?" Then I just proceed with them, asking questions of this sort as we go along the web. With webbing, the children see us organize the information right in front of them on the board. For example, when they are calling out colors, I am writing those down:

"Black, blue, green, those could all be colors of what?"
"I know, colors of cameras!"
"So I will write that down here."

And then somebody might give me another idea about buttons. I would ask,

"Would that go in colors of cameras?"
"Oh, no, Ms. Taylor, that is a part of the cameras."

Then I might say, "So let's make a new section called parts. What other parts do you know about?"

I help them organize their thoughts. Sometimes you might have a child who dominates the discussion and seems to have all the information. I want this child to be heard, but I also say, "Other people have ideas too, and I will get to yours in a minute. First I want to hear from Jane." And we always have the opposite too: children who don't give me enough information. Because I want to hear from everybody, I might say to the one being quiet, "Timmy, do you know anything about cameras?" I am obviously not going to put him on the spot because if he knows nothing, that is okay. I might say something like, "We are going to learn about cameras with our expert, Mr. Jeff, and I bet you will know something after he comes. He will tell you something." We try to encourage them to share as much as we can, but if they don't have anything to say, that is okay. I have found that it works best if they raise their hand if they want to share, and I pick and choose a little bit. If one person is dominating, then I just say, "It's someone else's turn to talk. I will try to write down everyone's ideas." I do not usually write down names beside what the children say when we are doing initial web. I feel that this is a documentation of what everyone knows.

Next we make a list of questions. I do write names beside those. For example, Montgomery says that there is a little thing that you look into to take pictures. But then she asks, "How does that red button work?" She may ask that question again later, when we ask children what they learned. So in the questions I feel I am documenting individual growth.

HOW LONG was Phase I in total? Total class time was about 4 days. We first started thinking of cameras as a possible topic on a Thursday. On Monday we had to add more cameras to the classroom, and on Tuesday the children's photos came back from the processor and went into a collage. By Wednesday we were already webbing with the children. This was a very fast-moving project. Sometimes that happens when you have a high level of interest. I find this phase goes faster when children have had experience doing projects. When we get that list of questions, we are done with Phase I.

PHASE II: INVESTIGATING

My favorite part of the project is the first part of Phase II, when children are beginning to investigate, our classroom has real artifacts, and either we are planning our field-site visit or we are returning from one. I like trying to anticipate where the project is going to go and how I am going to help the children learn more about the topic. I also am starting to think about how the children might share what they have learned in Phase III. I use the Project Planning Journal (at the end of this book) to guide Phase II, especially for organizing field-site visits and experts. I use the list of questions generated in Phase I to plan for Phase II.

One of the first things I did upon entering Phase II was to gather some found materials such as soap boxes, paper towel tubes, strings, milk caps, and so on. Then we set real cameras out on the art table as models. We challenged the children by asking if there was a way that they could create their own camera using these materials. By asking questions about their camera representations, we encouraged them to include some of the following items: buttons, lenses, battery compartments, and other relevant parts.

Integration of Learning Standards

During this phase we also try to integrate as many standards as we can and still keep the work authentic. We revisited the teacher's anticipatory planning web, where we had listed the Illinois Early Learning Standards and anticipated concepts that we have been working on. We looked for opportunities where these might be used authentically in the project. For example, in literacy, *Identifies with labels and signs* is a standard. We added a camera shape with the parts labeled to the writing area and to the word wall, and we created labels for pieces from the camera take-apart area. The children could copy the labels on blank diagrams.

In small groups we showed the children how they could measure the length of the film and see which camera has longer film (*Demonstrates a beginning understanding of measurement*). Children took apart the cameras and looked at the different parts (*Uses simple tools and equipment for investigation; Engages in active play using fine motor skills*). We made some "eye spy" books with pictures we had taken (*Understands that pictures and symbols have meaning and that print carries a message*).

Visiting Experts

We used community resources and parents as experts and guides in this project. The first expert we contacted was a parent. I knew Mary Dunaway was an expert with cameras, based on our home visit and getting to know her during the school year. In fact, she was a professional photographer. I asked her if she could come into the classroom to take pictures with the children. Our parent expert was very excited about doing this and had no issues or concerns at all.

I did not expect this visit to be as big an event as it turned out to be. I thought Ms. Dunaway would just come in and explore cameras with the children, but I asked her what she would like to do. To my surprise, she wanted to set up a whole camera studio to show the students how everything works. She brought in all the materials: her backdrop, her camera, her assistant, and props. The children also brought their own props, such as a teddy bear. Ms. Dunaway took the children to the "studio" two or three at a time and showed them the whole process of how to take a picture, including how to focus the camera (see Figure 6.4). She took individual pictures of the children with their toy props, and then they each took a portrait of their toy. It was a wonderful experience. From this visit I realized that we need to focus on parents and community experts as people—what they can do, and what they are willing to do—and not have predetermined ideas about what should happen.

The other expert who visited our classroom was from our local camera shop, Peoria Camera Shop, Inc. When I called, the owner was hesitant and asked if we really wanted

FIGURE 6.4 • Parents, such as this photographer mother, have much to share with children in project work.

FIGURE 6.5 • The camera expert helps a child focus a camera to take a picture. Experts like Mr. Jeff enrich the project and motivate children to learn.

to share cameras with children. I used the questions in the Project Planning Journal to focus our phone discussion. I also told him what the children already knew and what I wanted to expand on. I used the initial web of "what we know" to give him a little background information. Because the camera expert had this information, he could come prepared to make sure the children got their questions answered.

As a class, we would use "what we want to know" as our interview questions. When the expert came, the children would be prepared for him by having their questions written on papers attached to clipboards, and they would draw or write on the papers to help them remember what they were asking.

When I finished talking to Jeff Jaramillo from the camera shop, he was very excited about coming to visit. I asked him what he would like to do, and I wrote in my Project Planning Journal: "Mr. Jeff will bring several types of cameras and accessories. We will walk on the trail in the woods, and he will guide us in the picture taking process." It is very rare to find an expert willing to spend a whole day with children, but Mr. Jeff did. He brought in real cameras and accessories to share with the children.

When he arrived, the children took to him right away. They clung to him and asked many questions, which he treated very seriously. He was inspired by them and how much they wanted to know and how excited they got about

opening the cameras and looking inside. He sat with the children, telling them the names of the parts of a camera and how they worked. When we walked the trail, he showed the children how to focus on objects and take a photo (see Figure 6.5).

After Mr. Jeff came to visit, we added even more real cameras in the house corner and then set up the camera take-apart table. The children wanted to learn more about the special cameras that Mr. Jeff had brought, and we had a display table with different kinds of cameras and books that we had acquired.

Field-Site Visit

We were able to go to see a darkroom for our field-site visit. We contacted the Peoria Art Guild because we had heard that they had a functioning darkroom. We followed the planning process for field-site visits in the Project Planning Journal; however, because the Guild had many visitors, it had a pretty typical, preset field trip procedure. There was a specific plan of activities the Guild staff would go through with the children in the darkroom. At first our guide was not enthusiastic about answering the children's questions,

FIGURE 6.6 • The children were fascinated with the developing process in the darkroom they visited. Here children learn the purpose of the squeegee.

but toward the end she picked up on the children's excitement about being there and started to show us more things related to their questions (see Figure 6.6).

Classroom Layout and Schedule

During the Camera Project, investigation and representation took place throughout the school day. Each day during learning center time, we typically have an activity at the art table that teachers plan and children may choose to do. We also have a round table, where we like to put literacy-type activities such as diagramming, journaling, and writing books, letters, and notes. For the Camera Project, in the block area we put books by the artist Andy Goldsworthy, showing his photography of his environmental art, as well as related natural materials. When we do projects, we also keep everyday materials and supplies accessible. Our project permeates our classroom but does not overwhelm it. There are still doll play and puzzle assembly and free painting going on. Figure 6.7 shows how the room looked during this project.

We feel it is important to have a lot of artifacts related to the topic for rich project work. These are some of the things you would have seen in our classroom during this project: film (short and long), film that was not processed, processed film, film canisters, real cameras, camera books, a tripod, and a real squeegee. A digital picture frame displayed photos of the children throughout the day. Photos children had taken were all over the classroom and in photo books for them to see. In addition to the Andy Goldsworthy books, we had a book of Ansel Adams's photography. We also had some informational books about how to take photos and how cameras work, as well as manuals for cameras. These were not all in the classroom in Phase I, but were added as the project progressed.

Our walls were filled with documentation. We had a lot of charts and graphs that we had made as a group. The questions and webs with the words we had learned were displayed. We had our measuring chart on the wall with the different films we had measured. Any log that we wrote as a group, any kind of activity that we did, we displayed on our walls and throughout the classroom. The children created a word wall displaying information they had learned about the camera.

Hands-On Investigation

This project provided many opportunities for hands-on investigating by children. We posted Ms. Dunaway's photos around the room so the children could explore what their pictures were like. As I mentioned earlier, Mr. Jeff brought different kinds of cameras for the children to explore. They looked for things like the button to push, the lens, and how to focus. He left two cameras with us, including an old-fashioned one that pulls out.

We had a camera take-apart table, which was our biggest investigation area. This had real tools and space where three or four children could work and tear into the cameras—and they did! I have many pictures of them with their noses down in the cameras while using the tools, screwing in the screws, banging, and pulling (see Figure 6.8). They would take all the pieces apart and talk about what those pieces were and how they made the camera work. They took the red button out, and we talked about how that is what takes the pictures. It was then that the labeling started. A space was created to share the labeled parts. We also saw problem-solving at the take-apart table, when there were not enough tools for the children to take the cameras apart. Were they going to share a screwdriver, or were they going to ask for more? They decided to watch each other and take turns (see Figure 6.9).

The house corner evolved as well. After Ms. Dunaway's visit, the children created a studio in which they could use different kinds of cameras. After we went on our field trip to the darkroom, we added materials so the children could create their own darkroom.

Representation

Representation was difficult in this project, and I'm not sure why. Perhaps it was because when you get into cameras, there are intricate and complex parts inside that are not easy to draw. Although we normally do a lot of clay work during a project, clay was not a medium that worked well for representation in this case. We did have clay out and encouraged the children to use it, but they were focused on the internal structures of the camera, and became frustrated when they couldn't represent the tiny pieces. Problem solving

FIGURE 6.7 • The camera project permeates the classroom, with related activities occurring in a variety of areas and centers.

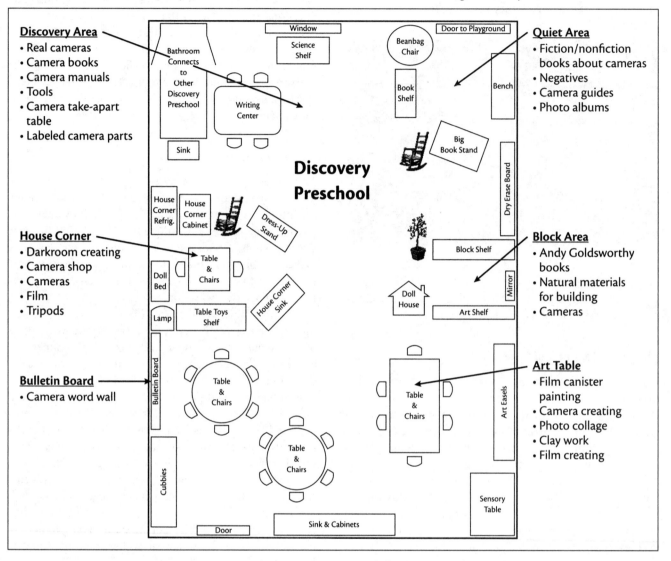

Discovery Area
- Real cameras
- Camera books
- Camera manuals
- Tools
- Camera take-apart table
- Labeled camera parts

House Corner
- Darkroom creating
- Camera shop
- Cameras
- Film
- Tripods

Bulletin Board
- Camera word wall

Quiet Area
- Fiction/nonfiction books about cameras
- Negatives
- Camera guides
- Photo albums

Block Area
- Andy Goldsworthy books
- Natural materials for building
- Cameras

Art Table
- Film canister painting
- Camera creating
- Photo collage
- Clay work
- Film creating

Labels within diagram: Window, Science Shelf, Door to Playground, Beanbag Chair, Bathroom Connects to Other Discovery Preschool, Writing Center, Book Shelf, Bench, Sink, Big Book Stand, Dry Erase Board, **Discovery Preschool**, House Corner Refrig., House Corner Cabinet, Dress-Up Stand, Block Shelf, Doll Bed, Table & Chairs, House Corner Sink, Doll House, Mirror, Lamp, Table Toys Shelf, Art Shelf, Bulletin Board, Table & Chairs, Table & Chairs, Table & Chairs, Art Easels, Cubbies, Sensory Table, Door, Sink & Cabinets

occurred when we made representations of cameras using found materials. If they couldn't get things to stick or something didn't look right, they would try another medium or a different approach. They couldn't get their camera lenses to work the right way. When the children encountered these problems, we tried to listen and help them clarify the problem. We might ask, "What have you tried? Can you think of another way you might do that? Do you want to look in the box and see if there is something that might work better?"

The children did, however, do a lot of representation by creating play environments. As I mentioned earlier, they created a studio and a darkroom in the house corner. After each expert's visit, we added something new. The children's studio had a camera on a tripod just like Ms. Dunaway's. Also, a little scenery turned up in the studio. When we put the cameras in the house corner, the children began taking pictures of each other acting out what they had learned in

the studio experience. "You sit here, and I am going to take your picture, and then we can switch." The role-playing was very rich.

The children had the idea of creating a darkroom and everything in it. They were really excited and told us everything they needed: "We need trays, tongs, some things here, and signs here." They remembered a lot from the field-site visit. They would say, "We have to put the light bulb up here because that is where the lights were hanging, and it has to be red." There was problem solving in this process. They realized that the kind of paint in the art area was not going to stick to the light bulb. They remembered using glass paint when they had made Christmas ornaments, so they wanted to get that out and see if it would work.

I suggested the children label things in the darkroom because there was some confusion from group to group about the process of developing photos. They were trying

FIGURE 6.8 • The opportunity to take apart a variety of cameras was an exciting component of the camera project. Parents and friends contributed broken or outdated cameras.

FIGURE 6.9 • Children solved the dilemma of too few screwdrivers by taking turns and watching one another. Learning to solve problems while working with others is one of the benefits of project work.

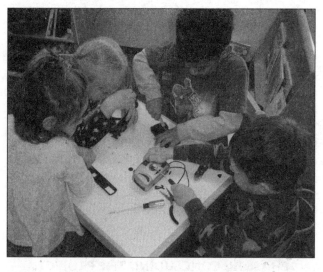

FIGURE 6.10 • Recreating the darkroom process in the house corner challenged children to learn about sequence and timing. Learning about the usefulness of academic skills and careful thinking occurs often in project work.

to get the trays in order: developer, fixer, stopper, fix remover, and water. They kept getting the order mixed up, so we encouraged them to go back to the photos from our field-site visit, look at them, and label the trays (see Figure 6.10). "Now think what you remember from this, and tell me the order." They then described the whole process they had observed in the darkroom and applied it to what they wanted to do.

"Which side of the table do we stand on?"
"When someone is developing pictures here, where do you stand, because it's going to matter in the order?"
"If you stand on this side of the table, you are going to go backwards."

They really thought about what they were doing and what the outcomes would be regarding their position in the space. This was so much more complex than the sequencing in typical preschool activities, for example, reading stories and talking about the story sequence or putting together puzzles. This is a good illustration of how much depth there is in project work, and because the engagement is so high, the children are motivated to think hard.

Parent Involvement

We had good parent involvement in this project. The studio experience was a parent contribution. Parents also brought items to the classroom. We also created a parent activity to encourage hands-on work at home. We asked the parents to take some pictures at home and make a book to show a day in the life of their child. We gave the children prepared books with blank pages so they had a concrete object to return. We felt that if we had just given the assignment, parents might not have been inclined to do it or might have been overwhelmed by trying to figure out how to do it. With a book the children brought home to be filled out and brought back, the activity was very structured. The parents and children knew what their task was and what it was to look like. We had an overwhelming number of books returned and enjoyed hearing stories about how the children told their families what they knew about the camera. The children enjoyed sharing their book with others.

PHASE III: CONCLUDING THE PROJECT

We felt the project was over when we noticed the children were not as interested in exploring cameras at the take-apart table anymore. There weren't as many children there each day during the learning center time. It had been busy, busy, busy, and then all of a sudden nobody was there. And in the darkroom it was basically the same way—they would play, play, play, and then again nobody was there. We knew that their interest in the topic was done. They had explored it to their full potential, and they were ready to move on to a new topic.

We sat down with the children in a group, and I told them that we felt we had learned all we could about cameras. I said to the children that now we needed to share what we learned with others: "How do we do that? What should we do?" Having not had a lot of experience with projects, the children didn't have that many ideas. We shared some of our ideas, such as a making book or having a camera show. They decided on the camera show.

The children invited students from other preschool and kindergarten classrooms to come to our classroom, and our children showed them the tripod with the camera and how to take a picture. They pretended to take the visitors' pictures and walked them through the darkroom and the process of developing photos. The children took their visitors to the take-apart table and let them explore cameras using real tools.

Documentation

Outside the classroom we have a space where we can display a lot of the documentation from our classroom. Obviously, we start with Phase I; I want the parents to under-

FIGURE 6.11 • This child-made sign designates the bulletin board to be used as a word wall. Even 3-year-olds are motivated to use letters and numbers.

stand the phases of our project in the documentation. In Phase I, I share the teacher's anticipatory web, as well as the children's questions. We reveal the documentation as the project goes along. Underneath each artifact I provide an explanation, such as, "This is why we are doing a Time 1 web with them; we want to know what they already know. This helps us plan our curriculum." I think it is important for others to see the teacher's anticipatory planning web. It shows parents that project work fits into our curriculum, is meaningful, and helps guide the curriculum so much better than a theme would. As we go through the project, I add new artifacts. After Mr. Jeff came, we displayed pictures of him and some of the work children did. We wrote about why it is so beneficial to have experts come in and share their knowledge. As we go through each phase, something new appears on the wall, so the display grows throughout the project.

Another form of documentation is the word wall, which was used by the children throughout the project to demonstrate and strengthen what they were learning and helped them to make their labels (see Figures 6.11 and 6.12).

FIGURE 6.12 • A 4-year-old created this label by copying the word lens from the word wall and taping a lens removed from a camera at the take-apart table to the card.

Throughout the project we also document for our assessment checklist and our portfolio. This particular project was rich in opportunities to observe and assess children's literacy, mathematical thinking, scientific thinking, and intellectual dispositions. In our classroom, we also document intellectual dispositions as part of our assessment. We are looking to see if children are investigating, if they are taking initiative, and if they are making sense of the world around them. The portfolio item in Figure 6.13 shows 4-year-old Lilly's disposition to not only find an answer to a question but also to write.

Children are also documenters. They documented what they were seeing and studying with drawings, photographs, and notes of answers to their questions. They used that documentation as they created the darkroom. Their representations and their creations also document what they have learned.

As part of culmination of the camera project, I usually "publish" panels to share the story of the project with others. For this project I decided to present the different roles that children assume in project work: explorer, researcher, documenter, and collaborator.

Teacher's Reflections

If I had to do this project over again, I would try to think of more ways to help the children represent. I felt that was an area in which we did not challenge the children enough. This was a good, basic project, but I think the children could have done more with representation and using their new knowledge to do that. Also, I would have liked to make a project history book with them reviewing what had happened, but when they were done with this topic, they were just done! I might have started doing a project history book earlier in the project. The work was very intense, and the project was consuming a lot of the children's time in Phase II. When we came to Phase III, they just seemed satisfied with what they had done, shared it, and moved on.

There were challenges in this project. The camera is a very complex topic, and it is difficult to find resources for children. We had a hard time finding experts who were able to bring it down to our children's level of understanding. For example, when talking about how the camera worked, an expert was talking about the light coming in and aperture openings, when the children just wanted to know which

FIGURE 6.13 • This child's question (*left*) became part of her portfolio, along with the answer (*right*), which she carefully recorded. Children's project work provides insight into the child's knowledge, skills, and dispositions. This 4-year-old is well on the way to literacy.

button to push! I know that photography is a very complex process and is interesting to many adults, but as teachers we have to make sure that what is shared about that complex process matches the children's prior knowledge and is put in a language that is understandable to the children.

I felt that the children took a lot of responsibility for their own work in this project. We supplied many materials, but the children took the initiative. For example, at the take-apart table, the children found camera parts, then wanted to label and display them.

The children were definitely strategic learners in this project. They developed strategies and skills and transferred those strategies and skills from one aspect to the next. As they studied the insides of the camera, they would say, "You have to push this button up here to make the shutter work inside in order to take a picture." They were getting basic knowledge of how turning the lens focuses the camera. They would then transfer that knowledge into picture taking, "Okay I have to look through here and focus it in," instead of just snapping a picture as they were doing before. I think they learned a lot about sequencing and the importance of observing the order in which things happen. This was important in the process of the darkroom. They seemed to say, "We need to have these in this particular order, and if you didn't do that correctly, we are in big trouble." They also learned the importance of labeling, when they took the pieces apart. Each time they took a part off, they would label it; otherwise they didn't know what it was for after they got it out of the camera.

I think adults learned a lot in this project too. Parents learned some strategies as they made the photography books at home. One child's book started with mom taking photos and then transitioned into photos the child took. The parent learned to give control over to the child and let the child explore. As a teaching team we were more collaborative. Because both my associate teacher and my student teacher were still learning the basics of project work, we worked through many issues together. That enhanced both the project and our skills.

As adults, we also learned a lot about the topic of cameras. All those fun big words! I thought I had a basic knowledge of cameras, but we learned some really interesting things about cameras that I don't think the average person knows. Bringing in all the different kinds of cameras was a big help, not only for the children's interests but also for the adults. I was right down there doing the same things as the children. I was pulling the cameras apart and looking at them and trying to find out how the stereo camera works as it takes two different pictures and puts them together. I still don't understand that. Just trying to figure out how film is processed was amazing to me. Watching the exposure and how many seconds it takes to expose a picture or the importance of how dark or light it is—I had no idea about those aspects. It was very engaging. All the work it takes to get a little picture! It was interesting for everyone.

LEARNING AS A JOURNEY

As presented in Chapter 1, the project approach is not a complete curriculum. It is an approach that constitutes one part of a curriculum for young children. One meaning of the word approach is "to come nearer to." Many of the teachers described in this book who have integrated projects into their classroom talk about how "they are working on it" or they "aren't there yet"—how they are coming closer to their vision of how children can learn and how a project can be an engaged learning experience. They describe the process of learning to do projects as a journey, one they think will not end soon but a journey they are enjoying. Lora Taylor shared her journey with you in this chapter. To experience the journey of Sallie Sawin, a teacher of toddlers, read about the Fire Hydrant Project in Chapter 7.

CHAPTER 7

· · ·

The Fire Hydrant Project
Adapting the Approach for Toddlers

OFTEN when a school or center becomes involved in the project approach, the teachers who care for the toddlers in that program will ask if the project approach can be used with their children. Since the first edition of this book came out, we have seen many toddlers actively involved in investigation. We have viewed documentation showing toddlers' growth in thinking and understanding, and have heard teacher reports of the enthusiasm with which parents receive reports of the toddler "projects." The activities occurring in these toddler classrooms have many of the characteristics of the project approach as defined by Katz and Chard (2000) and described in the flowchart and the examples in this book. They are certainly in-depth investigations of topics worth learning more about. Toddlers are actively involved in learning. Toddlers are investigating, and toddlers are representing. These toddler projects have the following characteristics in common with the project approach for older children:

1. Adults identify toddlers' interests. Toddlers show interest nonverbally and verbally. Toddlers can indicate they have a question by facial expression or gesture. They can verbally ask simple questions.
2. Teachers who see interest in objects or activities (such as balls or shoes) respond by bringing in resources and arranging for field-site experiences.
3. Toddlers learn words and concepts (such as *ball*) and apply those words and concepts in new situations.
4. Toddlers develop ways of investigating—such as touching, manipulating, dropping, pushing, or trying to put something through a hole—which they then apply to other objects or items and observe results. They build a repertoire of learning strategies. Teachers challenge toddlers by introducing new resources.
5. Toddlers recognize themselves in documentation and recall and reproduce experiences through play.
6. Toddlers create and interact with representations.
7. Teachers and parents of toddlers use documentation to communicate about toddlers' growth and to provide insight into growth in quality of thinking.

To understand that investigation by 1- and 2-year-old children can occur, it is helpful to see a project in action. The Fire Hydrant Project took place in a classroom for toddlers, 15 months through 2 years old, at the Center for Early Education and Care (CEEC) at the University of Massachusetts. CEEC provides full-day, full-year early education and care services for undergraduate, graduate, staff, and faculty families of the University. Sallie Sawin is the supervising teacher in this classroom and tells the story of the project. Cathy Savage is a co-teacher in the program.

PHASE I: GETTING STARTED

The toddlers' interest in fire fighting began in November, when the children in the classroom next door were investigating fire trucks. The toddlers wanted to investigate these as well. Viktor (2.6 yr) and Charlie (1.4 yr) tried on the firefighter gear, and fire fighting dramatic play began. The children in the next classroom had built a fire truck out of a large cardboard box. When our classroom had a chance to use the cardboard fire truck, ordinary objects became a hose, a house on fire, and another fire truck. Plastic fire hats quickly became necessary equipment for putting out fires.

Interest in the topic grew slowly. After observing the spontaneous fire fighting play, we made an anticipatory web about the fire truck, as this is what we interpreted the children to be most interested in. We brought other fire fighting artifacts into the classroom for the children to use in their dramatic play and added a number of books about fire fighting to the reading area.

A couple of months later, Viktor lined up a few classroom chairs next to each other and said, "I making fire truck." He used his cell phone to call the fire truck, and then put on a fire helmet (see Figure 7.1). He walked over to me and said, "Look, I fire truck." Ella joined Viktor on his fire truck and said, "We're firefighters." Viktor said, "I fire truck."

When we were on a walking trip through campus, we came to a fire hydrant that subsequently became the highlight of our walks. Viktor yelled, "Fire, fire!" the first time he

FIGURE 7.1 • After Viktor calls the fire truck, the other children respond to his call.

saw this hydrant. I said, "Yes, that's a fire hydrant." When we passed the same hydrant the next day, Viktor yelled out, "Fire hydrant!" I told him the names of the parts of the hydrant, explaining that firefighters use a hydrant wrench to open the hydrant. We asked, "What comes out of the hydrant?" The children did not know. They knew that hydrants were something the firefighters used, but their exact function was unclear. Thus began our investigation of fire hydrants.

We added a poster that labeled parts of a hydrant for the children to expand their vocabulary. The campus Fire Safety Officer, Rick Sawin, was invited to provide a fire hydrant demonstration for the children. He showed how the fire hydrant works by first opening it to show the children the inside. Ollie (2.5 yr) brought his own plastic pliers to help open the hydrant. "I bringed my pliers to help Rick," he said.

During the demonstration the children touched the hydrant and the tools. They got to look inside the open hydrant (see Figure 7.2). Rick attached a fire house to the hydrant, and the children felt how the hose changed in shape and weight as it filled with water. Then they watched the water spray out of the nozzle. At the end of the demonstration, Rick rolled up the hose. The children watched intently. Viktor paid very close attention to how the hose was rolled.

After the fire hydrant demonstration, we noticed changes in the children's dramatic play. The children now incorporated a hydrant into their play. They used pieces of hose to attach to chairs and shelves, which they pretended to be a hydrant. We decided that the children might appreciate an actual fire hydrant in the classroom to enhance and deepen their exploration and play. Since we could not come up with a real fire hydrant, I gathered a variety of plastic plumbing tubes, pipes, and connectors and built them into the shape of a hydrant. The children immediately unscrewed the end covers and pretended to attach pieces of hose. Viktor asked for a flashlight to shine into the hydrant just like he saw Rick do during the demonstration.

FIGURE 7.2 • Ella puts her hand inside to see if she can feel the water.

PHASE II: INVESTIGATING

Another Visit to the Fire Hydrant

We know toddlers learn from repeated exposures and being able to explore at their own pace. Therefore, it was clear that we should have another demonstration of the fire hydrant. When I discussed the second demonstration with Rick and the firefighters, they suggested bringing a fire engine, a deck gun, and a number of other fire truck "toys." We felt that too much information at one time would be confusing. We insisted the visit only include the fire hydrant and the tools that go with it. During the second demonstration the children were more involved. Maeve (1.3 yr) had joined the classroom the day before the demonstration. The day after the demonstration she was observed unscrewing the cap from the play hydrant and "attaching" a hose to it (see Figure 7.3). She was using memory recall to reenact what she had seen the firefighters do the previous day. She was representing her learning through dramatic play. During the fire hydrant demonstration, many of the children mostly watched and needed encouragement or prompting to touch the hydrant. Some children were very timid and did not want to get close at all, and a few were willing to explore the hydrant and talk to Rick. We soon realized that even the children who stood back and watched had learned about the fire hydrant. In their dramatic play they demonstrated their new knowledge and began to show evidence of wanting more information about the fire hydrant.

Cardboard Construction

The children had learned a great deal about the fire hydrant from the two demonstrations. They knew what it looked like, as well as the names and purpose of each part. We

FIGURE 7.3 • The day after the demonstration, Maeve, just over 1 year old, pretends to attach the hose to the play fire hydrant.

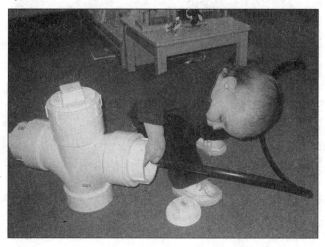

wanted to see how the toddlers could represent their knowledge of the fire hydrant. We set out cardboard boxes, plastic containers with screw-off tops, paper towel tubes, and large cardboard tubes to see what they might create.

We placed the construction materials on the floor and hung the fire hydrant poster nearby to help the children remember the different parts of the hydrant. With our guidance, the toddlers chose from the construction materials to represent the different parts of the hydrant. Using problem solving skills, fine-motor control, and great patience, the children built a fire hydrant together, with our support.

> *Ms. Sawin:* We need to stick this together. What can we use?
> *Ella* (2.9 yr): Tape.
> *Viktor* (3 yr): I want tape.
> *Ella:* I need a piece.
> *Isabelle* (2.5 yr): I want piece too!
> *Ms. Sawin:* Now we need something like this (pointing to a photo of the fire hydrant).
> *Viktor* (holding up the peanut butter jar): Here, Sallie.
> *Ms. Sawin:* How do we attach it?

The children sat and pondered this question for a while. I suggested that we cut a hole in the cardboard; then I cut a small hole and said, "It won't fit. What do we do?"

> *Viktor:* Push it! (He helped me push the jar into the box.)
> *Charlie* (1.10 yr): Hold it, hold it?

Ms. Savage gave Charlie a coffee creamer container to hold. I again pointed to the picture, this time drawing the children's attention to the arms on the side of the hydrant.

> *Ms. Sawin:* How can we make this part?

Charlie handed me the coffee creamer container.

> *Ms. Sawin:* Where should we put it on our hydrant?

Viktor pointed to the side of the hydrant. Sam (1.10 yr) wanted a turn. He pulled the coffee creamer through the cardboard.

Once the fire hydrant was completed to the children's satisfaction, we all sat back and looked at it. The children compared it to the picture of the real fire hydrant. When the children were satisfied that we had all the parts it needed, they began to play with it.

Papier-Mâché

We wanted a way to strengthen the children's fire hydrant so it would stand up to toddler use. Although we considered papier-mâché, at first we thought that this would be too messy and difficult for the toddlers. Then we decided that a mess could be cleaned up, and the activity would be a great tactile experience.

To papier-mâché the classroom fire hydrant, we had to tear a lot of newspaper strips. All of the children had a turn ripping the paper and putting it in the bin. The children helped make the paste for the papier-mâché. Viktor, Ella, and Isabelle mixed the paste to just the right consistency. They put the paper in the bowl with the paste, mixed it around, and then squeezed out the extra paste. Goooeey! The toddlers worked together until the hydrant was completely covered (see Figure 7.4).

When the papier-mâché was dry, we discussed painting the fire hydrant. We asked the group, "What color should we paint our fire hydrant?"

> *Ella:* Pink!
> *Ollie:* Yellow and blue!
> *Viktor:* No, it's red!

FIGURE 7.4 • Toddlers work together to accomplish their goal.

FIGURE 7.5 • Ms. Sawin uses a photo of the pump panel and talks with the children about the parts.

FIGURE 7.6 • Ollie digs through the box to find something to represent what he sees in the photo.

The group had been pondering the color choice for a few days when we decided that some direct "research" might help the children answer the question. The group set out to visit fire hydrants around campus. At each hydrant they stopped to notice its special features and talk about what it looked like. The children reminded us of the names of all of the parts of the fire hydrant that they had learned from Rick and the other firefighters.

A few days later we again asked the children, "What color should we paint our fire hydrant?" This time the children were all in agreement that the fire hydrant should be painted red.

And Another Visit to the Fire Hydrant

After two demonstrations and the construction of their own fire hydrant, the children had another question, which we observed during their dramatic play: "How does the water get into the fire truck hose to spray out the fire?" Once again, Rick and his student assistants were happy to answer the children's questions. This time they brought a fire truck to the fire hydrant to show the children, step by step, how the fire hydrant, hoses, and fire truck work together.

They showed the children how to connect the fire truck to the fire hydrant. The firefighters worked with the children individually, assisting them in investigating the part of the equipment that interested them the most. Water filled the hose while the children held the charged line. Again, some children were content to just watch. When the firefighters asked the children if they wanted to see anything else, some children asked to climb the ladder. Firefighter

Mike set the ladder up for the children. He helped each child safely climb.

The children learned that when the firefighters are done using the hose they have to walk the water out of the hose. To do this, they start at one end and lift the hose as they walk along the length of the hose to the other end. Viktor was eager to help walk the water out.

We thought the toddlers might be interested in connecting the hose to the engine, so we, as teachers, decided to help them build a representation of the part of the truck that connects to the fire hydrant: the pump panel. With toddlers in project work, representation is most often play. By constructing the panel with the toddlers' help, we were able to scaffold their thinking and create a play environment they would not have been able to construct on their own. This final construction pulled together all aspects of the fire fighting experience that the children had studied—fire hydrant, hoses, and fire truck—and enabled them to use what they learned as they developed play scenarios.

Building a Pump Panel

As a first step, I visited the local fire department and took photographs of the fire trucks, with close-ups of the pump panel. The fire chief cut a piece of real fire hose that was no longer usable into a length that would be manageable for the children and donated a box of old gauges and plumbing pieces for where the hose attaches to the truck. The next day we set out the box of gauges, knobs, and plumbing pieces for the children to investigate. Charlie (1.11 yr) picked up one of the gauges and said, "Look, clockies, I find clockies!" We put up two photos of pump panels. Pointing to each part of the pump panel, I named it for the children (see Figure 7.5). I explained that they were going to build a panel

FIGURE 7.7 • The photo of the panel the children had studied shows the dials and the knobs.

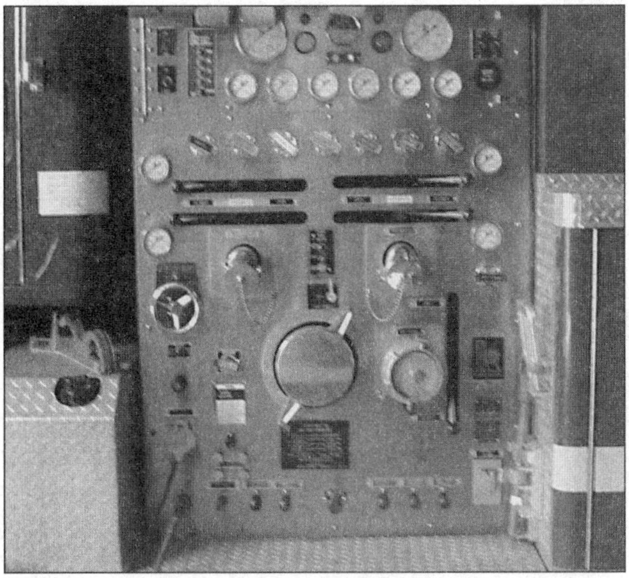

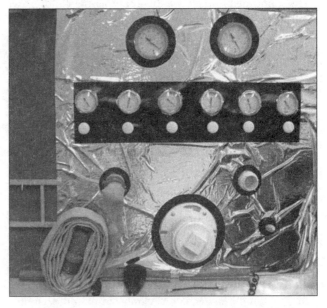

like the one in the picture. The children began to choose parts from the collection and thought about where to put each piece on the large piece of cardboard on the floor. This enabled them to participate in creating a three-dimensional representation that was also a play environment in which they could initiate their own learning (see Figure 7.6).

> *Ollie* (2.7 yr): My gauge right there.
> *Ms. Sawin:* Should they be right next to each other?
> *Ollie:* Yeah!

When all the pieces were laid out and the children were finished constructing their own pump panel (compare Figures 7.7 and 7.8), I took a photograph that I referred to later when I attached the pieces to a piece of wood so it would be sturdy enough for toddler use.

PHASE III: CONCLUDING THE PROJECT

During previous projects we had learned that a large group event does not work well for toddlers (too many people, too much noise, too many distractions). Instead, toddlers prefer to revisit what they have learned and share their new knowledge with familiar people in small groups or individually. We decided that the culminating activity for this project would be a photo display of the fire hydrant demonstrations, the constructions, and the children's fire fighting dramatic play on panels around the classroom. The children then used the photo panels to tell and retell their story to their friends, family members, and any visitors to the classroom.

When a new child, Aiden (2.0 yr), joined the classroom, Anayah (1.5 yr) pointed to the pictures of the fire truck dem-

FIGURE 7.8 • The toddlers' placement of the discarded dials and knobs on the play pumper panel is very similar to the placement of dials on the real panel they saw and on the one in the photo.

onstration to fill him in on what he had missed (see Figure 7.9). Revisiting the photos on display in the classroom provides opportunities for conversation, vocabulary reinforcement, and literacy development as children remember and recount the events of the fire hydrant demonstrations.

FIGURE 7.9 • Toddlers can identify themselves and events in photos. They appear to understand that the discussion is about their experiences and can share that experience with others.

Children's Development

During the weeks that followed the culminating photo panel display, the children's fire fighting dramatic play and vocabulary continued to develop. By observing the children, we continued to discover just how much the children had learned from their Fire Hydrant Project. When the project began in November, Charlie (1.9 yr) would say, "WHOOO, WHOOO," every time he saw a fire truck or when he played with a fire truck. His understanding of fire engines and hydrants, as well as his language, flourished during this investigation. By June, Charlie, now more than 2 years of age, had evolved considerably in his play. While playing dispatcher with our real fire radio and base microphone, he started dispatching engines to a fire. "You fire truck get going, you coming, get a fire truck, pumper, backhoe." Charlie made his own pumper truck with a matchbox truck and a real fire engine strobe light. He explained during this play scenario, "I make pumper truck with light." Sam tried climbing a toy ladder in the classroom. When he realized his feet were too big for the small ladder, he used a doll to climb the ladder. All the while he was singing, "Hurry, hurry, climb the ladder, climb, climb, climb, climb, climb!"

In Figure 7.10, taken in March, Viktor and Ella can be seen each engaged in fire fighting play but not with one another. Each holds his or her own piece of black plastic hose as they put out different fires. In Figure 7.11, taken in May, at the end of the project, their play has become cooperative as they assist one another in holding a real fire hose to put out a fire. Viktor is incorporating the wide leg stance that the firefighters use when they hold the nozzle. Ella picks up the middle of the hose, as she has seen the firefighters do, to help Viktor steady it because the water pressure is so strong.

When Viktor joined the classroom in August, he only spoke his home language of Bosnian. When we began the Fire Hydrant Project in March, he would say, "Fire, fire," when he saw something that he recognized as having to do with fire fighting. By June, Viktor was heard to say, "When I'm big like Rick, I can climb the ladder like Rick and spray the water, whoosh, and put out fire like Rick." His vocabulary and use of language to express his feelings, as well as his knowledge and ambitions, had grown tremendously during this investigation of a subject of interest to him.

Teacher's Reflections

The Fire Hydrant Project extended over many months of this school year. We had never engaged in a project quite this long before, but found that the pace of gradual exposure, numerous hands-on activities, and multiple visits to our fire hydrant provided the children an opportunity to new learn information, practice using it, and then add to this knowledge to extend and expand their understanding of this topic. Engaging in one area of focus for an extended period greatly enhanced the children's language development as well. Their vocabulary about fire hydrants and fire fighting grew more and more with each hands-on experience. Toddlers do not yet live in beginnings, middles, and ends, as was quite clear when fire hydrant and fire fighting play continued well beyond what we thought of as the conclusion of the project.

FIGURE 7.10 • When the Fire Hydrant Project began, the toddlers played side by side but did not interact.

FIGURE 7.11 • At the end of the project, the toddlers were joining together to create play scenarios using what they had learned about the fire hoses and the fire hydrant.

FIGURE 7.12 • At 18 months, this toddler is able to look at a hose and figure out which end attaches to the pumper panel.

Long after we had posted the display panels of the Fire Hydrant Project, and likely inspired by the panels, the children continued to look for fire hydrants on our walks around campus and to play fire fighting in dramatic play. Rather than assume that these young children could not present their learning in a representational way, we challenged the children (and ourselves) with a number of large-scale construction projects. We learned that toddlers are quite capable of recreating objects that they have had experience with when the work can done in a way that matches their fine-motor skills. Rather than ask them to balance a clipboard and pencil on their lap as older children may be able to do, we had the toddlers tear newspaper into long strips and paste the strips onto boxes taped together in the shape of a fire hydrant. As the children layered on the papier-mâché, they named each part, described what it did, and talked about their fire hydrant visit. It was quite clear in this project that dramatic play is a useful, even critical way, for toddlers to practice newly learned information. Exploring the fire hydrant with the Fire Safety staff provided the children with real-life scenarios to play and replay with their classroom hydrant, hoses, and pumper panel. By observing the children's dramatic play early in the project, we were able to discern the "gaps" in their knowledge about the topic. Later, as we observed the detail and complexity of their fire hydrant play increase, it was evident that they had learned a great deal. For example, Anayah (1.5 yr), after the third fire hydrant visit, used her new knowledge about the fire hose and pump panel, as she picked up the real fire hose, checked both ends to find which end had

the coupling necessary to attach it to the pump panel, and attached it (see Figure 7.12).

As we were new to the project approach, we were learning how to apply this pedagogical model to the toddler age level. As we determined ways to support the children's exploration of this topic, it was important for us to return to what we knew about toddler developmental levels to inform our decisions about how to approach each phase of the project. The toddlers' stages of development, as well as their interests, guided us throughout the project.

WAS THIS A PROJECT?

By revisiting the definition of a project quoted in Chapter 1, it is clear that the Fire Hydrant Project was indeed a project.

> A project is an in-depth investigation of a topic worth learning more about.... The key feature of a project is that it is a research effort deliberately focused on finding answers to questions about a topic posed either by the children, the teacher, or the teacher working with the children. (Katz, 1994, p. 1)

The toddlers had questions even if they couldn't ask them. They showed their interest and what they had questions about through their actions and the words that they could say. These toddlers, who were only 1 and 2 years old, did indeed use objects such as peanut butter jars to represent something that they had in their minds. They worked hard to solve problems, such as how to attach things or how to climb toy ladders when their feet were too big. Projects with toddlers look more like the flowchart in Figure 7.13 than the more elaborate chart in Figure 1.5. Significant time is spent in Phase I with a focusing event. Investigation in Phase II is encouraged by providing additional experiences and introducing items into the environment. Activities during this phase sometimes include making project books with photos of items for children to look at and carry around, introducing artifacts into the environment for children to explore, placing photos and documentation covered with plastic on walls and floors, conducting simple field-site visits where additional experiences with artifacts occur, and performing simple experiments in which toddlers can do things and observe their effects.

Investigation in projects with toddlers is almost always done as an individual activity or with very small groups of children. Culmination of projects with toddlers is, as Sallie Sawin described, more effectively done as a personal experience. The teacher summarizes what has happened and tells the story. It would be a mistake, however, to think that this story is not understandable to toddlers and that they do not take ownership of their accomplishments. But, as

FIGURE 7.13 · Flowchart of projects with toddlers

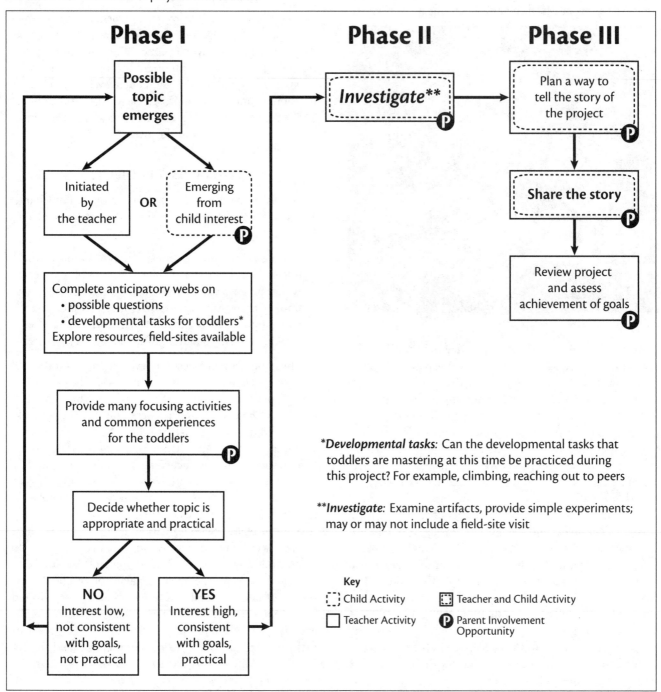

Ms. Sawin points out, it is important to let the toddlers' development guide the process. Rather than a push-down of preschool curriculum (even with a "calendar" for 2-year-olds!), using a project approach—which is child sensitive and builds on children's interest—can be a way to change the focus of a teacher in the selection of activities and experiences to provide for children of this age. Compared with more structured approaches, the project approach can be more appropriate for the toddlers' sense of time and sequence.

The work of teachers in infant/toddler centers in Italy (see Edwards et al., 1998; Gandini & Edwards, 2000; Lee-Keenan & Edwards, 1992) can serve as a further guide for practice.

WITH THE CLOSE of this chapter, we have followed two projects from start to finish. There are many variations in project work. The same project topics might evolve into very different experiences for children if they occur in another setting, with another set of children, or with another set of teachers. There are many factors that have an impact on project work, such as the availability of support for project work, the integration of standards and required curriculum, or the use of technology. In the next and final chapter, some of these factors and other issues in making project work happen in an early childhood program will be discussed.

CHAPTER 8

· · ·

Issues in Guiding Projects
with Young Children

ONCE TEACHERS ARE FAMILIAR with the processes of implementing projects and realize how they can support the development of knowledge, skills, and dispositions of young investigators, they then begin to integrate project work into their curriculum. In this chapter we address some of the main issues related to implementation of the project approach. Depending on the philosophy of the school or center, these issues may be more important for some teachers and programs than for others. Some of these issues concern curriculum requirements, achievement standards, integration of early literacy, involvement of parents in projects, and the use of technology in projects. Other issues involve the use of projects with specific populations—children with special needs and second-language learners—and the support of administrators for the project approach.

CURRICULUM REQUIREMENTS, STANDARDS, AND PROJECTS

Required Curriculum and Standards

Teachers of young children usually define their goals for the children and for their programs. These goals may be articulated in philosophical statements, teaching materials, or curriculum guides. For some teachers of young children, what they offer in their classrooms is determined by local or state curriculum requirements and/or academic standards. In such cases, many teachers are concerned about whether they can satisfy the requirements if they use the project approach. It may be helpful before discussing this issue to clarify the difference between curriculum requirements and achievement standards.

Curriculum is defined as an organized framework that delineates the skills and content that children are to learn. It includes the processes by which the curricular goals are to be achieved, what teachers are expected to do to help children reach these goals, and the context in which teaching and learning occur (Bredekamp & Rosegrant, 1995). The National Education Goals Panel (Goal 3 and 4 Technical Planning Group, 1993) distinguishes between two types

of standards: *content standards,* which specify what students should be able to know and do; and *performance standards,* which gauge to what degree content standards are met—that is, how skilled or competent the student must be.

The project approach is not the whole curriculum. It does not constitute the entirety of learning experiences the child has in the prekindergarten, kindergarten, or first-grade program. As presented in Chapter 1, there may be many other kinds of learning experiences under way in classrooms in which projects are also in progress. The project approach does not delineate the content that children are to learn. Nor does it prescribe the context for all learning that occurs within the classroom. It provides neither required curriculum content nor content standards.

However, implementing the project approach does not mean that content and subject matter that may be required are excluded from project work. On the contrary, project work provides a range of contexts in which most significant content and skill requirements can be addressed. Whether the content, subject matter, or topic of a project comes from the children or from the teacher, it can usually be related to both content and skills requirements. A characteristic of projects is the emphasis on in-depth investigation, which usually results in children learning a great deal about the topic under investigation. It is possible to incorporate many content goals and objectives into project work, in part because of the structure of the approach. The structure of the phases and the emphasis on questions for investigation enable teachers to plan how they can integrate content goals and assessment into the project experience. This approach contrasts with less-structured approaches to projects such as project work in the schools of Reggio Emilia, where content goals, performance standards, and early literacy skills are not emphasized.

When required curriculum delineates skills that the children are required to learn and practice, the project approach provides many opportunities to apply most academic skills, including speaking, reading, writing, listening, and counting. Some intellectual skills, such as observing, classifying, investigating, hypothesizing, and predicting, are practiced most easily, frequently, and purposefully throughout project work.

Performance standards indicate the level of skill or competence children must achieve. Assessment is usually based on specified performance standards. The specification of performance standards is also compatible with the project approach, especially if evidence of achievement can be gathered in authentic ways, as, for example, through good documentation, which provides rich, accurate evidence of children's knowledge and skills (Katz & Chard, 1996). Project documentation is often a more reliable indicator of children's capabilities than are standardized tests, because the high motivation associated with project work results in greater and more purposeful use of their knowledge and skills than standardized tests.

Using the Project Approach to Meet Standards

When project topics are selected on the basis of the guidelines provided in Chapter 2, the young investigators' learning experiences are often naturally consistent with most content standards and curriculum requirements. Here is a content standard from the National Science Education Standards (National Committee on Science Education Standards and Assessment, 1995):

Content Standards: K–4

SCIENCE AS INQUIRY

Content Standard A:

As a result of activities in grades K–4, all students should develop

- Abilities necessary to do scientific inquiry
- Understanding about scientific inquiry (p. 109)

Content Standard A is further clarified in a guide to the content standard:

Fundamental abilities and concepts that underlie this standard include

ABILITIES NECESSARY TO DO SCIENTIFIC INQUIRY

ASK A QUESTION ABOUT OBJECTS, ORGANISMS, AND EVENTS IN THE ENVIRONMENT. This aspect of the standard emphasizes students asking questions that they can answer with scientific knowledge, combined with their own observations. Students should answer their questions by seeking information from reliable sources of scientific information and from their own observations and investigations. . . .

PLAN AND CONDUCT A SIMPLE INVESTIGATION. In the earliest years, investigations are largely based on systematic observations. As students develop, they may design and conduct simple experiments to answer questions. (p. 122)

Teachers who have implemented projects with young investigators report that this content standard is achieved quite naturally in the course of good projects. An example of this is the Turtle Project in Linda Lundberg's kindergarten class at Parker Early Education Center in Machesney Park, Illinois. This project began when a turtle named George was given to the class. The following children's words and drawings about what they were observing are taken from a documentation panel for the Turtle Project.

For several months the children had been caring for George, who turned out to be a female turtle. In late November she began to act strangely.

What Happened:

The children noticed her digging a lot under her food dish. At times she practically tipped her dish over. We moved her aquarium into the meeting area.

What We Thought and Said:

- She is hungry (P.M. class wasn't feeding her enough).
- Some old food is under the dish and she is trying to get it.

What We Tried:

- We put food in the dish. George didn't eat it. [See Figure 8.1]

When the A.M. class came in, George was partly buried in her wood shavings.

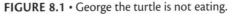

FIGURE 8.1 • George the turtle is not eating.

FIGURE 8.2 • George is digging in the wood chips.

FIGURE 8.3 • Aaron made a house for George, and Joe drew a picture of it.

What We Thought and Said:

- George is trying to make a nest.
- George is going to have babies.
- It is colder. We put on our coats.
- Maybe George is cold.
- He's digging in the chips to get warm.
- She was digging because she was too cold! [See Figure 8.2]

What We Tried:

- We dug our hands into the shavings and into the sand to see if it was warmer (some said yes, some said no).
- Aaron made a house out of paper for George. George went in. [See Figure 8.3]

What Happened:

The teacher brought in a log with a hole. George went into the log. George had to be awakened when it was bath time. George wasn't going to the bathroom in her tub anymore.

What We Thought and Said:

- George spends most of her time way inside the log and a little buried.
- George must have been cold and wanted to get warmer.
- The inside of the log was cozy and darker and warmer. [See Figure 8.4]

What We Tried:

- We looked in the book about turtles that we read earlier in the year.
- The children unanimously shouted "George is hibernating!"

This very brief documentation of a small part of the Turtle Project provides evidence that the children in this kindergarten classroom are well on their way to achieving

FIGURE 8.4 • George goes inside his log and hibernates.

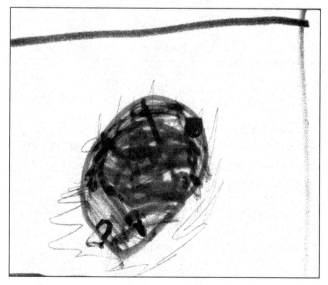

the kindergarten equivalent of Content Standard A, developing the abilities necessary to do scientific inquiry. The documentation shows how children are learning to ask questions about organisms and events in the environment and to plan and conduct a simple investigation. The children's words and drawings could also be collected for documentation of individual children's achievement of the content standard. These could be placed in portfolios. If performance standards were available (i.e., criteria and expectations of what would be considered "good" questions or observations), the children's work could be examined to document those performance standards. When examining recommended standards in various areas, such as literacy and mathematics, teachers can easily see that children are achieving these standards through projects. As teachers become familiar with content standards and curriculum requirements, they can incorporate the documentation of the achievement of these standards into projects.

Planning for Incorporation of Curriculum and Standards

Not all content standards or required curriculum will naturally emerge from projects and children's interests. However, it is possible to follow children's interests and still be assured that required curriculum is introduced and mastered. Many teachers have learned to follow the lead of children, engage them in learning, and still accomplish curriculum goals. One way to do this is to incorporate required curriculum and standards into the planning process. Many teachers have found the following suggestions from Helm (2008) helpful:

1. Gather together all statements of curriculum requirements, content standards, and performance standards that apply to the age group being taught.

2. Examine these statements and ask the following questions:
   - What are the knowledge, skills, and dispositions that children are expected to develop?
   - What should the children know and be able to do? If these are not clearly stated, make a separate list and ask for clarification.
   - Are performance standards indicated? For example, if the curriculum goal is for the kindergartener to learn to count, is that rote counting or counting actual objects? How many items should the child be able to count to meet the standard? 10, 20, 100, 1,000?

3. Once the curriculum requirements are understood, watch children for signs of interest that coincide with the curriculum content goals.

Consider the goals and standards when evaluating the appropriateness of a topic for your project. At the preschool through first-grade level, many of the content goals are stated very broadly. For example, the kindergarten science curriculum may indicate that children should learn about living and nonliving things. What living things do the children find interesting? Are they collecting caterpillars? Are they having many conversations about their pets? These topics have the potential to become projects in which curriculum goals can be easily incorporated. In other words, there is a high probability that children would learn many of the concepts specified in the required curriculum (such as what living things need to survive) in the process of their own self-directed investigation of these topics.

4. Make an anticipatory planning web, first by listing the concepts or content that relates to the project topic.

   The anticipatory planning web in Figure 8.5 shows how a teacher might make a web in response to children's interest in houses. The web shows these concepts in terms a prekindergartener's understanding—for example, that houses vary in styles, sizes, and shapes.

5. Examine the concepts placed on the web in step 4. Add to the anticipatory planning web the required curriculum objectives that could grow from these concepts.

   Curriculum objectives can then be added to the house web (see Figure 8.6).

FIGURE 8.5 • Teacher's anticipatory planning web by concepts (full web shown).

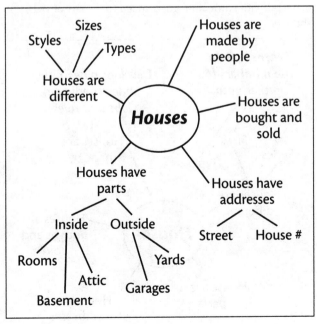

6. Examine the curriculum objectives added to the web in step 5. Add to the web how the achievement of goals and objectives may be documented.

A commonly used assessment system at the kindergarten level is the Work Sampling System (Meisels et al., 1994). In the Work Sampling System a checklist is used to record observations of children's development in seven domains of development. Teachers also collect portfolio items. Core items are specific portfolio items that represent particular areas of learning. Teachers in a school determine which items they are going to collect as core items and collect the same type of item three times a year. Core items coordinate with curriculum goals. An example of a core item is a sample of a child's emergent writing. By placing these items on the web, the teacher anticipates where documentation for the portfolio may be gathered to meet performance standards (see Figure 8.7).

Once the anticipatory planning web has been completed, the teacher can evaluate whether, on the basis of required curriculum, the topic would be the basis for a worthwhile project. It may not become a project if children's interest wanes. If it becomes a viable topic, then the teacher helps the children to form questions for the investigation and the process begins.

Thinking carefully about the relationship between the project topic and the required curriculum enables the teacher to introduce appropriate resources as needed and to take advantage of the learning opportunities that are pre-

sented. It helps the teacher to keep content goals in mind as he or she responds to the children during the project process. "Teaching on the fly" as described in Chapter 5 can be productive.

Seldom, however, does a project develop precisely in the way the teacher had anticipated. The children's interests are likely to narrow gradually, and the main focus of the investigation may shift to a small section of the web, or to a new concept not even shown on the anticipatory web. For example, a pet project may turn into an in-depth project about the work of a veterinarian. Teachers at this point may circle the section of the web that is the new focal point of the children's work, and then redraw lines. Sometimes the shift in focus has been so great that a new web is needed. Usually the first web can be cut apart, the new focal point can be placed in the center, and all those pieces of the first web that are still relevant can be rearranged around the new topic. Then the teacher can look at the web and see if there are any concepts or skills that are unlikely to emerge spontaneously from the project work. These can be introduced or taught separately from the project at other times of the day. The teacher may also decide that these concepts and skills might best be taught as a unit or a separate learning experience. Not all content or subjects are best studied through projects.

FIGURE 8.7 • Teacher's anticipatory planning web with concepts, curriculum goals, and assessment methods added (only part of web shown).

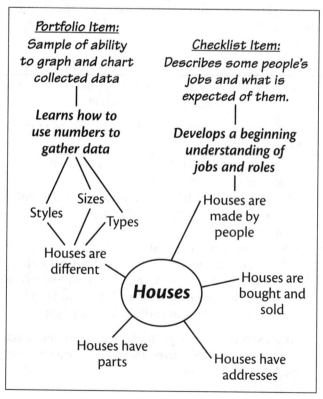

FIGURE 8.6 • Teacher's anticipatory planning web showing concepts with curriculum goals added (only part of web shown).

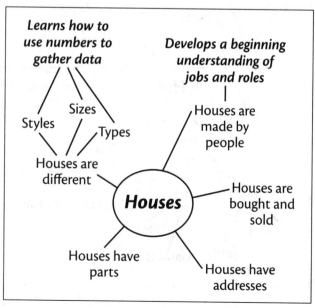

Integration of Early Literacy Experiences

One area of the curriculum that is more skills- than concept-based is the development of literacy—reading and writing skills. These skills are learned in many ways, but most children require some formal adult assistance to achieve mastery, and early experiences with books and writing are extremely important (National Association for the Education of Young Children [NAEYC], 1998). Children often learn new skills in reading and writing during the course of a project. Project work also affords many opportunities for reading and writing skills taught in other parts of the curriculum to be applied and therefore practiced. Activities in which children engage during project work are consistent with recommended teaching practices (NAEYC, 1998; Neuman et al., 2000). Some of these recommended strategies for the preschool years that occur naturally through projects include providing

- Print-rich environments
- First-hand experiences that expand children's vocabulary
- Opportunities and tools for children to see and use written language for a variety of purposes
- Opportunities for drawing children's attention to specific letters
- Opportunities for children to talk about what is read
- Opportunities to engage in play that incorporates literacy tools

Among the recommended strategies (NAEYC, 1998; Neuman et al., 2000) for the kindergarten and primary grades that occur naturally through projects are providing

- An intellectually engaging and challenging curriculum that expands knowledge of the world and vocabulary
- Experiences of being read to and independently reading informational texts
- Daily opportunities supported by the teacher to write many kinds of texts for different purposes
- Opportunities to work in small groups for focused instruction and collaboration with other children

In addition to recommended teaching strategies, it is helpful to look at developmental milestones in early literacy in relation to the project approach. The National Research Council's Committee on the Prevention of Reading Difficulties (Snow, Burns, & Griffin, 1998) has defined reading and writing skills that should be accomplished during the early years. Some of these accomplishments will require direct instruction for many of the children. However, many of these skills can be incorporated into project work and practiced through project activities. Some that are easily incorporated into project work are listed here.

3- and 4-Year-Old Accomplishments

- Recognizes print in the local environment.
- Understands that different text forms are used for different functions of print (e.g., a list for groceries is different from the list on a menu).
- Uses new vocabulary and grammatical constructions in own speech.
- Understands and follows oral directions.
- Is sensitive to some sequences of events in stories.
- Shows an interest in books and reading.
- Can identify about 10 alphabet letters, especially those from own name.
- Writes (scribbles) message as part of playful activity.
- May begin to attend to beginning or rhyming sounds in salient words. (p. 61)

Kindergarten Accomplishments

- Knows the parts of a book and their functions.
- Recognizes and can name all uppercase and lowercase letters.
- Understands that the sequence of letters in a written word represents the sequence of sounds (phonemes) in a spoken word (alphabetic principle).
- Recognizes some words by sight, including a few very common ones ("the," "I," "my," "you," "is," "are").
- Uses new vocabulary and grammatical constructions in own speech.
- Makes appropriate switches from oral to written language styles.
- Connects information and events in texts to life and life experiences to text.
- Retells, reenacts, or dramatizes stories or parts of stories.
- Listens attentively to books the teacher reads to class.
- Demonstrates familiarity with a number of types or genres of text (e.g., storybooks, expository texts, poems, newspapers, and everyday print such as signs, notices, labels).
- Correctly answers questions about stories read aloud.
- Independently writes many uppercase and lowercase letters.
- Uses phonemic awareness and letter knowledge to spell independently (invented or creative spelling).
- Writes (unconventionally) to express own meaning.
- Builds a repertoire of some conventionally spelled words. (p. 80)

First-Grade Accomplishments

- Uses letter–sound correspondence to sound out unknown words when reading text.
- Reads and comprehends both fiction and nonfiction that is appropriately designed for the grade level.

- Creates own written texts for others to read.
- Discusses prior knowledge of topics in expository texts.
- Uses how, why, and what-if questions to discuss non-fiction texts.
- Describes new information gained from texts in own words.
- Uses invented spelling or phonics-based knowledge to spell independently, when necessary.
- Produces a variety of types of compositions (e.g., stories, descriptions, journal entries) showing appropriate relationships between printed text, illustrations, and other graphics. (p. 81)

Projects are rich with potential literacy experiences leading to accomplishments because reading and writing enhance the investigation process and are used in clearly purposeful ways. Children's motivation to acquire skills seems to be strengthened when they themselves see their purpose and usefulness. As children use books for resources, they begin to recognize letters and words. Books become important sources of information for the young investigator. Literacy artifacts (periodicals, signs, instructions, menus) are also sources of information. Children acquire information from them; they copy words from them and put words on the models they create.

Projects also encourage children to write. They attempt to write because they have a purpose for writing: to communicate across time and with others. They write questions in order to remember them. They write words on pictures and label the parts of things. They write letters to field-site personnel and experts. They dictate or write captions for photos of the project process. Words on webs are dictated and in kindergarten and first grade are sometimes written by children. They write stories to tell what they learned and to describe field-site experiences. Project topics often appear spontaneously in journal entries. They make "word walls" of words that have importance to them because they tell about something in which the children have an intense interest. Writing becomes important to them because they see writing as a tool for their investigation.

Vocabulary develops throughout children's experiences. The concrete, hands-on nature of learning in project work makes words and concepts more easily memorable. Teachers report their own surprise at the number and complexity of words that children learn through projects, as in this list of words the kindergarteners learned in the Turtle Project:

turtle/tortoise	experts
plastron	large scale, small scale
carapace	shell (soft, hard,
bridge	top, bottom)
Native American	seasonal changes
leg rattles	hibernation
totem pole	reptile
emporium	soft shell turtle
three-toed box turtle	leaf turtle
mud turtle	ornate box turtle
stinkpot turtle	leopard tortoise
African side-neck turtle	sulcata tortoise

Kindergarten and first-grade teachers who include projects as part of their curriculum can maximize the impact of projects on literacy skills. These are some ideas for bringing reading and writing into the project experience.

1. Provide many books and periodicals related to the project for children's use for research.
2. Make "project dictionaries" by cutting photos, drawings, and words related to the project topic from periodicals, catalogs, and brochures. Place them in scrapbooks with labels so children can use them to copy words.
3. Make a project word wall listing words related to projects (see Chapter 4).
4. Look for ways young investigators can participate in purposeful writing and reading during the project. At the youngest age level this may be simply putting their names on a survey or placing a check or tally mark on a chart. At the kindergarten and first-grade level, as children develop writing skills, they can write their own lists and write their own questions and answers on their clipboards. They can either dictate or write letters to field-site personnel, thank you notes, and letters to other classrooms requesting help gathering supplies or inviting them to a culminating event.
5. Make sure clipboards and words are available for copying. Put a list of project words on children's clipboards for quick reference on field-site visits.
6. Draw children's attention to signs at field-sites. Ask experts to show children how they use writing and reading in their work. Borrow signs, blueprints, brochures, and other literacy artifacts from field-sites.
7. Have children revisit, redraw, and rewrite their work. For example, observational drawings can be photocopied, and the child can use one copy of the drawing for labeling parts.
8. Involve children in the writing of narratives of the project such as project history books, captions for photos and pictures, and wall displays.
9. Suggest possible topics for journal writing that relate to the project topic and especially to individual children's interest in different aspects of the project.

Besides bringing literacy into the project, kindergarten and first-grade teachers can also bring the project topic into other literacy experiences in the classroom. Mary Ann Gottlieb describes some of the ways she integrates the project topic into literacy instruction in her kindergarten classroom at Valeska Hinton Center:

I always have shared reading that correlates with the project. When we did the Zoo Project, we read the African folk tale of *The Ostrich and Crocodile* [Aradema, 1993] and *There's an Alligator Under My Bed* [Mayer, 1987]. I spend a week on each big book and use it as a reading activity for the week. If I don't have a big book that goes along with a project, then I write one. It may be fiction, folk tale, required reading curriculum—it usually just depends on what the topic is. I don't use a lot of nonfiction for shared reading because it doesn't have controlled vocabulary.

We make lots of little books that relate to the projects. It is a good way to reinforce vocabulary. In the Apple Project, I made an apple tree book that had just the parts of the tree. . . . I used a song as a shared reading activity: five green apples, four green apples, three green apples, etc.

In word lists for projects, I usually make the alphabet and record the words in alphabetical order that go along with the project. It is a graphic organizer; it focuses the children on the beginning letter so it reinforces letter–sound association for children who don't have that yet.

I have two journals for children—a learning journal and a daily journal. In the learning journal we wrote about what we learned about the zoo and about what we saw at the zoo.

We also use the journals for extension activities of the book that goes with the project. For example, we might write about what the children think would happen if there were one more page in the book.

Another way that reading and writing are used purposefully in projects is in documentation. Children see teachers write their words, they see teachers read their words, and they see the effect of the documentation on their parents and other adults. Children enjoy hearing their words read back to them and seeing the documentation of their project. Reading and writing enable teachers to capture what is happening in the classroom and communicate it to others. This is a valuable use of literacy skills, and the importance and the utility of reading and writing are not lost on even the youngest investigators.

INVOLVING PARENTS

In Chapter 1, the advantages of involving parents in projects were presented. There are ample opportunities for parent involvement in projects, and this involvement benefits the parent–child relationship as well as the child's education. A simple group invitation and regular sharing of documentation help to build enthusiasm and encourage parent participation in many classrooms. In some programs and

schools, however, involving parents doesn't just happen spontaneously in the project process. It takes patience and commitment on the part of the school staff. Some parents may feel uncomfortable in school environments. Going to school and being involved in learning experiences may not be part of the parent's cultural background or may be associated with discomfort for some. There may also be issues of transportation or work schedules. Classrooms in which young investigators are doing projects become communities of learners. Drawing parents into that community can contribute greatly to their children's education. Teachers are sometimes disappointed, however, when invitations to participate seem to be ignored or parents seem uninterested in the projects or documentation.

Topic selection is especially important if parents are reluctant to participate in the project process. Parents, just like their children, are more likely to respond to project topics that relate closely to their world and their interests. Adults, like children, appreciate understanding more fully and accurately their experiences and environment. They too enjoy looking closely at phenomena in their environments worthy of appreciation. Parents can become co-learners with their children.

Learning how the suction tube at the drive-up bank works can capture the attention of adults as well as children. Cultural relevance is, however, an important consideration. Parents, like children, are more likely to become interested and involved in a project on the auto repair shop down the street than on an ocean they have never seen.

Willingness to participate in the project may also depend upon how the invitation is extended. Reluctant parents will sometimes respond to a personal invitation for help rather than a duplicated letter to all parents. When requesting participation, it is also effective to ask parents to help with a specific activity. For example, asking a parent to "come in and show the children how you make tamales" or "help the children collect acorns in the park" is more likely to get a positive response than asking a parent to just "help out with the project" on Tuesday. For many parents, a phone call is usually more effective than a note.

The teacher also needs to be sensitive to the financial costs of a parent's participation. A parent may hesitate to cook a dish with the children or build a birdhouse if he or she has to supply the materials. When inviting parents to participate, the teacher can also request a list of materials or ingredients the parent will need and indicate that these will be made available in the classroom for their use.

Sometimes parents who have important knowledge or skills to share on a topic are reluctant to volunteer because they may think their knowledge and skills are inadequate to qualify them as experts. They may not think of themselves as experts or having expertise. Again, parents are more likely to respond positively when the request is clear and specific. For example, a parent may not see himself as someone who can "talk about fixing cars." When a note is sent home asking if anyone can come and show the children how "to change a tire on a car or truck," a parent may be more willing to participate.

Sharing the questions that children have generated helps parents see the level of expertise needed in the project. Parents are often surprised at how simple the questions are. Knowing the questions in advance gives them confidence that they will be able to answer them. When parents are asked to "speak to the class" or "share," they often think that means giving a speech. Giving speeches, even in front of small children, is a frightening prospect for many adults. It often helps to give a more specific invitation that explains what their role will be. "Could you come and show the seashells that you and Maria collected at the beach? We'll have you sit at the table and have a few children at a time come and talk to you." As parents get to know the children and feel comfortable in the environment, they often begin to address the whole group.

It is important to create an atmosphere of warmth when parents come into the classroom. Many teachers have a procedure for welcoming guests and helpers to their classroom in which the children participate. The teacher or a child shows the adults where to put their coats and where volunteers often work. The volunteer is introduced to the group, and the children are told how to address the volunteer. Children are taught to make a space for the volunteer in whatever group they are in at the time. It is also helpful if the children have laminated name tags that they can slip on whenever a parent or visitor comes to the classroom. Children respond better if the adult can call them by name, and the parent volunteer also can spell children's names if necessary. These name tags can also be used for field-site visits.

Sometimes teachers have a volunteer basket or tray where they put the materials and tools such as staplers, scissors, tape, and markers that the parent might need. Other teachers have carpenter's aprons with supplies in the pockets that volunteers are given when they come in. Most parents are reluctant to interrupt the teacher if they run out of things to do or need materials. Baskets, boxes, or aprons prepared for the volunteers communicate that their visit was anticipated and valued and that they, like others before them, have a place in the classroom. Giving the reluctant parent something to do immediately also makes the parent feel needed and that his or her time is being well spent.

It is helpful to have adult-size chairs in which parents can sit and work with the children. Early childhood teachers and young children are floor-sitters, but many parents are not used to sitting on the floor and feel uncomfortable if they are expected to do that. A chair for a 3-year-old is not appropriate for a 200-pound adult male.

When parents serve as helpers on field-site visits, following the guidelines in the Project Planning Journal and in Chapter 3 will make the experience not only more productive for children but better for parents. Parents will have a more successful experience and will feel encouraged to participate again when the teacher takes the time to prepare for their involvement. The teacher can brief parents using the checklist in the Project Planning Journal and carefully select children assigned to each adult. The teacher should keep the more challenging children in his or her own group. Documentation of the experiences at field-sites in photos and display panels should include not only what the children did but also what parents did. In this way, other parents can see how parents were involved and what they did.

For a variety of reasons, some parents are not able to assist with a project during the school day. These parents can be asked to contribute specific items for the project. We have worked with several teachers who have engaged young children in projects on shoes. In each case, parents have seemed more than willing to donate old shoes, boots, and slippers to the children's collection for study. Parents can undertake a particular activity at home and send documentation to school. For example, a report on an examination of the pipes coming into their kitchen or bathroom can be sent to the class. Documentation such as project history books can be sent home. If the program is multilingual, it is helpful to have all languages spoken by the group of children included in the project history book. Many programs are adopting digital communication strategies such as e-mailed newsletters, websites that share project work as it is ongoing, and photo sharing. These bring the project to life for parents, and even the busiest parent can keep up on the intellectual pursuits of their young investigators.

Care should also be taken to schedule culminating events at the most convenient times. Having a culminating event in which children must be present and where parents are encouraged to bring extended family members often brings parents to school. Once there, they can view documentation and talk with other parents about the project.

It is especially difficult to get parents involved in a project if this is the first project for a class or even a school. Once parents become involved in a first project, they understand the process and often become more responsive and involved in subsequent projects. Pam Scranton contrasts the Fire Truck Project, the first project for that classroom, with the Vet Project, done by the same young investigators later in the year.

Our parents had really bought into the project approach. There were so many donations from parents for the vet clinic. They had experienced projects, they knew what they were about, what the children were trying to do. They brought things in. Our parents brought in stethoscopes, white nurses' coats which the children labeled vet coats, empty bottles that the children covered and labeled "cow vitamins," old brushes and combs for the grooming center, empty shampoo bottles. One mother brought in an old hose sprayer from the sink. That was a main part of the washing spot that the children made. One mother supplied us with all the boxes we needed. The children brought in stuffed animals for the patients. When we did the Fire Truck Project I had to request everything, but on the Vet Project the parents understood what it was about and spontaneously brought these things in. I never made a list. The children made a list of what they wanted and told the parents. It was wonderful to see that happen. The children were dying to build this vet office. The children became the catalysts for the parents.

The teacher who is having difficulty getting the participation of parents in a project can take heart from Ms. Scranton's story. Documentation, patience, and the building of a history of projects can bring parents into the learning community.

UTILIZATION OF TECHNOLOGY

Many of the teachers whose projects are described in this book have become highly competent at utilizing technology in the project process. New technology skills used by these teachers have ranged from less sophisticated skills, such as how to use the photocopy machine to capture Time 1/Time 2 webs, to more elaborate skills, such as making multimedia presentations on the children's project work to put on websites. Although cost is a constraint for many early childhood programs, we are seeing more and more kindergarten and first-grade programs with access to interactive whiteboards. Internet access is common—if not in the classrooms, then located somewhere in the building. A few prekindergarten programs are using document cameras and digital microscopes. Much of this technology enables children to study and explore topics at greater depth than they were able to before. In many cases, the projects provided an impetus for the teachers to make great leaps forward in their own technological skills. Teachers often reported working with and learning from parents. Together they used technology to improve the quality of the learning experiences in their classrooms.

The technology resources most frequently used by teachers in project work appear to be the digital camera, scanner, and photocopier. Photocopy machines are used by teachers of young investigators in instruction and in documentation. Photocopies of artifacts and photos, in black-and-white and in color, are used to make project dictionaries, to illustrate words on webs, and in narratives and displays. Children's drawings and webs are copied mid-process so that the sequences of the drawing process can be captured. Teachers copy children's drawings so the children can label them without writing on their original work.

Overhead projectors continue to have a place in early childhood classrooms. Some teachers make color transparencies using their digital photos of field-sites and project them onto walls so children can revisit and experience the site again. These can also be used as backdrops at culminating events. Children can draw on overhead transparencies, which can be projected on large paper so the children can trace them for murals. This enables young investigators to manipulate their drawings on the overhead projector and place them on the mural where they want them to be. Scanned drawings and an LCD projector can also be used in this way, but it requires more adult management.

Tape recorders and video cameras are becoming smaller and smaller. Small video cameras, not much bigger than a deck of cards, can be carried in a pocket on field-site visits. "Point and shoot" capability enables children to use them and to capture not just what they saw but also what they heard. When the class returns to the classroom, a USB connection enables instant playback of the video. Digital segments can be uploaded to websites or included in presentations. Still photos can be printed from the video. Plug-in charging keeps the cameras charged for 2 hours and eliminates the need for batteries. This kind of technology is enhancing not just documentation of project experiences but also study and investigation by children. Some of the promising technology applications that can be used for project work include:

- Document cameras, also known as docucams, that enable a group of children to look at each other's work, see larger versions of pictures, and study real objects from different perspectives. Images can be stored.
- Digital microscopes that display magnified images at high quality. For example, children can examine the pistil of a flower and see pollen grains or can see the organisms in water. These can also be viewed by many children at the same time.
- Digital contact with experts and other programs throughout the world through e-mail, webinars, or shared meeting areas.
- Interactive whiteboards that combine the features of a whiteboard with an interactive computer screen.
  - When functioning like a giant computer monitor, it provides easy viewing of online videos, web content, and, with the addition of a webcam, interaction with anyone in the world.
  - When functioning as a whiteboard, it can be used by the children and teacher to write, draw, rewrite, save, and print any of the children's project work, including webs.

Although some people think of computers and the use of these newer technologies as inappropriate for younger children, when they are used to enhance children's investigations and representations, they can be not only very appropriate but also highly motivating to young children and empower them to take even more control of their learning in project work.

USING THE PROJECT APPROACH WITH SPECIFIC POPULATIONS

We are often asked if the project approach is appropriate for all children. Questions usually focus on the appropriateness for young children who are 3 and 4 years old, or children with special needs, or children who come from backgrounds that have provided only limited educational experiences. Sometimes teachers indicate that they believe the project approach is appropriate for children from advantaged homes but not for children who are growing up in poverty and who need practice on skills. The implication is that not all children are capable of doing in-depth investigation or that projects take time away from other badly needed direct-instruction experiences. One teacher examining drawings and observations of 4-year-olds in a project commented that these children were obviously gifted and that is why they were able to do the work they did! However, this was not the case. The children were actually in an early childhood program designed for children at risk of academic failure.

As discussed in Chapter 1, the project approach may be especially meaningful for children growing up in poverty, and many of the projects in this book come from intervention programs for young children at risk of school failure, many of whom are also poor. In the following sections we will address the appropriateness of using projects with two particular groups of children—those with special needs and second-language learners.

Children with Special Needs

Many teachers think that projects are not appropriate for children with special needs, or children with "special rights," as they are described in the schools of Reggio Emilia (Smith, 1998). However, we have observed many projects done in classrooms where children had special needs, both self-contained classrooms and others with full inclusion. Rebecca Edmiaston (1998), who has studied the use of projects in inclusive environments, concluded that the project approach is particularly well suited to meet the needs of all young children. She lists five reasons for this claim. The first is that projects are collaborative; that is, they encourage children and teachers to work collaboratively and all children to contribute in their way. Second, projects are based on children's interests. She tells this story of a project in an inclusive environment.

In a class meeting children in an inclusive kindergarten were exploring "shoes" as a possible next project. To the casual observer a young child with disabilities was squirming around on the floor looking at his feet and apparently was not engaged in the group discussion. His behavior probably would have been described as "off-task." However, his teacher recognized that he was tracing the lines on the soles of his shoes as the other children were identifying questions they had about shoes. She pointed out to the children that he was examining the pattern on the bottom of his shoes. His activity captured the interest of the others and they quickly began to examine their own shoes and those of their peers. As a result, several children became very interested in how patterns and different colors and words were imprinted on tennis shoes. Children made representations of the bottoms of their shoes and some even tried to make their own shoes. The child with special needs was able to address one of his educational goals, identifying similarities and differences, through his interest in the different patterns he found on the bottoms of shoes. (p. 1:20)

In project work, children's interests are encouraged and the learning experience can be shaped to meet all children's needs. Third, in projects not all children do the same things. Projects include a variety of experiences and activities. They do not require that every child participate in every experience, so individual abilities are taken into consideration and individual educational plans (IEPs) can be integrated. Fourth, much work in projects is undertaken in small groups, which makes it easier to be sure that individual goals are met and that the child with special needs can be included. Fifth, the rich documentation and the emphasis on documenting the children's activities and experiences in the variety of ways that children learn and express themselves facilitate the emphasis on their strengths. Throughout this book, we have shared ways that teachers determine interests through observation, encourage verbalization from children who are not yet verbal, and support children to use a multitude of ways to investigate. These are all good techniques for use with children with special needs.

Second-Language Learners

Projects can be very helpful for another group of children: those who are learning a second language. In U.S. schools, this primarily includes children who are learning English and native-English-speaking children who are learning second languages in bilingual or foreign language immersion programs. Many experiences that occur in the typical process of a project are compatible with recommendations for second-language learners. Teachers can use the project approach to help them meet language goals for these children. Pérez and Torres-Guzman (1995) emphasize the importance of authentic literacy events in the early years—reading and writing that is meaningful and purposeful. They also recommend beginning with children's interest and planning around a "theme": "Students' interests are the best place to begin curriculum planning" (p. 70). Others stress the importance of cultural sensitivity in second-language instruction (McLaughlin, 1995; NAEYC, 1995). Focusing projects on the children's immediate environment and the interests of the children and their families helps achieve this goal. Pérez and Torres-Guzman's recommendations also include purposeful collaborative learning and culminating activities, which occur as a natural part of the project process.

Many of these recommendations are rooted in the importance of hands-on, concrete experiences for learning. Christian (1994) says that for bilingual classrooms "experiential or hands on learning works especially well because students can get meaning from experience as well as from language" (p. 10). Christian also suggests that graphic representation techniques such as webbing, small-group discussions, and direct experience on field trips help children pick up relationships that might be missed because of language differences. These experiences also reinforce new vocabulary and concepts. Rebecca Wilson, who teaches a dual-language Spanish/English kindergarten, identifies some of the advantages she has found in including projects in her curriculum:

Projects help with literacy development in both languages. Children use books and resources in both languages, and they work hard to understand what they say because they want to learn about the topic. When we make up questions for experts they have to think in the language of the expert so they can communicate.

There are many places a child can fit into the project. Children at all different stages of development in their language can find something to do and contribute to the work of the project.

Being a non-native Spanish speaker, I've found that the project also pushes me to use more complex words and sentences in Spanish because the children want to know exact names for things. This helps my Spanish speakers continue their development in their language, which is important, and enriches my English speakers' experiences. For example, in the Garden Project I learned and used names for many different kinds of garden tools—words that I had not learned before—for example, three-tined cultivator. I have come to rely on my parents as resources for this knowledge. In the Garage Project, I had to ask a father to tell me the Spanish words to describe the mechanic's car lift which the children were creating in their garage. My need for parents to help in this way has also made

them a part of the process. Parents are interested in the projects and in what we are doing.

Wong Fillmore (1985) recommends strategies for children who are just learning to speak English. Many of these are already part of the project approach or are easily incorporated. Some of Wong Fillmore's strategies that are included in the recommended strategies for projects and second-language learners follow:

1. *Use demonstrations.* These can occur during field-site visits and classroom visits by experts. Bringing artifacts (such as tools) into the classroom for children to use or incorporate into dramatic play increases the understanding of what was demonstrated.

2. *Model and role-play.* Role-playing how to ask questions of visitors, as suggested in Chapter 3, provides valuable language practice. Creating dramatic play environments encourages role-play and the use of language related to the topic (see Chapter 4), especially if children are involved in creating the environment or play structure.

3. *Provide new information in the context of known information.* Discussing what is known about a topic and using graphic organizers such as webs, lists, and word walls enable children to connect new words and concepts with what they know and what they are experiencing. These are especially helpful for children with limited English proficiency. It is most effective if there is a clear distinction between the two languages in the graphic organizers such as the word wall shown in Figure 4.10, which has English words related to the garage on one side and Spanish words on the other.

4. *Repeat words, sentence patterns, and routines.* The extended time frame of projects and the in-depth nature of the investigation support repetition. There is time for children to repeatedly use words, phrases, and sentences in a meaningful way until they become part of the children's language. Incorporating songs, storybooks, and rhymes that relate to the topic also provides repetition of words.

5. *Tailor questions for different levels of language competence and participation.* In the project, children's questions can be as simple as those with yes/no answers or as complex as "How do they . . . ?" Teachers can encourage all children to participate in thinking of questions, asking them, and recording answers.

Taking care to include these strategies as part of the project activities can help the teacher achieve language goals for second-language learners. It also enhances the benefits of the project when the teacher uses the project experiences as a focus for any individual or small-group support provided for second-language learners.

ADMINISTRATORS' SUPPORT OF THE PROJECT APPROACH

Learning to use the project approach with young children is a complex process. Teachers face many challenges unique to projects at this age level that teachers of older children implementing the approach do not have to address. Many administrators are recognizing the advantages of the project approach for the children in their school or center and are beginning to encourage teachers to attempt to learn the process. Cathy Wiggers is such an administrator. She has directed an early childhood program in which the project approach was initiated and served as principal in an elementary school where project work is encouraged. She supports project work because she thinks it brings about good-quality learning in which children become engaged in the work and aspire to do things well. She likes the way children have the opportunity to become decision makers and take responsibility for their accomplishments. She also sees that in projects children develop their literacy skills as they use reading and writing for many purposes. She knows, however, that learning to do projects with young children is a challenge.

> Sometimes teachers have difficulty transitioning from their instructional plan to truly following the child's lead and letting them determine the direction the study will go. Recognizing children's interest and going with them in that direction can be a challenge. Teachers have to learn to be supporters, to scaffold children's learning—knowing when to step in and support and when to remain an observer.

Some of the ways administrators can support teachers in their learning how to implement the project approach is by providing professional development courses and workshops on the project approach on site, arranging for mentor teachers to work with teachers new to projects, and encouraging small groups of teachers to meet for sharing and dialogue. It is very helpful for teachers if principals and center directors participate in project approach training with their staff so they can more fully understand the strategies and the benefits to the children. Cathy Wiggers, like many directors and principals, makes a point of visiting classrooms during work time to see the projects and listen to children talk about their work. Providing planning time for developing projects is also important. Teachers need time to plan together and discuss the projects going on in their classrooms. Administrators can also provide support by assuring that field-site visits can be made when needed for investigation, video equipment is available for use, and teachers have cameras and film. Administrators can also set up systems in which teachers can obtain supplies quickly as the project evolves.

Taking the time to support teachers and projects can have many beneficial effects. These are changes that Ms. Wiggers, as an administrator, has noted:

> When teachers learn to do projects they do more of an in-depth analysis of the learning that is taking place in their classroom. When they see the higher level thinking their children are doing, they raise their expectations for their children. I've seen more sharing and discussion with colleagues as teachers problem-solve and study together how to reach higher levels of learning in their classroom. This affects their teaching in a positive way. Teachers ponder more deeply how they support children and their learning. They have a greater passion for how children learn.

CLOSING THOUGHTS

The descriptions of many of the projects featured in this book might prompt readers to ask if the time and energy devoted to them were warranted, given the topics under investigation. After all, very little of the knowledge gained in projects at the toddler, preschool, kindergarten, and first-grade level could not be "picked up" by most children as they grow to adolescence: Sooner or later most individuals acquire as much knowledge of the nature of cameras, fire hydrants, or the work of a veterinarian as they need for competence in their daily lives. So, one could ask, why bother? These topics can hardly be thought of as "core knowledge" required by children for full participation in mainstream culture. However, close reading of the projects in Chapters 6 and 7, as well as the other projects referred to in this book, suggests a number of answers to that question.

First, most of the important inborn intellectual dispositions are expressed and thereby strengthened through projects, rather than ignored or set aside by excessive emphasis on rote learning, drill, and exercises. The disposition to observe and to formulate questions to be answered is strengthened by the investigation of what is to the children an interesting phenomenon. When a teacher invites children to predict what the answers to their questions are likely to be, their dispositions to hypothesize are expressed; when the teacher encourages them to share the bases of their predictions, their dispositions to reflect on their own hunches are expressed. When children return to the classroom after a field-site visit and compare their findings with their predictions, their dispositions to check the facts, to be empirical, can be developed. The list of these kinds of learnings is potentially very long, and they are all "life skills" not usually included on school district or state tests.

Second, looking at the ability of such young children to engage in their first experience of representing numbers through tallying and graphing parts of an object of real interest to them, we can easily recognize how this can help them understand the representational function of mathematical symbols and the purposes they can serve. In this context, mathematical operations are intellectual engagements rather than rote learning or counting for the sake of reciting numbers from 1 to 10, as in many academically oriented curricula.

Third, considering how the children in the Camera Project solved the problem of too few tools for everyone to take apart cameras at once, we can see that they were learning another life skill not covered on any standardized performance test: They were learning to manage their own experiences and work with others. Throughout projects like this one, a variety of social skills are called on as the work progresses, and the children exchange ideas and opinions; share responsibility for posing questions to experts; and offer each other suggestions and corrections, as well as encouragement to try something again. All of these occur during genuine encounters about something that matters to the children. There are many more examples of intellectual and social dispositions and competencies, as well as academic skills, that are strengthened during good project work.

We want to emphasize the central issue of the quality of the work undertaken in projects. Like any other classroom procedures or processes, projects can be done well or poorly. Good-quality projects are those focused on worthwhile topics that constitute the content of their work; they involve children in important processes such as setting the research agenda that takes them in depth into the topic and preparing products that are detailed representations of the results of their investigation experiences. Most teachers with whom we have worked indicate that it takes a few project experiences before they develop full confidence in the children's abilities to take initiative and responsibility and to persist in their investigations. Once this confidence has been acquired, the teachers become co-investigators in that they are learning from their experiences with the children about how best to provide the environments in which the children can flourish and grow. They also report that while the work is intense, it is both interesting and satisfying for the children and for themselves.

With the emphasis on standards and accountability that determines much of what happens in our schools today, we would like to draw attention to the importance of the kind of experiences children have doing projects. We suggest that instead of attempting to judge the value of an educational experience on the basis of the standard of test scores, it is more appropriate to ask ourselves: What are the *standards of experience* that we want all of our children to have? Thus, when we decide to evaluate or assess a program for young children, we might ask: What kind of *experiences* is each child having much of the time? Or perhaps we should ask: What does it feel like to be a child in this environment day after day after day? To use these questions as a basis for assessing the appropriateness of programs for young children requires coming to agreement on which experiences are thought to be essential to yield the kinds of short-term *and* long-term outcomes we want for children. The following is our list of some important "standards of experience" that could guide what is provided for all young children in all programs, much of the time. We suggest that young children should frequently have these experiences:

- Being intellectually engaged, absorbed, and challenged
- Having confidence in their own intellectual powers and their own questions
- Being engaged in extended interactions (e.g., conversations, discussions, exchanges of views, arguments, planning)
- Being involved in sustained investigations of aspects of their own environment worthy of their interest, knowledge, and understanding
- Taking initiative in a range of activities and accepting responsibility for what is accomplished
- Knowing the satisfaction that can come from overcoming obstacles and setbacks and solving problems
- Helping others to find out things and to understand them better
- Making suggestions to others and expressing appreciation of others' efforts and accomplishments
- Applying their developing basic literacy and numeracy skills in purposeful ways
- Developing feelings of belonging to a group of their peers

This list is derived from general consideration of the kinds of experiences that all children should have much of the time that they spend in our educational settings. It is based on philosophical commitments as well as the best available empirical evidence about young children's learning and development. While young children can benefit from some academic experiences, excessive emphasis on direct instruction in academic skills overlooks the kinds of experiences that are most likely to strengthen and support young children's *intellectual* dispositions and their innate thirst for better, fuller, and deeper understanding of their own daily encounters with life. In other words, we are suggesting that young children should be helped to acquire academic skills *in the service of their intellectual dispositions,* and not at their expense. We suggest also that teachers working together may want to modify the list we have offered, based on their knowledge of the particular community they are serving.

In studying the project approach in toddler, prekindergarten, kindergarten, and first-grade classrooms, we have, above all, been most impressed with the enthusiasm of children, parents, and teachers. In project after project, documentation has captured the energy and the kind of deeply engaged learning experiences that occur in good projects. Teachers seem to become reenergized by watching their young investigators. Many do not just become co-learners with the children, but often embark on their own journeys. By observing, listening, and documenting, they become investigators not only of the project topic but of how children learn.

We have seen the project approach change teachers and teaching. As administrator Cathy Wiggers has said, "Learning to do the project approach affects all areas of teaching, not just project work." That is perhaps the greatest benefit of projects—that learning and teaching continue to be adventures for all investigators, young and old alike.

References

American Academy of Pediatrics. (2006). Clinical report: The importance of play in promoting healthy child development and maintaining strong parent–child bonds. *Pediatrics, 119*(1), 182–191.

The American heritage dictionary (3rd ed.). (1992). Boston: Houghton Mifflin.

Aradema, V. (1993). *The ostrich and crocodile.* New York: Scholastic.

Barrell, J. (2006). *Problem based learning: An inquiry approach.* Thousand Oaks, CA: Corwin Press.

Beneke, S. (1998). *Rearview mirror: A preschool car project.* Champaign, IL: ERIC Clearinghouse on Elementary and Early Childhood Education.

Beneke, S. (2004). *Rearview mirror: Reflections on a preschool car project* [DVD including video and electronic version of Beneke's 1998 book *Rearview mirror: A preschool car project*]. Champaign, IL: ECAP Publications, University of Illinois at Urbana-Champaign.

Berk, L. (2008). *Child development.* Boston: Allyn and Bacon.

Berk, L., & Winsler, A. (1995). *Scaffolding children's learning: Vygotsky and early childhood education.* Washington, DC: National Association for the Education of Young Children.

Berliner, David C. (2009). *Poverty and potential: Out-of-school factors and school success.* Boulder, CO, & Tempe, AZ: Education and the Public Interest Center & Education Policy Research Unit. Retrieved September 15, 2010, from http://epicpolicy.org/publication/poverty-and-potential.

Blakemore, S., & Frith, U. (2005). *The learning brain: Lessons for education.* Oxford, UK: Blackwell.

Bodrova, E., & Leong, D. (2006). *Tools of the mind: The Vygotskian approach to early childhood education* (2nd ed.). Englewood Cliffs, NJ: Prentice-Hall.

Bredekamp, S., & Rosegrant, T. (1995). *Reaching potentials: Transforming early childhood curriculum and assessment* (Vol. 2). Washington, DC: National Association for the Education of Young Children.

Brenneman, K., Stevenson-Boyd, J., & Frede, E. C. (2009, March). Math and science in preschool: Policies and practice. *Preschool Policy Brief, National Institute for Early Education Research, Issue 19.*

Bryson, E. (1994). *Will a project approach to learning provide children opportunities to do purposeful reading and writing, as well as provide opportunities for authentic learning in other curriculum areas?* Urbana, IL: ERIC Clearinghouse on Elementary and Early Childhood.

Cadwell, L. (1997). *Bringing Reggio Emilia home: An innovative approach to early childhood education.* New York: Teachers College Press.

Cadwell, L. (2003). *Bringing learning to life: The Reggio approach to early childhood education.* New York: Teachers College Press.

Carle, E. (1984). *The very hungry caterpillar.* New York: Putnam Publishing.

Catherwood, D. (2000). New views on the young brain: Offerings from developmental psychology to early childhood education. *Contemporary Issues in Early Childhood, 1*(1), 23–35.

Chard, S. C. (1994). *The project approach: A practical guide, I and II.* New York: Scholastic.

Chard, S. C. (1998a). Drawing in the context of a project. In J. H. Helm (Ed.), *The project approach catalog 2* (pp. 1:11–1:12). Champaign, IL: ERIC Clearinghouse on Elementary and Early Childhood Education.

Chard, S. C. (1998b, July 11). *Representation and mastering the medium.* Message posted on Projects-L Listserv. Champaign, IL: ERIC Clearinghouse on Elementary and Early Childhood Education.

Charles, C., Louv, R., Bodner, B., Guns, B., & Stahl, D. (2009). *Children and nature 2009: A report on the movement to reconnect children with nature.* Santa Fe, NM: Children & Nature Network.

Children's Defense Fund. (2005). *Child care basic.* Washington, DC: Author.

Christian, D. (1994). *Two way bilingual education: Students learning through two languages.* Santa Cruz, CA: National Center for Research on Cultural Diversity and Second Language Learning.

Clements, R. (2004). An investigation of the status of outdoor play. *Contemporary Issues in Early Childhood, 5*(1), 68–80.

Darling-Hammond, L. (2010). *The flat world and education: How America's commitment to equity will determine our future.* New York: Teachers College Press.

DeVries, R., Reese-Learned, H., & Morgan, P. (1991). Sociomoral development in direct-instruction, eclectic, and constructivist kindergartens: A study of children's enacted interpersonal understanding. *Early Childhood Research Quarterly, 6*(4), 473–517.

Dickinson, D. K. (2002). Shifting images of developmentally appropriate practice as seen through different lenses. *Educational Researcher, 31*(1), 26–32.

Dodge, D. T., Colker, L., & Heroman, C. (2002). *Creative curriculum for early childhood* (4th ed.). Washington, DC: Teaching Strategies.

Donaldson, M. (1978). *Children's minds.* Glasgow: Fontana.

Edmiaston, R. (1998). Projects in inclusive early childhood classrooms. In J. H. Helm (Ed.), *The project approach catalog 2* (pp. 1:19–1:22). Champaign, IL: ERIC Clearinghouse on Elementary and Early Childhood Education.

Edwards, C., Gandini, L., & Forman, G. (Eds.). (1993). *The hundred languages of children: The Reggio approach.* Stamford, CT: Ablex.

Edwards, C., Gandini, L., & Forman, G. (Eds.). (1998). *The hundred languages of children: The Reggio approach—advanced reflections* (2nd ed.). Stamford, CT: Ablex.

Epstein, J. (1995). School/family/community partnerships: Caring for the children we share. *Phi Delta Kappan, 76*(9), 701–712.

Gandini, L. (1993). Fundamentals of the Reggio Emilia approach to early childhood education. *Young Children, 49,* 4–8.

Gandini, L. (1997). Foundations of the Reggio Emilia approach. In J. Hendricks (Ed.), *First steps toward teaching the Reggio way* (pp. 14–25). Upper Saddle River, NJ: Prentice Hall.

Gandini, L., & Edwards, C. D. (2000). *Bambini: The Italian approach to infant/toddler care.* New York: Teachers College Press.

Gandini, L., Hill, L., Cadwell, L., & Schwall, C. (2005). *In the spirit of the studio: Learning from the atelier of Reggio Emilia.* New York: Teachers College Press.

Goal 3 and 4 Technical Planning Group. (1993). *Promises to keep: Creating high standards for American students.* Washington, DC: National Education Goals Panel.

Grant, M. M. (2002). Getting a grip on project-based learning: Theories, cases, and recommendations. *Meridian: A Middle Schools Computer Technologies Journal, 5*(1). Retrieved May 1, 2010, from http://www.ncsu.edu/meridian/win2002/514/index.html.

Harlan, J. (1984). *Science experiences for the early childhood years.* Columbus, OH: Merrill.

Heidemann, S., & Hewitt, D. (2009). *Play: The pathway from theory to practice* (Rev. ed.). St. Paul, MN: Redleaf Press.

Helm, J. H. (2008). Got standards? Don't give up on engaged learning! *Young Children, 63,* 14–20.

Helm, J. H., Beneke, S., & Steinheimer, K. (2007). *Windows on learning: Documenting young children's work* (2nd ed.). New York: Teachers College Press.

Helm, J. H., Berg, S., & Scranton, P. (2004). *Teaching your child to love learning: A guide to doing projects at home.* New York: Teachers College Press.

Helm, J. H., Berg, S., Scranton, P., & Wilson, R. A. (2005). *Teaching parents to do projects at home: A toolkit for parent educators.* New York: Teachers College Press.

Helm, J. H., & Helm, A. (2006). *Building support for your school: How to use children's work to show learning.* New York: Teachers College Press.

Henderson, A., & Berla, N. (Eds.). (1994). *A new generation of evidence: The family is critical to student achievement.* Washington, DC: Center for Law and Education.

Hendricks, J. (Ed.). (1997). *First steps toward teaching the Reggio way.* Upper Saddle River, NJ: Prentice Hall.

Herberholz, B., & Hanson, L. (1994). *Early childhood art.* Boston, MA: McGraw-Hill.

Holt, B.-G. (1989). *Science with young children* (Rev. ed.). Washington, DC: National Association for the Education of Young Children.

Hyson, M. (2008). *Enthusiastic and engaged learners: Approaches to learning in the early childhood classroom.* New York: Teachers College Press.

Illinois State Board of Education, Division of Early Childhood. (2002). *Illinois early learning standards.* Springfield, IL: Illinois State Board of Education.

Jones, B., Valdez, G., Norakowski, J., & Rasmussen, C. (1994). *Designing learning and technology for educational reform.* Oakbrook, IL: North Central Regional Educational Laboratory.

Katz, L. G. (1993). *Dispositions, definitions, and implications for early childhood practice.* Champaign, IL: ERIC Clearinghouse on Elementary and Early Childhood Education.

Katz, L. G. (1994). *The project approach.* Champaign, IL: ERIC Clearinghouse on Elementary and Early Childhood Education.

Katz, L. G. (1995). *Talks with teachers of young children: A collection.* Stamford, CT: Ablex.

Katz, L. G., & Chard, S. C. (1989). *Engaging children's minds: The project approach.* Norwood, NJ: Ablex.

Katz, L. G., & Chard, S. C. (1996). *The contribution of documentation to the quality of early childhood education.* Champaign, IL: ERIC Clearinghouse on Elementary and Early Childhood Education.

Katz, L. G., & Chard, S. C. (2000). *Engaging children's minds: The project approach* (2nd ed.). Stamford, CT: Ablex.

Kellert, S. R. (2005). *Building for life: Designing and understanding the human–nature connection.* Washington, DC: Island Press.

Kindler, A. L. (2002). *Survey of the states' limited English proficient students and available educational programs and services 2000–2001 summary report.* Washington, DC: National Clearinghouse for English Language Acquisition and Language Instruction Educational Programs. Retrieved September 12, 2010, from http://www.ncela.gwu.edu/files/rcd/BE021853/Survey_of_the_States.pdf.

Knapp, M. (Ed.). (1995). *Teaching for meaning in high-poverty classrooms.* New York: Teachers College Press.

LeeKeenan, D., & Edwards, C. (1992). Using the project approach with toddlers. *Young Children, 47*(4), 31–35.

Louv, R. (2008). *Last child in the woods: Saving our children from nature-deficit disorder.* Chapel Hill, NC: Algonquin.

Machado, J. (1995). *Early childhood experiences in language arts: Emerging literacy.* Albany, NY: Delmar.

Marcon, R. A. (1992). Differential effects of three preschool models on inner-city 4-year-olds. *Early Childhood Research Quarterly, 7*(4), 517–530.

Marcon, R. A. (1995). Fourth-grade slump: The cause and cure. *Principal, 74*(5), 6–17, 19–20.

Marcon, R. A. (2002). Moving up the grades: Relationship between preschool model and later school success. *Early Childhood Research and Practice, 4*(1). Retrieved May 10, 2010, from http://ecrp.uiuc.edu/v4n1/marcon.html.

Mayer, M. (1987). *There's an alligator under my bed.* New York: Dial Books for Young Children.

McLaughlin, B. (1995). *Fostering second language development in young children: Principles and practices.* Santa Cruz, CA: National Center for Research on Cultural Diversity and Second Language Learning.

Meisels, S. J., Jablon, J. R., Marsden, D. B., Dichtelmiller, M. L., Dorfman, A. B., & Steele, D. M. (1994). *An overview: The work sampling system.* Ann Arbor, MI: Rebus Planning Associates.

Miller, L. B., & Bizzell, R. P. (1983). Long-term effects of four preschool programs: Sixth, seventh, and eighth grades. *Child Development, 54*(3), 727–741.

National Association for the Education of Young Children. (1995). *Responding to linguistic and cultural diversity: Recommendations for effective early childhood education.* Washington, DC: Author.

National Association for the Education of Young Children and the International Reading Association. (1998, May). *Learning to read and write: Developmentally appropriate practices for young children*. Washington, DC: National Association for the Education of Young Children.

National Committee on Science Education Standards and Assessment. (1995). *Education standards*. Washington, DC: National Research Council.

Nebraska Department of Education. (2008). *Nebraska early learning guidelines: Connecting children to nature*. Lincoln, NE: Nebraska Department of Education Early Childhood Training Center. Retrieved September 12, 2010, from http://ectc.education.ne.gov/ELG/nature_education.pdf.

Neuman, S., Copple, C., & Bredekamp, S. (2000). *Learning to read and write: Developmentally appropriate practices for young children*. Washington, DC: National Association for the Education of Young Children.

Neumann-Hinds, C. (2007). *Picture science: Using digital photography to teach young children*. St. Paul, MN: Redleaf Press.

New, R. (1990). Excellent early education: A city in Italy has it! *Young Children, 45*(6), 4–10.

New, R. (1991). Early childhood teacher education in Italy: Reggio Emilia's master plan for "master" teachers. *The Journal of Early Childhood Teacher Education, 12*(37), 3.

Partnership for 21st Century Skills. (2010). *A framework for 21st century learning*. Retrieved March 6, 2010, from www.21stcenturyskills.org.

Pelo, A. (2007). *The language of art: Inquiry based studio practices in early childhood settings*. St. Paul, MN: Redleaf Press.

Polman, J. (2000). *Designing project-based learning science: Connecting learners through guided inquiry*. New York: Teachers College Press.

Pérez, B., & Torres-Guzman, M. E. (1995). *Learning in two worlds*. White Plains, NY: Longman.

Rankin, B. (1992). Inviting children's creativity: A story of Reggio Emilia, Italy. *Child Care Information Exchange, No. 85*, 30–35.

Ravitch, D. (2010). *The death and life of the great American school system: How testing and choice are undermining education*. New York: Basic Books.

Rosenow, N., Wike, J. R., & Cuppens, V. (2007). *Learning with nature idea book: Creating nurturing outdoor spaces for children*. Lincoln, NE: National Arbor Day Foundation.

Schweinhart, L. (1997). *Child-initiated learning activities for young children living in poverty: ERIC Digest*. Urbana, IL: ERIC Clearinghouse on Elementary and Early Childhood Education.

Smilansky, S., Hagan, J., & Lewis, H. (1988). *Clay in the classroom: Helping children develop cognitive and affective skills for learning*. New York: Teachers College Press.

Smith, C. (1998). Children with "special rights" in the preprimary schools and infant–toddler centers of Reggio Emilia. In C. Edwards, L. Gandini, & G. Forman (Eds.), *The hundred languages of children: The Reggio Emilia approach—advanced reflections* (2nd ed.; pp. 199–214). Stamford, CT: Ablex.

Smith, G. (2002, April). Place-based education: Learning to be where we are. *Phi Delta Kappan, 43*, 584–593.

Smith, L. (1997). "Open education" revisited: Promise and problems in American educational reform. *Teachers College Record, 99*(2), 371–415.

Smith, N. R., & the Drawing Study Group. (1998). *Observation drawing with children: A framework for teachers*. New York: Teachers College Press.

Snow, C. E., Burns, M. S., & Griffin, P. (1998). *Preventing reading difficulties in young children*. Washington, DC: National Academy Press.

Sobel, D. (2005). *Place-based education: Connecting classrooms and communities*. Great Barrington, MA: Orion Society.

Taylor, A. F., & Kuo, F. E. (2006). Is contact with nature important for healthy child development? State of the evidence. In C. Spencer & M. Blades (Eds.), *Children and their environments: Learning, using and designing spaces*. Cambridge, UK: Cambridge University Press.

Topal, C. W. (1983). *Children, clay and sculpture*. Worcester, MA: Davis Publications.

U.S. Bureau of the Census. (2008). *Income, poverty, and health insurance coverage in the United States: 2008*. Report P60, n. 236, Table B-2, pp. 50–55.

Vygotsky, L. S. (1978). *Mind in society: The development of higher mental processes* (M. Cole, V. John-Steiner, S. Scribner, & E. Souberman, Eds. & Trans.). Cambridge, MA: Harvard University Press.

Wexler, B. (2008). *Brain and culture: Neurobiology, ideology, and social change*. Cambridge, MA: MIT Press.

Wong Fillmore, L. (1985). Second language learning in children: A proposed model. In R. Eshch & J. Provinzano (Eds.), *Issues in English language development*. Rosslyn, VA: National Clearinghouse for Bilingual Education. ERIC Document No. ED 273 149.

Zull, J. (2002). *Art of changing the brain: Enriching the practice of teaching by exploring the biology of learning*. Sterling, VA: Stylus.

Index

About the Authors

JUDY HARRIS HELM assists schools and early childhood programs in integrating research and new methods through her consulting and training company, Best Practices, Inc. She began her career teaching first grade, then taught, directed, and designed early childhood and primary programs as well as training teachers at the community college, undergraduate, and graduate levels. She is past state president of the Illinois Association for the Education of Young Children.

Dr. Helm is a national and international speaker and trainer on project work, engaged learning, and documentation and assessment. Included among the seven books she has authored, coauthored, or edited are *Young Investigators: The Project Approach in the Early Years*; *The Power of Projects*; *Windows on Learning*; *Teaching Your Child to Love Learning: A Guide to Doing Projects at Home*; and *Teaching Parents to Do Projects at Home*. She also provides consultation on school design and is currently principal design consultant for two new birth through eighth-grade 21st Century Community Learning Centers, which will feature project work and engaged learning.

LILIAN G. KATZ is Professor Emerita of Early Childhood Education at the University of Illinois (Urbana-Champaign), where she is also Co-Director of the Clearinghouse on Early Education and Parenting. She is author of more than 100 publications, including articles, chapters, and books about early childhood education, teacher education, child development, and parenting.

Dr. Katz was founding editor of the *Early Childhood Research Quarterly*, and served as Editor-in-Chief during its first six years. In 1989 she wrote *Engaging Children's Minds: The Project Approach* (with S. C. Chard; released in its second edition in 2000), which has served as a basic introduction to the project approach. Dr. Katz has lectured in all 50 U.S. states and in 54 countries. She has held visiting posts at universities in Australia, Canada, England, Germany, India, Israel, the West Indies, and in many parts of the United States. Dr. Katz is Editor of the only online peer-reviewed bilingual (English/Spanish) journal in the field: *Early Childhood Research & Practice*.

Project Planning Journal

Name of Teacher _____

Project Title _____

Project Dates _____ to _____

School/Center _____

Age Level _____

from

Young Investigators
The Project Approach in the Early Years
(2nd edition)

By Judy Harris Helm and Lilian Katz

Introduction to the
Project Planning Journal

• • •

THE PROJECT PLANNING JOURNAL serves two purposes. The first purpose is to support and encourage teachers while they are learning how to do a first project. Along with the chapters in this book, *Young Investigators: The Project Approach in the Early Years,* the Journal provides step-by-step guidance through the decisions that a teacher has to make in doing a first project with young children. It helps teachers prepare, plan, and implement a project with young investigators in their own classroom.

A second, unplanned, purpose for the Journal was discovered as teachers who already knew how to guide projects with young children began to use it as a convenient way to organize their thinking and record information. It enabled them to keep track of their planning tasks, the events of a project, and their documentation. For busy teachers, it provided reassurance that they were preserving the key information about each project. More important, the Journal appeared to provide a place and a purpose for reflections. These reflections were often then shared with colleagues.

The Project Planning Journal is designed to be reproduced by teachers for use in various ways. (It may be photocopied from the book or printed from a PDF version that is available for free download from www.tcpress.com.) Some teachers put copies into three-ring binders and add pages for additional notes, scrapbook pages, or pocket folders for photographs. The main task in each phase of the project is presented, questions to consider are listed, and Teacher Journal boxes (highlighted with **TJ** icons) are provided for teacher reflection. Areas and activities that offer good opportunities for parental involvement are identified with **P** icons. Some principals and directors of programs prepare such notebooks for their staff to encourage project work. As Project Planning Journals accumulate with second and subsequent projects, teachers, as well as centers or schools, can build a data bank of their project experiences. This encourages teachers to look back on their own development as teachers guiding projects and provides ideas and support for teachers new to project work.

On page 3 of this Journal appears the handout "How We Are Learning: An Introduction to the Project Approach." This handout can be given to parents at the beginning of the year to explain project work. It can also be sent or hand-delivered by teachers to field-site staff and given to experts before visits. The handout can also be included as a take-away when project work is displayed.

The project flowchart described in Chapter 1 (Figure 1.5) is reproduced on page 4 of this Journal to assist in planning and to remind teachers of the structure of the project approach. Teachers report that revisiting the flowchart and then finding the corresponding pages in the Project Planning Journal provides a sense of direction and focus to their daily planning. Sections of the flowchart are reproduced throughout the Journal to serve as landmarks to show where specific activities fit into the larger picture. If you are working with toddlers, you will want to study the flowchart for toddlers that appears on page 5 of this Journal (reproduced from Figure 7.13) and review Chapter 7 regarding planning activities to match the knowledge and skills of toddlers. Comparing the flowcharts side by side will provide additional insight into how project work can be adapted to serve the younger set.

The Project Planning Journal is a guide, a road map for a journey. Projects, like journeys, do not always take the direct route. There may be side roads followed, detours taken that enrich and delight. This book, this Journal, and the flowcharts show the lay of the land, where roads lead and where one might go. These guides are not like a blueprint for a building that must be carefully and precisely followed. Where the journey goes and where the children and teacher end up are decided by them together.

How We Are Learning:
An Introduction to the Project Approach

What is the project approach?

The project approach is a method of teaching in which an in-depth study of a particular topic is conducted by a child or a group of children.

How is it different from others ways of learning?

Our children study one topic for a long time period. The topic is selected partly because they were interested in it and it is meaningful to them and their lives. The children will go into great depth and often at a level higher than many adults would expect for this. The teacher integrates content knowledge like math, reading, and science into the project.

How is a project planned?

The children make many of their own plans with the teacher's help. Plans usually include an on-site visit and/or interviews with experts. An expert is anyone who knows a great deal about the topic of study.

How will children learn?

Children use a variety of resources to find answers to their questions. These include traditional resources like books. They also conduct in-depth investigations on site visits. The children plan questions for interviews and have assigned tasks for trips or for interviewing experts. They make field notes and draw or write on site. They make plans for building structures and play environments that will help them sort out what they are learning about the topic.

Children do their own problem solving with the teacher structuring problems and assisting in finding solutions and resources. Children will redraw and rewrite as their knowledge grows. Some of the ways that they will record their learning are project books, posters, murals, artwork, graphs, charts, constructions, and journals.

How does the teacher know if children are learning?

The teacher collects children's work, observes what they do, and analyzes their work. This is called documentation. The curriculum goals of the school or center are reviewed and documentation is planned to be sure that children are learning concepts and skills specified in the goals. Often a display will be prepared that shows what students are learning.

Is this the only way these children are learning?

The project approach is one way among a variety of ways that children learn. The project integrates much of the same knowledge and skills presented in more formal ways in the classroom. Projects have the added advantage of providing an opportunity for children to apply and use what they are learning as they solve problems and share what they know. It provides opportunities for developing group skills such as working with others and challenges children to think, which supports brain development.

How can others help with projects?

Realize that children have their own questions and are learning to use you and many resources to find answers. Take their questions seriously, and listen to what they have to say. Provide space and opportunities for them to draw or photograph what they are studying. Children learn best when many senses are involved, so anything that they can touch, see up close, or hear is helpful. Things that can be borrowed for study in the classroom are valued and appreciated, especially parts of machines, tools, samples of products, and so forth. We hope you will follow up, view our documentation, and find out how children have processed what they have learned.

Phases of a Project

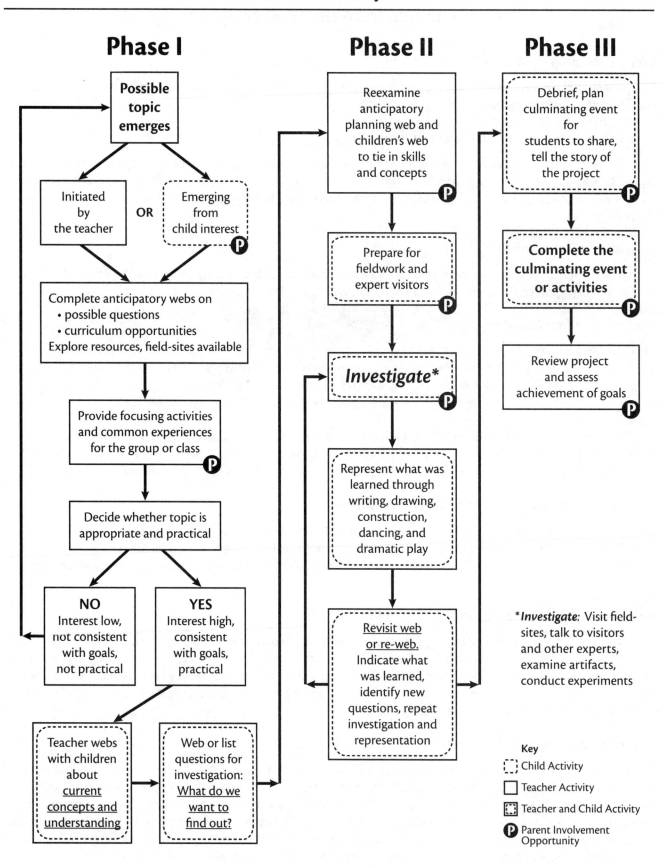

Phase I

Possible topic emerges

Initiated by the teacher

OR

Emerging from child interest Ⓟ

Complete anticipatory webs on
• possible questions
• curriculum opportunities
Explore resources, field-sites available

Provide focusing activities and common experiences for the group or class Ⓟ

Decide whether topic is appropriate and practical

NO
Interest low, not consistent with goals, not practical

YES
Interest high, consistent with goals, practical

Teacher webs with children about <u>current concepts and understanding</u>

Web or list questions for investigation: <u>What do we want to find out?</u>

Phase II

Reexamine anticipatory planning web and children's web to tie in skills and concepts Ⓟ

Prepare for fieldwork and expert visitors Ⓟ

*Investigate** Ⓟ

Represent what was learned through writing, drawing, construction, dancing, and dramatic play

<u>Revisit web or re-web.</u> Indicate what was learned, identify new questions, repeat investigation and representation

Phase III

Debrief, plan culminating event for students to share, tell the story of the project Ⓟ

Complete the culminating event or activities Ⓟ

Review project and assess achievement of goals Ⓟ

*__Investigate__: Visit field-sites, talk to visitors and other experts, examine artifacts, conduct experiments

Key

⌐⌐ Child Activity

☐ Teacher Activity

▣ Teacher and Child Activity

Ⓟ Parent Involvement Opportunity

Young Investigators, 2nd ed., Copyright © 2011 by Teachers College, Columbia University

Phases of a Project with Toddlers

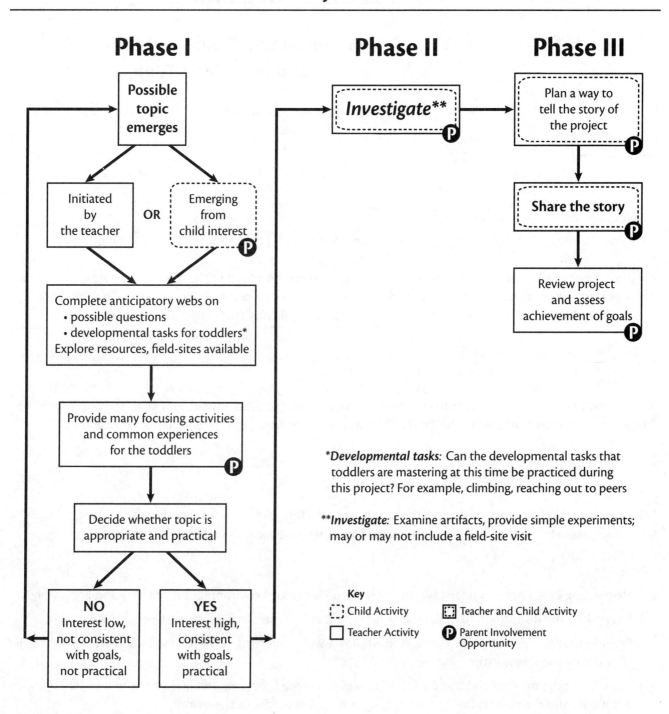

Phase I

Possible topic emerges

Initiated by the teacher **OR** Emerging from child interest **P**

Complete anticipatory webs on
• possible questions
• developmental tasks for toddlers*
Explore resources, field-sites available

Provide many focusing activities and common experiences for the toddlers **P**

Decide whether topic is appropriate and practical

NO
Interest low, not consistent with goals, not practical

YES
Interest high, consistent with goals, practical

Phase II

*Investigate*** **P**

Phase III

Plan a way to tell the story of the project **P**

Share the story **P**

Review project and assess achievement of goals **P**

Developmental tasks: Can the developmental tasks that toddlers are mastering at this time be practiced during this project? For example, climbing, reaching out to peers

**Investigate:* Examine artifacts, provide simple experiments; may or may not include a field-site visit

Key

⌐⌐ Child Activity   ⊡ Teacher and Child Activity

☐ Teacher Activity   **P** Parent Involvement Opportunity

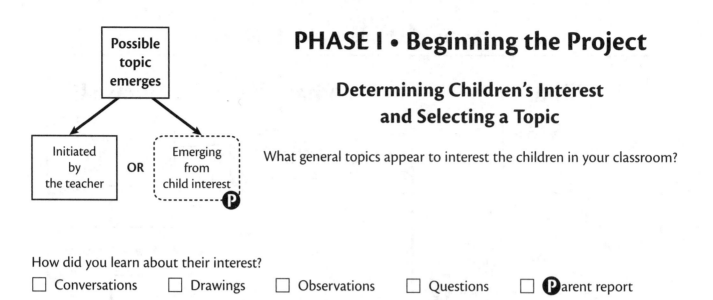

PHASE I • Beginning the Project

Determining Children's Interest and Selecting a Topic

What general topics appear to interest the children in your classroom?

How did you learn about their interest?

☐ Conversations ☐ Drawings ☐ Observations ☐ Questions ☐ **P**arent report

If a student-initiated topic does not emerge, the curriculum can be examined for broad topic areas. Is there an event or learning experience coming that could be used as a starting point? A walk around the school and neighborhood will often result in identifying something in the vicinity that might interest your children.

What are your curriculum goals for the children this year? Attach a list of curriculum goals to your journal. Are there some topics that are both of interest to your children and a part of your curriculum goals?

Select a few topics of interest and apply the criteria for selection of a topic for a project (see Chapter 2). If this topic were to develop into a project, would the experience have value for children?

Will it

☐ Help young investigators understand their own experience and environment more fully and accurately?

☐ Strengthen the disposition to look closely at phenomena in their environments worthy of appreciation?

☐ Provide ample opportunity for children to employ a wide variety of interactive skills and dispositions while conducting the investigation?

☐ Provide opportunity for children to develop insight into the functions and limitations of a variety of different media and develop skillfulness in applying the various media to their work?

What topics that your children find of interest meet the criteria for topic selection?

Make an Anticipatory Planning Web

Make a web to see if the project can be integrated with your curriculum. If you do not have a required curriculum experiment with some of the anticipatory webs described in Chapter 2. If you do have a required curriculum, follow the webbing process described in Chapter 6.

TJ *Teacher Journal: Planning Web*

Copy your anticipatory planning web here.

TJ *Teacher Journal:* | Take time to reflect on your selection of this possible topic.
Topic Selection | Record your thoughts.

What are your reasons for selecting this topic?

What possible directions could it take?

What content or skills would be strengthened?

What do you know about this topic? What would you like to know about this topic?

Trying Out a Topic and Getting Started

The project can begin in several ways: Children express an interest, teacher introduces a topic, or a topic is agreed upon by children and teacher (Katz & Chard, 1989). For young children, it is helpful to spend some time introducing the topic.

Topic: _____   **Date Phase I Began:** _____

Establish Common Ground

The main idea is to establish a common ground among the children by pooling the information, ideas, and experiences they already have about a topic. Build a shared perspective. During preliminary discussions, the teacher encourages talking about the topic, playing, and depicting current understanding in many ways. (Katz & Chard, 1989, p. 82)

The younger the children and the more diverse the group, the more time the teacher may need to spend creating a common understanding. Teachers may provide several experiences for children relating to the topic. Children will need enough knowledge about the topic to develop questions for investigation.

What event can be used to focus the children's attention on this topic?

☐ Book   ☐ Video   ☐ Related objects   ☐ Discussion   ☐ Dramatic play

Notes/Results:

P Is there an opportunity to involve parents in focusing events?

What do the children already know about this topic? How can their knowledge be recorded?
For ideas on how to access children's prior knowledge, see Chapter 2.

☐ Web   ☐ List of questions   ☐ Drawings/constructions   ☐ Recording discussions

Notes/Results:

Extend Children's Interest and Build a Common Vocabulary

What resources can be used to stimulate interest and clarify questions?

☐ Books ☐ Construction materials ☐ Visitors ☐ Artifacts ☐ **P**arent contributions

Notes/Results:

How are the children showing what they already know about the topic? How are they beginning to explore the topic?

☐ Drawings/sketches ☐ Paintings ☐ Constructions ☐ Play ☐ Language products

What can be done to encourage representation?

Notes/Results:

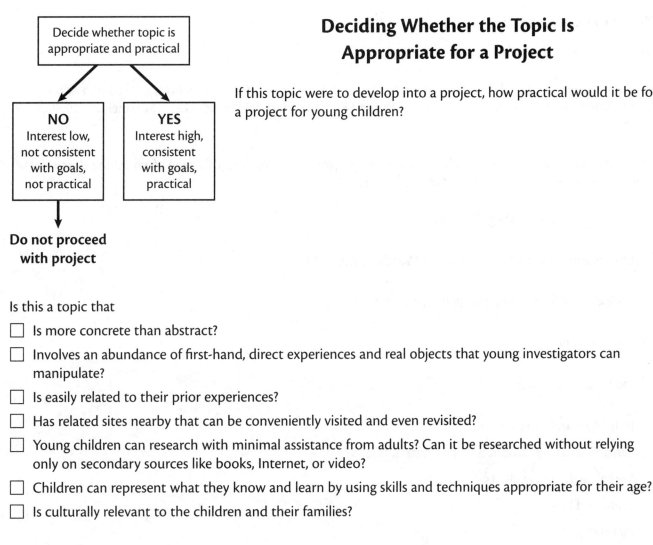

Deciding Whether the Topic Is Appropriate for a Project

If this topic were to develop into a project, how practical would it be for a project for young children?

Is this a topic that

- ☐ Is more concrete than abstract?
- ☐ Involves an abundance of first-hand, direct experiences and real objects that young investigators can manipulate?
- ☐ Is easily related to their prior experiences?
- ☐ Has related sites nearby that can be conveniently visited and even revisited?
- ☐ Young children can research with minimal assistance from adults? Can it be researched without relying only on secondary sources like books, Internet, or video?
- ☐ Children can represent what they know and learn by using skills and techniques appropriate for their age?
- ☐ Is culturally relevant to the children and their families?

Is this topic still a topic of interest?

- ☐ No, because children's interest in this topic has waned.
- ☐ Yes.

Does this topic have merit for curriculum integration?

- ☐ No, it does not fit curriculum goals.
- ☐ Yes.

If the answer to either of the above questions is no, you can continue to explore the topic as a teacher-directed unit or move on to other topics. Wait for a better topic for a project.

If both answers are yes—the children are interested and this has promise of being a valuable learning experience—then proceed with the project.

Plan for Documentation

Take time now to think about documentation.

Review the following list of ways to document. For more information on documentation see Chapter 6 and consult *Windows on Learning: Documenting Young Children's Work* (Helm, Beneke, & Steinheimer, 1998a, 1998b).

What types of documentation can be used for this project? Come back to this page often during the project. Write down what has been collected for each type.

☐ Project narratives: Telling the story

☐ Observations of child development: Watching the child

☐ Checklists of knowledge and skills in curriculum

☐ Anecdotal notes

☐ Individual portfolios

☐ Individual and group products:

Written language products: Signs, letters, books

Verbal language products

Webs and lists

Pictures

Representational pictures: Time 1 and Time 2 pictures, symbolic pictures

Music and movement

Constructions: Play environments, sculpture, blocks, or building toys

☐ Self-reflections of students

Are there characteristics of this topic that make one type of documentation more effective than another?

Are there school or center personnel who can be asked to help with documentation?

ⓟ Are there parents who can help with documentation (i.e., photographing, taking dictation, videotaping)?

This documentation planning sheet should be completed as the project progresses (see Chapter 5).

"Collection Task" refers to taking photos, writing down conversations, and so forth. If the teacher aide does this task, then plan for someone else to cover the teacher aide's task that would normally be done at this time. For example, a parent may prepare the snack. Think ahead and prepare materials and equipment.

Anticipated Project Events	Possible Types of Documentation	Equipment or Materials Needed	Collection Task Assigned To	Coverage of Collector's Tasks

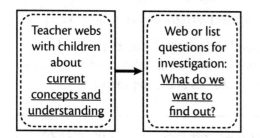

Determining What Children Know and What They Want to Find Out

In a large or small group, talk with children about what they know about the topic. What concepts and understanding do they already have about the topic? How will you record it?

☐ Webs   ☐ Lists

Notes/Results:

With the children, record what they want to know about the topic. What initial questions have been generated for possible research?

☐ Webs   ☐ Lists

Notes/Results:

Reexamine
anticipatory
planning web and
children's web
to tie in skills
and concepts

Ⓟ

PHASE II • Developing the Project

Project Topic: _____

Focus of the Topic: _____

Date Phase II Began: _____

Reexamining the Instructional Planning Web

Now that a topic has been selected, reexamine the planning web. What curriculum goals will integrate into the project? Are there experiences that should be provided at times other than project work times? If the topic has changed significantly from the anticipatory web and there is a required curriculum, consult Chapter 6.

TJ *Teacher Journal: Looking Ahead* | What can the children gain from this experience? What content and skill development do I hope to see? What dispositions do I hope will be strengthened?

Prepare for
fieldwork and
expert visitors

(P)

Preparing for Investigation

The emphasis during this phase is on introducing new information and finding answers to questions. This phase can include visiting field-sites, talking with visitors who bring real objects to the classroom, and examining books, photographs, or artifacts. Children are encouraged to follow their interests and find answers to their questions.

How can the investigation become focused?

☐ Discussion   ☐ New web   ☐ List of questions   ☐ Assigned tasks

Notes/Results:

What additional resources should be brought into the classroom to enable and support in-depth study?

☐ Books   ☐ Artifacts   ☐ Visitors

☐ Websites   ☐ Construction materials   ☐ **(P)**arent contributions

Notes/Results:

What skills might the children need help with? These skills are described in Chapter 3 with suggestions for practicing and integrating these skills. These skills are also learned during the project.

☐ How to pose a question to an adult

☐ How to tally data

☐ Observing and talking about what they observed

☐ Observational drawing and field sketching

☐ Using construction tools and materials such as tape, glue, staplers

☐ Using clay

☐ How to use camera or video

How can the children best be prepared for field-site experience?

☐ Discussion   ☐ Practicing skills   ☐ Reminders   ☐ Rehearsal

Notes/Results:

Planning for Field-Site Visits

Arrange Transportation

Do I need to arrange for transportation to a site? Do I need permission slips from parents?

Communicate with Field-Site Personnel

How will I prepare the field-site personnel to maximize investigation opportunities for my children?

☐ Phone call   ☐ Pre-trip visit by teacher   ☐ Reminder letter   ☐ "How We Are Learning" handout

Checklist for discussion with site personnel (see Chapter 3 on preparing site personnel)

☐ Safety issues involved in this site visit
☐ Importance of child investigation and direct first-hand experiences
☐ Importance of real objects, especially those with which children can interact by using their senses
☐ Overview of what the children currently know and understand
☐ Overview of what the children are interested in learning (share some of the questions they might ask)
☐ Explanation of how children will record what they see, what they think, and what they find out (tape recording, video, clipboards, writing, photographing)
☐ Opportunities for demonstration of a task or activity
☐ Possible items or scenes that children may sketch or record
☐ Artifacts (tools, equipment, products, etc.) that can be borrowed and kept in the classroom for further investigation
☐ Importance of having a guide or host with experience in communicating with young children

Notes from discussion:

Plan and Prepare for Adult Helpers/Chaperones Ⓟ

How many children will go on the visit? _____   How many adults are needed? _____

What preparations should adult helpers have?

☐ Phone call   ☐ Request letter   ☐ Meeting   ☐ Reminder note   ☐ "How We Are Learning" handout

Checklist to cover with adult helpers:

☐ Safety issues involved in this site visit
☐ Information about particular children who might require special assistance
☐ Importance of child investigation and direct first-hand experiences
☐ Importance of children interacting with real objects and using their senses
☐ Overview of what the children currently know and understand
☐ Overview of what the children are interested in learning (share some of the questions they might ask)
☐ Explanation of the importance of seeing adults model drawing, writing, or recording
☐ Explanation of how they can help children record what they see, what they think, and what they find out (tape recording, video, clipboards, writing, photographing)
☐ Possible demonstrations of tasks or activities, and items or scenes that children may sketch or record
☐ Artifacts (tools, equipment, products, etc.) that may be borrowed and brought back for further investigation
☐ Time schedule

Gather Materials and Supplies for the Field-Site Visit

Materials and supplies needed:

☐ Clipboards

☐ Recording equipment: ☐ Camera   ☐ Camcorder   ☐ Tape recorder

☐ Paper, pencils, art materials

☐ Bags, boxes, or other containers for materials collected

☐ Other

Organize the Children Ⓟ

How will children be organized for the experience?

☐ Children assigned to specific adult   ☐ Groups with a specific task   ☐ One large group

How will responsibility for children be assigned to adult helpers?
List adults who are helping and list children by groups.

```
Investigate
```
Ⓟ

TJ Teacher Journal: Field-Site Visit	Write a narrative about what happened during the field trip. Where did the children go? What did the children see and do? With whom did they interact? What were the highlights of the experience?

Arranging for Visiting Experts

Will the visitor come into the classroom? Do I need to schedule a room or space?

Communicate with the Visiting Expert

How will I prepare the expert visitor to maximize the opportunities for investigation for my children?
(See also Chapter 3)

☐ Phone call   ☐ Reminder letter   ☐ "How We Are Learning" handout

Checklist for discussion with visiting experts.
☐ Safety issues involved in this visit. Will items brought into the classroom be safe for children to explore?
☐ Importance of child investigation and direct first-hand experiences
☐ Importance of real objects, especially those with which children can interact by using their senses
☐ Overview of what the children currently know and understand
☐ Overview of what the children are interested in learning (share some of the questions they might ask)
☐ Explanation of how children will record what they see, what they think, and what they find out
   (tape recording, video, clipboards, writing, photographing)
☐ Opportunities for demonstration of a task or activity
☐ Possible items for the expert to bring that children may sketch or record
☐ Artifacts (tools, equipment, products, etc.) that can be borrowed and kept in the classroom for further
   investigation
☐ Importance of using language that young children can understand

Notes from discussion:

Plan and Prepare for Adult Helpers ⓟ

Would it be helpful to have additional adults in the classroom when the visit occurs?

How many adults are needed? _____

What preparations should adult helpers have?
☐ Phone call   ☐ Request letter   ☐ Meeting   ☐ Reminder note   ☐ "How We Are Learning" handout

Checklist to cover with adult helpers:
☐ Safety issues involved in this visit
☐ Information about particular children who might require special assistance
☐ Importance of child investigation and direct first-hand experiences
☐ Importance of children interacting with real objects and using their senses
☐ Overview of what the children currently know and understand
☐ Overview of what the children are interested in learning (share some of the questions they might ask)
☐ Explanation of the importance of seeing adults model drawing, writing, or recording
☐ Explanation of how they can help children record what they see, what they think, and what they find out
   (tape recording, video, clipboards, writing, photographing)
☐ Possible demonstrations of tasks or activities, and items or scenes that children may sketch or record
☐ Artifacts (tools, equipment, products, etc.) that may be borrowed and kept for further investigation
☐ Time schedule

Gather Materials and Supplies Needed When the Visiting Expert Comes

☐ Clipboards

☐ Recording equipment: ☐ Camera   ☐ Camcorder   ☐ Tape recorder

☐ Paper, pencils, art materials

Plan Interactions with the Visiting Expert Ⓟ

How will children be organized for the experience?

☐ Children assigned to specific adult   ☐ Groups with a specific task

☐ Children individually approach or observe the visitor   ☐ One large group

How will responsibilities be assigned to adult helpers? If adult helpers will be assisting with groups of children, list the groups here.

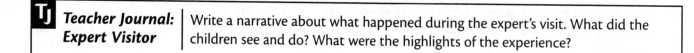

Teacher Journal: Expert Visitor | Write a narrative about what happened during the expert's visit. What did the children see and do? What were the highlights of the experience?

Representing What Was Learned

Represent what was learned through writing, drawing, construction, dancing, and dramatic play	**How will children review their experiences and fieldwork?** ☐ Discuss sketches ☐ Review photos ☐ Time 1/Time 2 drawings ☐ Dictate experience ☐ Revise webs ☐ Answer questions on list ☐ Scrapbook ☐ Display Other:

How can children be encouraged to use secondary sources?

☐ Introduce books   ☐ Add to choices in room   ☐ Encourage play, creation of play environment

How can the children represent what they have learned about the topic?

☐ Drawings/sketches   ☐ Paintings   ☐ Constructions   ☐ Play   ☐ Language products

What do I need to do to encourage representation?

How can the following experiences be provided through this project?

☐ Problem solving: What can children figure out on their own?

☐ Application of construction skills such as taping, gluing, organizing materials.

☐ Working together as a group.

☐ Using a variety of ways to represent what they are learning and to communicate, such as drawing, building, dramatic play, writing, constructing, musical expression, and so forth.

TJ *Teacher Journal: Children's Dispositions*	Write a narrative about the children's dispositions and the development of their investigation skills. What dispositions are you seeing expressed during their project work? Are the children actively engaged in the project?

Revisiting the Children's Web and List of Questions

Revisit web or re-web. Indicate what was learned, identify new questions, repeat investigation and representation

What have children learned? Did they find the answers to their questions?

Are there new questions for investigation? How might they be answered?

What would be helpful for the children to have?

- [ ] More resources such as books
- [ ] Additional experts to visit
- [ ] Additional field-site visits
  - [ ] Same site revisited
  - [ ] Different site
- [ ] Revisiting of documentation of field site
- [ ] More representation opportunities

What additional experiences can be provided?

Determine When to Culminate the Project

- [ ] Are the children satisfied with their new knowledge?
- [ ] Would further investigation require skills the children do not have (such as advanced reading and writing)?
- [ ] Are children just losing interest in the topic?

If the answers are *yes*, then the project is probably ready for culmination.

Debrief, plan culminating event for students to share, tell the story of the project

PHASE III • Concluding the Project

In the third phase children bring work to completion and summarize what has been learned. It is important that children are able to "elaborate what they have learned so that its meaning is enhanced and made personal" (Katz & Chard, 1989, p. 84).

Sharing with Others What We Have Learned

What evidence of children's learning can be gathered and discussed with them?

☐ Drawings/sketches ☐ Paintings ☐ Constructions ☐ Language products

☐ Final webs ☐ Lists ☐ Play

Discuss the project with the children. What do the children think they have learned?

With whom would they like to share their project?

How might the children share what they have learned?

☐ Exhibit

☐ Role-play in play environment

☐ Make histories of the project

☐ Write reports

☐ Plays, dramas, music

☐ Make individual scrapbooks or files

☐ School presentation

☐ Open house for parents **P**

☐ Presentation for parents

☐ Take home books

☐ Community displays

Reviewing the Documentation

What types of documentation have I used to document this project? Review the following list of varieties of ways to document (see Chapter 5; also Helm et al., 1998a, 1998b).

☐ Project narratives

☐ Observations of child development

☐ Checklists of knowledge and skills in curriculum

☐ Anecdotal notes

☐ Individual portfolios

☐ Individual and group products:

    Written language products: Signs, letters, books

    Verbal language products

    Webs and lists

    Pictures

    Representational pictures: Time 1/Time 2 pictures, symbolic pictures

    Music and movement

    Constructions: Play environments, sculpture, blocks, or building toys

☐ Self-reflections of children

Consider the Next Project

Is there another topic that has emerged for further investigation?

Would this topic be a topic to investigate now or at a later time?

Evaluating the Project:
Learning How to Do It Better

TJ *Teacher Journal:* | Review the project. What have you learned about topic selection? Was this
Project Evaluation | a good topic? Why did it work or not work for children's investigation?

Review page 15 (Phase II). Did children gain the content knowledge and skills that you hoped they would?

What did you learn about Phase I?

What did you learn about Phase II?

What did you learn about Phase III?

What would you do differently in the next project?

What suggestions do you have for other teachers working with the same age group or topic?

Evaluate Engagement in Learning

Apply the concepts of engaged learning to your project (see Chapter 5).

1. *Did the children take responsibility for their own work or activity?*
   - ☐ Did they show that they have a voice in what they study?
   - ☐ Did they take charge of the learning experience and explain or show the teacher what they wanted to do?

2. *Were children absorbed and engrossed in their work?*
   - ☐ Did they find satisfaction and pleasure in their work?
   - ☐ Were they developing a taste for solving problems and understanding ideas or concepts?

3. *Were children strategic learners?*
   - ☐ Were they developing problem-solving strategies and skills?
   - ☐ Did they apply what they learned in one experience to a similar experience?

4. *Were the children becoming increasingly collaborative?*
   - ☐ Did they work with other children?
   - ☐ Could they talk about their ideas to others?
   - ☐ Were they fair-minded in dealing with those who disagreed with them?
   - ☐ Did they offer each other support, suggestions, and encouragement?
   - ☐ Did they recognize their strengths and the strengths of others?

5. *Were tasks in the projects challenging and integrative?*
   - ☐ Were they complex, requiring sustained amounts of time over days or even weeks?
   - ☐ Did tasks require children to stretch their thinking and social skills in order to be successful?
   - ☐ Were children learning how literacy, math, science, and communication skills are helpful?
   - ☐ Were all children encouraged to ask hard questions, to define problems, and to take part in conversations?

6. *Is children's work from the project being used to assess their learning?*
   - ☐ Is there documentation of how children constructed knowledge and created artifacts to represent their learning?
   - ☐ Is there documentation of achievement of the goals of the curriculum?
   - ☐ Does the documentation include individual and group efforts?
   - ☐ Does the documentation make visible children's dispositions in the project such as to solve problems, to ask questions, and so forth?
   - ☐ Does the documentation include drafts as well as final products?
   - ☐ Were children involved in the documentation process and encouraged to reflect on the documentation?
   - ☐ Were children encouraged to generate criteria, such as what makes a good observational drawing or a good question?

7. Did you, as a teacher, facilitate and guide the children's work?

☐ Did you provide a rich environment, rich experiences, and activities?

☐ Did you encourage sharing of knowledge and responsibility?

☐ Did you adjust the level of information and support based on children's needs?

☐ Did you help children link new information to prior knowledge?

☐ Did you help children develop strategies to find out what they want to know?

☐ Did you model and coach?

☐ Did you feel like a co-learner and co-investigator with the children?

TJ **Teacher Journal:**
Final Narrative

Write a final narrative on this project. Was this project an engaged learning experience for you and your children? What might you have done differently to increase engagement? Closing thoughts:
